GOOD BUSINESS

GOOD BUSINESS

The *Talk, Fight, Win* Way
to Change the World

BILL NOVELLI

Foreword by
JIM CLIFTON
Chairman and CEO, Gallup

Foreword by
JO ANN JENKINS, CEO, AARP

JOHNS HOPKINS UNIVERSITY PRESS
BALTIMORE

Johns Hopkins University Press
2715 North Charles Street
Baltimore, Maryland 21218-4363
www.press.jhu.edu

Library of Congress Cataloging-in-Publication Data

Names: Novelli, William D., author.
Title: Good business : the talk, fight, win way to change the world / Bill Novelli ;
foreword by Jim Clifton, chairman and CEO of Gallup ; foreword by
Jo Ann Jenkins, CEO of AARP.
Description: Baltimore : Johns Hopkins University Press, 2021. | Includes index.
Identifiers: LCCN 2020020195 | ISBN 9781421440422 (hardcover) |
ISBN 9781421440439 (ebook)
Subjects: LCSH: Social marketing.
Classification: LCC HF5414 .N68 2021 | DDC 658.8—dc23
LC record available at https://lccn.loc.gov/2020020195

A catalog record for this book is available from the British Library.

*Special discounts are available for bulk purchases of this book. For more information,
please contact Special Sales at specialsales@press.jh.edu.*

Johns Hopkins University Press uses environmentally friendly book materials, including
recycled text paper that is composed of at least 30 percent post-consumer waste,
whenever possible.

To my grandchildren: Dominic, Juliana, Nathan, Christopher, Victor, Julia, and Leo. You have the promise and the opportunity to do great things, most especially to do well by doing good. I'll cheer you on.

To my kids: Peter, Alex, and Sarah. Thanks for growing up to become my friends, for being good parents, and for making a difference.

And, of course, this dedication is to Fran, the girl from Missoula, my lifelong partner and true compass on this fascinating journey.

CONTENTS

FOREWORD

Millennials really are different. So is Generation Z.

Here is what the firm I work for—Gallup—uncovered. Compared with baby boomers and other generations, millennials and Gen Z want a job that *matters* more than they want a job with the highest paycheck. They want a job that honest-to-God might change the world a little, or a lot, on any given day. These generations seek mission and purpose. Money is still important, but "my purpose" has moved ahead of it to become the number-one thing they want from a job. We all need to write that into our leadership playbooks.

And it goes deeper. Millennials and Gen Z want a job that matters because if their job matters, it means their *life* matters. The two generations have a very different mission and purpose from my boomer generation.

This is a good thing. The data are overwhelming: A purpose-filled workforce will outperform a purposeless workforce. This new "will" is one of America's and the world's greatest new opportunities. Millennials and Gen Z are saying, "I need to work at an organization with a soul." We should be able to deliver that. If we do, national and global productivity will boom overnight—which we all need right now more than anything. It will create a surge in GDP and job growth like never before.

You are about to read a book about a guy who was born with a will to change the world. Bill Novelli has packed his life mission into each job he has had. He has always wanted to have a job that matters—and a life that matters. He was ahead of his time.

In this book, Bill tells how he took it upon himself to create that soulful job. Bill and I were around the same age—about 25—when he was starting his career and seeking fulfillment in New York. At the time I was in Lincoln, Nebraska, working with zero mission and purpose—as were probably 99 percent of other 25-year-olds. One of the first projects Bill observed at the famous Madison Avenue ad agency where he worked was a campaign promoting a new brand of cigarettes. If the campaign was successful, it would suggest that smoking is for beautiful, elegant people—and more people would smoke. But Bill knew smoking made people sick. He knew the ad campaign his colleagues developed would enrich investors at the expense of human health. He began to wonder: What if I built a firm that created campaigns to *help* people—such as a campaign to stop people from smoking?

Being a dandy entrepreneur, Bill—along with his friend Jack Porter—started a public relations firm that became a famous American enterprise: Porter Novelli. This was likely the first PR or advertising firm based on the core value of *deep purpose first*. If an ad campaign or client didn't have a deep purpose, Porter Novelli didn't do it. If the assignment didn't make the world a better place, Porter Novelli didn't take it on. Bill and Jack built the first Madison Avenue firm with a soul. Bill went on to build the first campaign that *discouraged* smoking—reducing the number of people who started the habit as well as changing the image of smoking from an activity of the successful and elegant to one of dead-enders.

It worked. Bill and his teams played a key role in the massive decline in smoking. He achieved his will of the workplace. He changed America and the world. His job mattered so his life mattered.

Bill demonstrates that you can find purpose through almost any outlet. He created high-mission work for himself through business and free enterprise as well as by helping lead the global humanitarian organization CARE and then running one of the biggest and most influential nonprofit organizations in the world—AARP. Now a popular professor at Georgetown University, Bill teaches the purpose of leadership. Determining life's rich purpose, he says, is up to you. Leading a life that matters is up to you. Managing a team or running a company or nonprofit with a soul can't be legislated—it is up to *you* to give it that soul.

Through great real-life stories, this book by Bill Novelli makes a profound statement—that all organizations in America and the world need to take their mission to a higher level to meet the new will of the world's workplace. You are the one he is talking to. If you don't lead the charge to change the soul of organizations, no one else will.

JIM CLIFTON
Chairman and CEO, Gallup

When Thomas Jefferson wrote in the Declaration of Independence that one of our unalienable rights is the pursuit of happiness, he wasn't using the phrase the way we might think of it today. He wasn't talking about a pursuit of pleasure or entertainment; he was referring to pursuing the good life. He meant developing our individual talents and skills to our fullest potential to do good work. Happiness, to Jefferson, was achieved by contributing to the greater social good as a productive member of a community, enabling the well-being of others. In other words, we achieve happiness by fulfilling our purpose in life to the best of our abilities.

As someone who has been involved for over a quarter century in the leadership of organizations deeply committed to work that improves the quality of people's lives, I realize how closely people's sense of meaning and fulfillment is tied to their work. I have had the great good fortune of doing work that is consistent with my own internal sense of calling. I know how vital it is to be engaged in work that allows us to express our gifts, in support of causes we are passionate about, with people who share our values and aspirations. That's why I'm so excited about this book.

Bill Novelli discovered his purpose early in his career: to make significant contributions to solving the world's major social problems. And the pursuit of this purpose has guided his career, and his life, ever since. In this book, Bill shares his extraordinary journey to show us how we can use our own gifts, passions, and values in our work to find meaning and fulfillment while attacking the world's major social problems; in other words, how to do well by doing good.

He shows us how "a marketing guy" went from an entry-level position selling soap at consumer goods giant Unilever to selling ideas, issues, and causes by creating one of the most successful public relations firms in the world (Porter Novelli) while helping to develop the discipline of social marketing. He tells us how his passion for finding solutions to major social problems led him to leave his successful PR firm to pursue a career in public service full time, first at CARE, then at the Campaign for Tobacco-Free Kids, AARP, and the Coalition to Transform Advanced Care. And he shares his work at Georgetown University, where he is not only teaching the next generation of leaders how to do well by doing good, but also working with corporations and nonprofit organizations through Georgetown Business for Impact to improve business performance while creating social value.

I first met Bill when he was chief executive officer (CEO) of AARP. Little did I know then that I would one day hold that same position. At the time, I was the chief operating officer at the Library of Congress and had just been appointed to the board of AARP Services, Inc., AARP's for-profit subsidiary. It didn't take long to realize that Bill and I were both attracted to AARP by the powerful social mission of its founder, Dr. Ethel Percy Andrus, to involve older people in society and help them age with independence, dignity, and purpose. This was her calling and would be her true legacy—to help people live a more fulfilling life as they grow older. By pursuing what he calls a talk, fight, win strategy, Bill contributed significantly to that legacy (see chapters 4 and 5).

Today, AARP is an organization of nearly 38 million people aged 50 and older. As CEO, I see that more and more of our members want to keep working past traditional retirement age because they want to continue to contribute to society and find meaning in their own lives, and work does that for them. But it doesn't matter whether we're just graduating from college or coming to the end of a lifetime of service to an organization or cause; the same powerful impulse to express who we are through what we do remains alive at every point in our lives.

If that describes you, I'm confident that you will gain many valuable insights and lessons from following Bill's journey within these pages. You'll learn that discovering and fulfilling our purpose in life is the key to living the good life we all seek. And you'll learn that we don't have to make a choice between doing well or doing good. We can and should be doing both. In fact, that's what the pursuit of happiness is all about.

JO ANN JENKINS
CEO, AARP

GOOD BUSINESS

INTRODUCTION

I'm a marketing guy. When someone asks me what I know, or what I trained in, I say "marketing." That's what I do. Back in the 1960s, when I graduated from the University of Pennsylvania, my ambitions were not much different from those of many of the graduate students I teach today at Georgetown University. I wanted to go to New York, land a good job with a big company, make a splash, work my way up to the corner office, and earn a lot of money.

I had five offers coming out of graduate school, and I decided on Unilever, a major packaged-goods firm (then known in North America as Lever Brothers). I began by selling detergents, fabric softeners, dishwashing liquids, and other products. Though I was doing well at Unilever and had worked my way up to brand manager, I decided to move to a hot New York ad agency, Wells Rich Greene, run by Mary Wells, possibly the most successful and flamboyant woman ever to preside over a Madison Avenue agency. In those days, to make it big in my trade, it was considered smart to work both sides of the business—the client side (Unilever) and the ad agency side—so this seemed like a good career move.

I thrived at WRG, where I worked on the Ralston Purina and Bristol Myers accounts. I was still selling packaged goods. It wasn't soap and laundry products any more; now it was hair cream, dog and cat food, and kids' cereals. One of our target segments for a cat food was FHOHICOH (female head of household in cat-owning households). It wasn't much different from targeting detergent buyers, but I had climbed a few rungs higher on the corporate ladder.

Despite my progress, I felt like something was missing. A famous football coach reportedly said, "You have to be smart enough to play the game, and dumb enough to think it's important." My colleagues and competitors were plenty smart, but I just didn't think the work was all that important. I wanted something more, which I vaguely identified as social relevance.

The turning point came the day I returned from a client meeting with two test products in plastic bags, one a new kids' cereal and the other a new soft, extruded dog food. A young copywriter came into my office, announced that he was working on ad concepts for the cereal and asked to see the product. As a joke, I pulled out the dog food and tossed it to him. Without much of a glance, he caught it and said, "Yeah, we can sell that."

That was a big moment for me. I realized I was ready to change directions, but how and where? Luckily, I was assigned a new client, the Public Broadcasting Service. It was the first time PBS had retained an ad agency to build viewership for public television. One of my initial tasks was to attend a press conference featuring Joan Ganz Cooney, a creator of *Sesame Street*. I was fascinated by her *Sesame Street* approach to learning. She was an educator, yes, but I also saw her as a marketer. That's when the light bulb went on. The thought struck me that marketing principles and practices could be applied to ideas, issues, and causes just as effectively as to the products I had been promoting.

For me, this was a big idea that offered the social relevance I'd been looking for. It was also the first step in changing the direction of my career from marketing packaged goods to marketing social causes. It led me to discover my purpose: to make significant contributions to solving the world's major social problems. The pursuit of this purpose has guided my career ever since.

My career has now spanned some 50 years. My personal journey has included business marketing at a worldwide consumer goods company (Unilever), making it at a hot New York ad agency during the Mad Men era, cofounding and building a large international public relations agency (Porter Novelli), running CARE USA in 40 developing countries, fighting and helping win the war against the tobacco industry, leading the largest nonprofit organization in America (AARP), cofounding a national coalition to reform how advanced illness and end-of-life care is delivered in the United States, and creating and overseeing Georgetown Business for Impact—a center for partnerships with companies, nonprofits, and government to create economic *and* social value—as well as teaching in the MBA program at Georgetown University. I've gone from being a commercial marketer to a social marketer, to a PR maven to running large nonprofits and social advocacy organizations, to an educator. At my core, though, I'm still a marketing guy.

When I began my career at Unilever, the idea of doing social good as a corporation or as a businessperson was an afterthought—something to pursue after succeeding at making money. But what I discovered that day at the *Sesame Street* press conference, and have proven over my 50-year career, is that you can make a positive social difference. Whether you are in business, government, or civil society; whether you are just starting out as a newly minted graduate, at midcareer, or in an encore period of your life, you can make a dent in the universe. In other words, you can *do well* (creating economic and financial success for yourself and your company or organization) by *doing good* (helping to solve the world's and society's major problems).

Back in my brand management days at Unilever, the company's annual report was a worldwide story of products and profit that contained hardly a word about sustainability or social impact and no mention of the triple bottom line (people, planet, profit). The business model has changed a lot since then. In *Fortune* magazine's issue on 50 "Change the World" companies a few years ago, editor-in-chief Clifton Leaf wrote that Paul Polman, the now former chief executive officer (CEO) of Unilever, said his company was driving forward successfully largely *because* of its sustainable living plan.

I once attended a conference of up-and-comers, executives of various companies whom McKinsey—the management consulting firm that hosted the conference—had identified as likely to become CEOs in the next five years. I was invited to talk about social impact. After my remarks the chief operating officer of a Fortune 100 company stood up and said, "We can't always do what we love, so we have to learn to love what we do." Really? Is that how we want to live our careers and our lives?

At lunch at that same McKinsey conference, I sat next to a senior executive from another big corporation. I asked her if her company had a purpose. She said, "A purpose? We sell bleach!" Then she thought about it a bit more and said, "Well, we do have a sort of statement about how every day we try to help our customers in some small way." That's really not enough. It won't differentiate that company from its competitors. It won't do much for the bottom line. And it won't make much difference to her or society.

The imperative to labor at what you may not love is less and less true today. People are learning to find more social reward—along with financial reward—in their daily work, and companies are engaging employees through a variety of strategies that create social good as well as profit. As you'll see in this book, social good can *create* profit.

Today's business leaders are tapping into the power of purpose. They're building social and environmental strategies into their core businesses to improve financial performance, gain a competitive edge, attract and keep talent, and achieve economic success for their shareholders as well as success for other stakeholders and for society. When they can do that, they're doing well by doing good, and it's their sweet spot.

There are many terms of art for this approach. "Corporate social responsibility" is often used, but some companies view this label as out of date. The "triple bottom line"—people, planet, profit—is still a popular expression, especially among younger people. "Sustainability" is a common term but usually applies more narrowly to creating *environmental* change and stewardship. "ESG" (environment, social, governance) is gaining in popularity. "Corporate philanthropy" is often considered a subset of a broader mix. There is no universal descriptor.

Today this way of doing business is often described as creating "shared value," a term popularized by Michael Porter and Mark Kramer in their landmark 2010 article in the *Harvard Business Review*. Diminished trust in business, said Porter and Kramer, was a serious problem that could undermine competitiveness and reduce economic growth. They concluded that we need a new model—one of shared value—and that companies must take the lead in bringing business and society back together.

The new model they posited is not about charity but rather self-interested behavior: creating economic value by creating social value. They argued for expanding the pie, not merely redistributing the slices. In the Porter-Kramer concept, the roots of shared value lie in business's having a successful "community," not only to create demand for goods and services but also to provide critical public assets and a supportive environment. They believe that a community needs successful businesses to provide jobs and wealth creation opportunities for its citizens.

They identified three ways that shared value is created: reconceiving and reimagining products and markets, redefining productivity in the value chain, and building supportive industry clusters at the company's locations. The gist of all this is that profits involving a social purpose represent a higher form of capitalism that will enable society to advance more rapidly while allowing companies to grow and prosper.

The shared value argument is compelling. Just about every businessperson I know has read the article. The idea of doing well by doing good wasn't a new concept, but Porter and Kramer synthesized it, branded it, and expanded it in a powerful way. After the article appeared, Steve Lohr in the *New York Times* wrote this:

> Corporate social responsibility efforts have always struck me as the modern equivalent of John D. Rockefeller handing out dimes to the common folk . . . small gestures at the margins of what companies are really trying to do—make money. Shared value is an elaboration of the notion of corporate self-interest—greed, if you will. The idea that companies can do well by doing good is certainly not new. Shared value . . . points toward "a more sophisticated form of capitalism," in which "the ability to address societal issues, is integral to profit maximization instead of treated as outside the profit model."

In the phrase "doing well by doing good," the word "by" is important. It means that a company can improve its bottom line—shareholder value—*as a consequence of* creating positive results for other stakeholders and for society.

So there's money in all this. It's not just a moral imperative, not just the right thing to do, although many think that that is justification enough. But businesses are supposed to perform financially. In doing well by doing good, we have an important pathway to business success. A few years ago Babson College and the consulting firm IO Sustainability reported that corporate social responsibility (or whatever you choose to call it) can create business value by

- improving how shareholders view performance (share price and market value);
- increasing sales and revenue;
- reducing risks and protecting or improving a company's license to operate;
- growing and protecting brands and reputation;
- enhancing competitive positioning;
- deepening customer relationships; and
- improving commitment and engagement of employees.

Porter Novelli developed and issued its Porter Novelli / Cone Purpose Premium Index, a study of the top 200 companies in the United States. Its findings show that purpose is an important driver of overall reputation. Nine out of ten companies with strong reputations also have strong purpose scores. And consumers value corporate purpose: the attributes they rank highest are being responsible, caring, advocating for issues, protecting the environment, and giving back to important causes.

Roy Spence, the head of the ad agency GSD&M, which did outstanding work for AARP when I was CEO there, made a similar argument in his book *It's Not What You Sell, It's What You Stand For*. In the book Roy calls for a strong and unique purpose as a way to make a difference in the marketplace and create a path to high performance for your company. A strong purpose, he argues, drives corporate decision-making and is a determining factor in allocating resources, attracting employees, planning for the future, and creating customer preference for your company.

Simon Sinek, the noted author, speaker, and management consultant, also supports this view. He believes that people don't buy what you do, they buy why you do it. He argues that highly successful companies succeed because they have found—and they communicate—their "why." In other words, they know their purpose and use that to drive success, regardless of what kind of business they're in.

As compelling and attractive as all this sounds, none of it is a magic solution for outstanding corporate performance or for going to heaven. It is not a substitute for strong management, high-quality products and services, effective marketing and sales, and solid operational practices. But it is a powerful opportunity, if seized upon, to succeed.

As Porter and Kramer point out, public trust in business is declining. Trust in other institutions is on the decline as well, including government, the media, nonprofits, and, in the United States as in many other countries, elected officials. The late US senator John McCain liked to say that trust in Congress is now down to a few friends and blood relatives.

As for business, lack of trust is due to many factors. There have been scandals, like Volkswagen's cheating on pollution tests; Wells Fargo's practice of signing up customers for credit cards without their knowledge or permission; and Uber's "step on toes" marketing, poor treatment of its drivers, and harassment of women employees. The public is also concerned about companies' impacts on the environment, including water contamination, air pollution, and harmful mining and other extraction practices.

The simple fact is that in today's world, the public has come to expect—even demand—that companies do good by taking a positive stand on social issues, supporting communities, and investing in causes and social problem solving. And many, if not most, companies have come to understand this.

Don't get me wrong, I am a capitalist. Winston Churchill supposedly said that democracy was the worst form of government, except for all others. Capitalism is not perfect either, but it is the most successful and effective economic and social system ever devised for creating wealth and social progress. That said, we need balance and fairness, and we need to make things better. And balance and fairness need to include socioeconomic and racial equity.

Porter and Kramer and other proponents of the economic value of doing well by doing good have come to deeply influence business thinking. The idea that profit is everything never really did ring true. As Margaret Blair, a professor at Vanderbilt Law School, said, "We don't build companies to serve Wall Street. We build corporations to provide goods and services to a society and jobs for people." Companies have always had the responsibility, as well as the opportunity, to be good corporate citizens.

Larry Fink, the chairman and CEO of Blackrock, the global investment management company, has a strong sense of corporate purpose and responsibility, and the firm's $6.5 trillion in assets under management give him a bully pulpit from which to speak. Fink sent an open letter asking corporations to think beyond the bottom line and consider the community as well. He wrote that "society is increasingly looking to companies, both public and private, to address pressing social and economic issues . . . from protecting the environment to retirement to gender and racial inequality, among others."

Earlier, he had sent another open letter saying that "every company needs a framework to navigate this difficult landscape, and . . . it must begin with a clear embodiment of your company's purpose in your business model and corporate strategy. Purpose is not a mere tagline or marketing campaign; it is a company's fundamental reason for being—what it does every day to create value for its stakeholders." In bold print, Fink went on to say, "Purpose is not the sole pursuit of profits but the animating force for achieving them. Profits are in no way inconsistent with purpose—in fact, profits and purpose are inextricably linked."

Employees' intensity of connection to their organizations is based on their commitment and ability to achieve *work* performance goals, to be sure. But the connection is also related to the opportunity to do some good. Social responsibility ranks high in employee engagement. In a report on how workplace giving is changing, America's Charities found that employees "want their giving experiences to be engaging, empowering, and catalyzing. These new expectations are causing employers to . . . find new ways to meaningfully engage Millennials in giving their time, talent, and money."

In 2019 Gallup produced an important new book called *It's the Manager*, by Gallup chairman Jim Clifton and Jim Harter, based on the organization's largest global survey of the future of work. They found that what millennials (indeed, virtually all employees) want and value in their business careers is not a boss but a coach. And they want purpose. Gallup created a useful coaching guide that focuses on what employees see as their purpose and goals and what they want their development and their future to look like.

Universities get this picture because their students demand it. Young people have a strong interest in making things better. That's probably been true of each generation, but it's especially the case today. Business schools know they have to do more than just teach students finance, accounting, marketing, strategy, and other competencies.

What is the role of business education in today's society? Two professors, Mie Augier and Arjay Miller, writing in *BizEd*, summed it up well in a 2017 article titled "Rooted in a Sense of Purpose":

> We know that it's easier to teach students how to make money than how to solve social problems. After all, problems such as climate change, education, and healthcare are too complex for an algorithm to handle. But if schools can add dimensions of social conscious-

ness to their existing core curricula, they can help students think through how they and their organizations can help address large social issues on a regional, national, or global scale.

As this idea takes hold, the way business schools are ranked will also change. Traditionally, business school performance has been judged on criteria like graduating students' starting salaries, faculty publications, and where and how fast students get jobs after graduation. We now see evaluations based not just on financial success but also on how well graduates contribute to the world—in other words, contributions to doing well by doing good.

Business students are for the most part hard-eyed realists. They believe in free enterprise and the rewards of capitalism. After all, these *are* business schools. But today's students also want to know the business case for sustainability, and they are interested in socially beneficial business practices. They care about business and public policy and society. When we started our social purpose program at Georgetown nearly a decade ago, one of our students—in learning about the business of doing well by doing good—remarked, "Especially with issues like the climate, there's a huge business opportunity there, and there's going to be a huge market for solving it. Earlier, we were relegated to charity or do-gooderism, but now we know it can also make you money."

More recently, I got e-mail messages from two students. The first said, "The vision you presented for embedding corporate social responsibility in the DNA of companies will likely stick with me throughout my career, as I seek opportunities to implement these concepts in my future roles." The second wrote, "I have student debt. I want to pay if off and make a good living. But I also want to stay engaged. I don't want to lose my sense of purpose."

These are the workers and future executives that Fink referred to and that companies want and need. According to a survey by PwC, the professional services firm, business leaders worldwide say that attracting and keeping skilled younger workers is one of their biggest talent challenges. In other surveys both employers and young graduates say that an education in social responsibility, as well as leadership and business ethics, is important.

While corporations are combining financial and social performance and results, the sector that has traditionally been oriented toward social impact is *civil society*—nonprofits and nongovernmental organizations (NGOs), universities, faith-based organizations, associations, and others that are all striving to make a difference, from saving the planet to saving souls. Although I have spent about half my career in the corporate world, I've spent the other half mostly starting and working in nonprofits large and small. I know how committed and dedicated the management and employees of these groups truly are. They are vitally engaged in how to create and sustain social change. This is who they are and what they do. It's in their DNA and their reason for being.

In our Georgetown Business for Impact center, we have a large program—New Strategies—dedicated to helping nonprofits build and broaden their revenue bases. Some 250 nonprofit CEOs and development officers come through this program every year to work on attracting corporate support, creating cause marketing and social media campaigns, enhancing data analytics, improving earned income, practicing impact investing, and other strategies. Over 1,000 nonprofit leaders have participated in New Strategies to date, and the entire program is paid for by major corporations that want their nonprofit partners to do well. This is corporate-nonprofit partnership at its best. Curt Weeden, formerly the head of corporate philanthropy for Johnson & Johnson, created New Strategies and brought it to us at Georgetown. He is focused on bridging the gap between companies and nonprofits and creating successful partnerships for the benefit of both.

Those who work in the civil society sector are also doing well by doing good. They are creating financial results (revenues to apply to their mission and their cause) as well as social and environmental success for all stakeholders. The difference is that rather than turning profit over to shareholders, the money remaining at the end of the year is counted as a net asset—that is, a fund for developing new endeavors and for future spending on the organization's mission. And those committed to the civil society sector no longer have to take vows of poverty. Their salaries may not be as high as in the private sector, and bonuses certainly aren't, but today nonprofit and other employees can earn a decent living, provide for their families, and prepare for the future.

As you'll read in subsequent chapters, five civil society organizations have played critical roles in my career: CARE, the Campaign for Tobacco-Free Kids, AARP, the Coalition to Transform Advanced Care (C-TAC), and Georgetown University. There have been many others in my life that I will also reference, such as Kaboom! and the American Cancer Society.

In addition to the private sector and civil society, we need *government* to create policies and adopt and fund innovative approaches to advance economic and social progress. All three sectors need to be in sync and work together. But today, as I mentioned, trust in American government and its capacity to deliver is at a serious low point. The politics of government are in messy, nasty gridlock. You can get a laugh anywhere in the country with the line, "I'm from Washington, and I'm here to help." President Ronald Reagan is famously quoted as saying that "government is the problem" in a speech about the economic recession in the early 1980s. The full quote is "In this present crisis, government is not the solution to our problem; government *is* the problem," but the shorter nugget—government *is* the problem—caught on and has been repeated countless times. Politicians and many others call for smaller government without saying whether they mean eliminating Social Security administrative judges assessing disability claims or getting rid of Environmental Protection Agency scientists.

Today a career in government is often thought of as unrewarding, and government employees are perceived as largely unrewarded. In the United States there are constant ideological attacks on government service at every level. We have had government shutdowns over immigration and other partisan issues. It is almost a national pastime to complain about government red tape—federal, state, and local—and perceived government employee indifference to public and customer service across the board. Under these circumstances, who would want to be a government employee?

But dedicated government service is critical to the performance and success of corporate and civil society, and I have seen how government can pave the way for economic and social progress. I was proud to serve in a government agency that did so: the Peace Corps. And government can be an effective partner with others. When Jack Porter and I began Porter Novelli, the first initiative we worked on was the National High Blood Pressure Education Program. It was managed from within government by the National Heart, Lung, and Blood Institute at the National Institutes of Health. Nonprofits, such as the American Heart Association, were enthusiastic partners. So were pharmaceutical companies, which saw the expansion of high blood pressure detection and treatment as a way to build business. This program was a true partnership, and it was one of the most effective national health education programs in American history.

Students at Georgetown sometimes come to me and ask some variation of a profoundly important, yet strikingly innocent, question. "What's the path to success?" Of course, for most of us there is no linear path. There wasn't for me. Our path is what we make it, and that journey can be winding and uncertain, maybe risky, and hopefully enormously gratifying. Make *your own* path, I tell the students; you have the skills, talent, and commitment to make it a unique and successful one. And if you're in late career or even "retired" (that word always belongs in quotes because it doesn't mean what it used to), you still have opportunities and a pathway ahead.

I wrote this book because I believe that regardless of whether you work in corporate America, the civil sector, or government; whether you are just beginning your career, in the middle, or contemplating retirement; whether you are an executive, a middle manager, or a worker bee, you can make a difference in the world by pursuing your passion and fulfilling your purpose—and that you, personally, and your company or organization will profit.

Once at an awards dinner in his honor, the TV journalist John Chancellor recounted that his father had warned him not to go into journalism because he'd never make any money. Chancellor replied, "I don't care; I just want to have an interesting life." And he got one. He put a spotlight on current events, including with his bold coverage of the forced integration of Central High School in Little Rock, Arkansas, in 1957, when he was pursued by angry segregationists. Not only did John Chancellor have an interesting life, he made a difference—and, because he was very good at what he did, he made a lot of money. There's absolutely nothing wrong with making money. I did, by marrying my passion for marketing with my purpose, and as a result I and the organizations I worked for all profited.

I teach a course in the MBA program at Georgetown called Principled Leadership for Business and Society. One of the most popular readings among the students in that class is "How Will You Measure Your Life?" by Clayton M. Christensen. It was published in the *Harvard Business Review* in 2010, but the article is timeless. Christensen asks three key questions: (1) How can I be sure that I'll be happy in my career? (2) How can I be sure that my relationships (with spouse and family) become an enduring source of happiness? (3) How can I be sure I'll stay out of jail (a serious question with ethical dimensions)? Among his conclusions, Christensen says we must identify our purpose in life. His own yardstick for measuring his life is how much he has contributed to others. My goal, over a long career, has been to make significant contributions to solving major social problems. I call that my purpose.

Incidentally, Christensen also believes that no other line of work is as important as management in making contributions and allowing you to achieve your goals. He calls it a "noble profession." I'm good with that, too.

My journey has been a long and winding one. Along the way, I developed a sense of direction and learned a lot of important lessons. I hope that by sharing my journey and those lessons with you here, I can show you that we can all do well by doing good. We can all make significant contributions to solving the world's major social problems. And, perhaps most important, by working together to pursue our passions and fulfill our purpose, not only will we all profit, we will create a better world for our children and grandchildren.

CHAPTER ONE

FINDING MY PURPOSE

From Selling Soap to Selling Causes

When it rained, I sudsed. It was a humbling way to begin my career in business, but that was the reality. When I graduated with a master's degree from the Annenberg School for Communication at the University of Pennsylvania in 1964, I had the same goal as many others in that era: get a good job (with benefits, including health insurance and a pension, ideally at a big company), climb the corporate ladder, and make a career of it. The thought of starting my own firm or being an entrepreneur never entered my mind or was mentioned in the classroom. Today entrepreneurship is a magic concept for many students. Talk to five MBA students at Georgetown, where I am now, and you'll hear six ideas for start-ups.

I had five good job offers and chose Unilever, then known in North America as Lever Brothers. I wanted to go to New York, and Unilever was where I learned the basics of marketing and business. But first I learned humility.

Before landing at our fancy Manhattan headquarters at Fifty-Third and Park Avenue, called Lever House, I went through sales training—learning the business from the bottom up by working retail. After a week's orientation, I was given a station wagon (the ancestor vehicle to today's SUV) full of products and promotional materials and a sales bag (I still have it) and sent off into the Syracuse district in upstate New York. I was on the ground and among real people, our customers and consumers.

Unilever had a large product line, and each salesman (there were no saleswomen in those days) was responsible for all of it. Our mainstay was laundry detergent. I had two suits, which I alternated day by day. As I worked the shelves in supermarkets and slogged through warehouses, sometimes with my super-aggressive sales manager, Norm Rosenblatt, I collected detergent powder in my cuffs and pockets. So, when it rained, I sudsed. Not very dignified, but a good way to learn the business.

It all started for me back in Bridgeville, Pennsylvania, near Pittsburgh. I loved sports, especially football, and had dreams of playing in college. We were Pittsburgh Steelers people. Still are. My brother Jerry named his dog after the Steelers quarterback Ted Marchibroda. At our high school football banquet, my mother revealed that fact to Marchibroda himself, the featured speaker. He tried to act pleased. Later, when the Steelers changed QBs, Jerry renamed his dog Rudy (after Rudy Bukich).

I had always wanted to be a football player, ever since I got a real helmet for Christmas—not the kind you could fold up and put in your pocket. I like to say I was small but made up for it by being slow (actually, I had some speed). In the 10th grade I had had a nasty football injury, a serious indentation in my forehead. My mother almost fainted when she saw it. As I was wheeled into surgery at Mercy Hospital in Pittsburgh, a nun asked, "Are you William?" I said yes, and she responded, "We'll pray for you."

I recovered and kept playing through high school. In my senior year, several alumni took some students from the Pittsburgh area on a recruiting trip to Penn, an Ivy League school in Philadelphia. This was the first time I laid eyes on Penn's hallowed Franklin Field, and I was awestruck. At a dinner for us held at the university museum, an old alum (probably about 60) stood up and said, "I hope you boys are accepted and decide to come to Penn." He added, "I gave *my* son two choices; he could go to Pennsylvania or he could go to hell." I chose Penn—a decision that shaped my life.

At first I wasn't sure I belonged there. At freshman orientation they gave us a list of 50 books we should have read in high school. I had read five of them. For the first month I didn't even unpack. But I soon came to realize that I did belong. I wasn't a star, but with hard work and some growing confidence, I could hold my own in the classroom, on the field, at social events, and at my job waiting on tables in the freshman commons.

On the first day of football practice there were some impressive bodies in the locker room. One big, good-looking guy said to nobody in particular, "Baron Weeks . . . what a name for a football player." I asked the guy next to me who that was, and he said, "That's Baron Weeks."

Our freshman squad was big and talented. But injuries, academics, and other forms of attrition got in the way, and by my senior year we had only 11 seniors on the team. Penn had won the Ivy League championship my freshman year and then fired the coach. The school had been downsizing its football program to prepare for Ivy League competition and had gone through some losing seasons. By the time we were successful, it was too late for Coach Steve Sebo. Penn foolishly decided to let him go.

Our new head coach, John Stiegman, came from Rutgers, and he introduced the single wing, an offense so antiquated that it was actually thought to be an advantage, although the players didn't share that view. The theory was that opposing teams would be unfamiliar with the system and wouldn't have time to prepare. The reality was that as a team we never got comfortable or skilled with the single wing and never made it work effectively.

But it worked for me. Before Stiegman arrived, Penn coaches had recruited for the T-formation, with talented quarterbacks and running backs. But the single wing required players who could run and pass. I was just proficient enough at both to get to play a good bit.

I got knocked out in a game against Yale. I tried to make a tackle and ran into a blocker's knee. I spent the rest of the game trying to remember my plays and why my head hurt so much. Today I can joke about all this. A few years ago I was driving to work and heard on the radio that older men who played football in their youth had a far greater risk of dementia than those who didn't. I was so upset I almost drove off the road, but by the time I got to work I'd forgotten all about it.

I also played lacrosse at Penn and was elected co-captain my senior year. Sports—the competition and teamwork—helped shape my life in business and everything else. We all grow up, but we carry with us the lessons of our youth. To this day, I almost never miss a homecoming game at Franklin Field, and I root for the Quakers as hard as ever.

It was also at Penn where I met my future and forever wife, then Frances Bickell. An education major, she had a part-time job in the football office. She would type endless streams of letters that began "Dear Student Athlete" and knit sweaters for her boyfriend back home in Missoula, Montana. He was not a football player.

I participated in student government as the election chairman. Pete McCarthy, a teammate, was in student government with me, and we got into a controversy with the school newspaper, the *Daily Pennsylvanian*. We controlled the paper's budget, and we withdrew the funds and closed it down. It was a dumb, authoritarian thing to do, and we were roundly criticized in the Philadelphia newspapers.

I oversaw student elections, and some freshmen decided to run a fictitious candidate, Otto Schmink, for their class president. They had fun campaigning around campus. My roommate, George Edelstein, who later became a brilliant lawyer in the Antitrust Division of the Justice Department, had a solution to the problem: "Let's beat them up and tear down their signs!" Schmink won. More jibes from the city papers. Maybe this is why I have never had an interest in becoming a politician.

As an undergraduate, I was an acceptable, though not outstanding, student. I majored in English with a focus on journalism, and I liked to write. After graduation, unsure what career I wanted to pursue, I decided to go to graduate school at Penn's Annenberg School for Communication. There I studied mass media and propaganda, took a course called TV Lab (television program production) to which I brought Fran on inexpensive dates, and enrolled in a marketing program in the Wharton School. I really took to marketing. I read David Ogilvy's 1963 book *Confessions of an Advertising Man*, which helped inspire me to launch a career in marketing and advertising. Ogilvy's focus on consumer research, product positioning, effective persuasion, and Madison Avenue derring-do portrayed an exciting way to crack the business world and to compete and win. Ogilvy was above all a fierce competitor.

After we graduated, Fran and I got married in her hometown of Missoula, Montana. I soon came to love Montana, which has become my adopted state. I've made many good career decisions with my feet dangling in creeks in the Bitterroot Valley. Fran's brother, Larry, became my lifelong hiking buddy. Montana's winters are tough, but as they say, if it didn't get cold in Montana, the Californians would never go home.

Selling Soap

Ogilvy believed that to succeed in business, you had to learn the business from the ground up. That's just what I was doing working retail at Unilever. Once I was calling on a wholesaler and had to get in line to see the buyer. Waiting on a bench in front of me were four Procter & Gamble salesmen, each responsible for a different line of business: detergents, dentifrices, food, and so forth. I realized how tough P&G was and came to appreciate the company even more over the years.

Lever had a product called Spry, a cooking lard that competed with P&G's Crisco. One day Norm Rosenblatt, my sales manager, caught up with me in a supermarket and said our unit was not going to make its numbers for the month unless we did something extraordinary. "Like what?" I said. "I already did it," said Rosenblatt. "I ordered a carload of Spry [some 700 cases, as I recall] to be shipped to your customer, Norm Oretskin, here in Binghamton." Oretskin operated an independent supermarket in competition with all the chains. "Now," said Rosenblatt, "we just need to tell him about it and figure out how he's going to move it off the shelves." Norm Rosenblatt was a selling machine—but a carload of Spry, without telling the customer?

We sat down with Oretskin in his office, and Rosenblatt told him straightaway what he'd done. A carload of Spry was coming his way. The reaction was almost violent. Oretskin stood up and began to shout, "Unorder it right now, you *&%$ morons. I'll call your boss's boss's boss, and you're dead!"

Rosenblatt was calm. He had a plan to offer it on sale. "Your customers love sales, and so do you. We'll build a giant end-aisle display, and this stuff will fly out the door." An hour later we were still arguing (at least they were; I wasn't saying a word). Pretty soon, some scotch came out of the cabinet, and the argument went on and on. Finally, Norm Rosenblatt, the super-salesman, won the day. He had calmed Oretskin, figured out the merchandising plan, and sold the order, and we were on our way. As we got to our cars, he smiled and said, "We made our numbers. Now that's salesmanship." You couldn't get that from Ogilvy's book.

After sales training, I discovered just how competitive marketing was at Unilever back in New York. The assistant brand managers, of which I was one, and the secretaries sat at metal desks in big, open bullpens on each marketing floor. The secretary in our group was Pearl Gold, a supremely competent woman who today would probably have an MBA and be running a division or a whole company. Pearl would spend time on the phone managing her kids after school while filing with the other hand.

My challenge was to compete with the other assistant brand managers—all confident, hard-charging young guys in white shirts from top schools—to earn my way into one of the carpeted offices occupied by brand managers and group brand managers (the corner office was held by a division vice president). I made it—at the time, the youngest in company history—and in the process learned my trade.

It wasn't easy. I was assigned to a couple of minor brands and to the development of a new product: a dry laundry bleach. There were files passed on from previous forays into the bleach business, meetings with research and development (R&D), the running of endless numbers on the bleach market and our hypothetical product, and interactions with the ad agency assigned to this new product—Ogilvy & Mather. One afternoon the great man himself, David Ogilvy, was invited to lecture the assistant brand managers in our Household Products Division on his "scientific principles" of marketing. We were a cheeky lot, and we challenged him on his research and just about everything else. Ogilvy gathered up his materials and left in a huff. Maybe he wasn't so scientific, but he was still my guy. I admired his style and his success.

Lever had tried before with a product called Reward. P&G now had Stardust in the market. Colgate had Action. Was our bleach going to be a capsule or loose powder? If a powder, should it be packaged in a conventional carton-type container or perhaps a new plastic one? We conducted focus groups, worked on names, argued with the R&D people, talked to Sales, looked at ad concepts, fooled around in the test kitchen, and kept running the numbers. This is how I spent my time.

I learned that ad agencies don't like new products, because they often can't make money on them. I relearned that later when I went to Wells Rich Greene and worked on new products for Ralston Purina.

There were many delays. In my notes I would often write: "No bleach activity today." I had time on my hands, which is scary when you're in a hurry to prove yourself. I hid out in the library reading old marketing plans and a book called *Promotional Decision-Making: Practice and Theory*. Finally, the project was scuttled.

Some time later, a new VP took over: Bob Anderson, who had been at P&G, was the best packaged goods marketing guy I have ever met. He was also tough, bordering on nasty. Bob called me into his office and said, "I want to go into the bleach business." Déjà vu. He gave me a carton full of back data from Nielsen and told me to write a report on how to crack the market.

I labored over that proposal for several weeks before turning it in. A week went by. It came back to me from Bob's corner office—by office mail, even though he was right down the hall. It was marked up in green, the color Bob used to be distinctive. My opening sentence in the report read something like, "Ninety-five percent of all bleach sales are in supermarkets." Bob had written in the margin, "No shit." I decided I'd better update my resume.

In any event, I was trying to come to grips with a conflict beginning to form in my mind. I was in the job I wanted, in the company and city I wanted, and yet I wasn't sure about it all. Was I in the right place and doing what I wanted to do? I had some doubts.

It was Bob who put me on a fast track to brand manager, and I got my office. Bob knew how to embarrass people, and he worked at it. One time I put in many hours to plan and prepare for a meeting with an ad agency. When the meeting finally came to pass, Bob ended it after five minutes. The problem: the agency's creative director couldn't articulate the brand strategy to Bob's satisfaction. Another time, Bob stepped into my office and said loud enough for everybody in the bullpen to hear him: "Your sales and revenue projections are late." I said I was sorry, but I was reworking them to take them down. "Take them down?" he bellowed. "I can hire a monkey to take them down. I hired you to take them *up!*"

I wasn't the only one called on the carpet in this intense environment. One of our brand guys was summoned to the president's office (reached via special elevator). The president told him he had seen a commercial for the brand on television the previous evening. "Yes sir, what did you think?" my colleague asked. The president said, "I think it's somewhere between useless and downright harmful." "Wow," I said when I heard about it. "What did you say?" The brand manager replied, "What could I say? At that point I argued for useless." Maybe if he had tested his TV spot, he could have argued for useful.

I had several group brand managers along the way, and they were all solid marketing people. Most of them had served in World War II or Korea or both. At that time the country was in the midst of the Vietnam War, and when I would go to lunch in the cafeteria with my older colleagues, I got an earful. The war, and the turmoil at home to protest the war, were on the news every night. These older guys believed in America to their core. They hated hippies, whom they considered dirty, disrespectful, and, maybe worse, unemployed. But now they were also beginning to doubt their own government as well. The war was a quagmire, and they had many doubts about it all—so did Fran and I. It wasn't easy to reconcile working on bleach and other mundane products with the social cataclysm that was happening across the world and right there in the streets of Manhattan.

One day Alex Hoffman, a group brand manager I greatly admired, called me into his office to go over some numbers Personnel (what we now call Human Resources or Talent Management) had given him. Unilever had an excellent pension program, Alex said, and he painted a picture of my future. After two years at the company, I had become vested in the plan, he explained, and vesting would occur at a rate of 4 percent a year. After 27 years with the company, I would be fully vested in the pension program, and when I turned 65 in 2006, I could retire with hundreds of thousands of dollars (I forget the exact number, but it sounded big at the time). That's the way it worked. Climb the ladder, earn a pension, retire.

But I continued to wonder if I was on the right career path. So I took a bold step—I sent in a preliminary application for a White House Fellowship. In truth, I wasn't sure what a White House Fellow did, but I was curious and felt I had something to offer. When Bob Anderson found out about it, he came to see me. "Why did you do that?" he asked. "You're doing well here. What's the problem?" I couldn't really tell him what the problem was, but I was working on finding the answer.

Switching Sides

After several years at Unilever I switched from the client side of the business to the agency side. Headhunters had called with job offers, mostly in brand management. For a time I was under serious consideration by McKinsey. But after several conversations, they said they didn't think I was cut out for the consulting world, and I heartily agreed. So I left Unilever to move to the ad agency Wells Rich Greene, run by Mary Wells. She was innovative, glamorous, and a magnet for creative talent. She married one of her clients, which of course engendered a lot of comments about client service.

The agency's signature was to make advertising fun and humorous. Although many of WRG's clients were second and third in their categories and looking for breakthrough advertising, the agency's clients also included Procter & Gamble, Ralston Purina, and other major companies.

Dick O'Reilly, who had been a senior executive at SSC&B, an ad agency that worked for Unilever, recruited me to come to Wells Rich Greene to bring some marketing discipline to the creative shop. I liked the people and the energy but didn't always succeed with the discipline. Mary encouraged off-the-wall creativity. Seeing a copywriter riding his bike around the 15th floor of the General Motors building on Fifth Avenue (our offices then) or watching an art director wrestling on the floor with a copywriter over a storyboard told you it was a creative place. But there were also good marketing people there. One of my accounts was Bristol Myers's Score hair gel for men. It was advertised on pro football quarterback Joe Namath's TV talk show, among other places, because the brand's tagline fit with Namath's image as a lady-killer—"Score, if you're going to play." We had a new Score TV spot planned. Without letting me know, the creative team had produced it, and they brought it to me already done. It was a guy walking through hair follicles like he was going through the jungle. It wasn't even on strategy (what would Bob Anderson say?). I took the creative guys and the TV spot to Mary to figure out what to do. She said, "Well, that's a piece of crap." Then she turned to me and said, "Take it to the client, and let's get it on the air." I didn't like the ethics of that. Weren't we, including Mary as president, supposed to exercise quality control? I could see that she didn't want to eat the production cost of the commercial, but what did we owe our client?

We had an opportunity to win McDonald's business. Irv Sloan, a senior account guy, and I worked hard on the presentation. The agency's creative reel was always our best selling point (with the exception of the Score commercial). We made the presentation at McDonald's in Chicago at 9 a.m. on the appointed day. Mary was late. Finally, she walked in, strode in front of everybody right up to the McDonald's marketing vice president and said, "Last night I ate dinner at McDonald's. You make the best hamburgers in the world. I make the best advertising in the world. We've got to get together." Then she sat down. We didn't get the business. It went to Needham Harper & Steers, an agency that eventually played a major part in my future.

Although I did well at WRG and enjoyed working on the Ralston Purina and Bristol Myers accounts, I was still looking for something more relevant. My college buddy George Edelstein was now out of law school and trying antitrust cases for the Justice Department; I was promoting cat food. What should I do? I talked it over with Fran and thought about some kind of change. The young copywriter I mentioned in the Introduction, who mistook the dog food for a kids' cereal, was added incentive. So was working on the PBS account and hearing Joan Ganz Cooney talking about *Sesame Street*. My idea of applying marketing to issues, causes, and ideas didn't seem like the way to pay the bills and feed a young family, but it was powerful for me.

Selling Causes: From Madison Avenue to Pennsylvania Avenue

One morning I read in the *New York Times* business section that the Peace Corps wanted to reposition itself and was looking for marketing expertise. Host countries welcomed the Peace Corps and the enthusiasm young Americans brought to their work. But these countries also wanted more older and experienced volunteers (nurses, agriculturalists, MBAs) and more people who looked like the citizens of the countries in which Peace Corps volunteers served. That same day, I called the headhunter named in the article and said I wanted to apply. There were hundreds of applications for that position, he responded, but he had the perfect job for me—at Avon. I explained that the Peace Corps, not Avon, was it for me, and a few weeks later he called to say I was a finalist and interviews were being set up.

The first person I met at the Peace Corps offices in Washington was Jack Porter, whom I knew from interviewing at Ogilvy & Mather when I was in grad school. Jack was about seven years older but had had a similar career—marketing and advertising in New York and London—and he had come to the Peace Corps as head of public affairs. He and I had a great talk, and he invited me to come work with him. My title would be director of advertising and creative services. The Peace Corps offices were in a nondescript building just across Lafayette Square from the White House.

It was 1970. I went home and talked to Fran. We were living in Princeton Junction, New Jersey, and had three small kids. Her response was "Let's go for it." That's Fran. Up for almost anything, Montana steady, she's our family's chief operating officer, a great mother, and now a terrific grandmother. She's smarter than I am and a liberal to my centrist perspective. Her one negative—or is it a positive?—is that she doesn't laugh at my jokes. I long ago gave up on reading her my draft speeches. "That's not funny . . . That isn't funny . . . What's that supposed to mean?" I have a button from a college reunion I keep as a lucky charm: "I met my wife at Penn."

So we packed up—young Peter and me in the U-Haul, and Fran, Alex, and Sarah following in our small car—and set out for Washington, DC, now often known as The Swamp. I was thinking about my emerging career goal: to make significant contributions to solving major social problems.

Jack and I built a strong team at the Peace Corps, and we were part of a great organization. Peace Corps volunteers are justifiably national heroes. I did a public survey of attitudes toward the Peace Corps and our volunteers. This was only a decade after the organization began, yet an extremely high percentage of Americans claimed to personally know current and returned Peace Corps volunteers. I didn't think that was possible. I concluded that the results really showed that people admired our volunteers and *wanted* to know them. It was strong support for what President Kennedy and Sargent Shriver had started years before. Today there are nearly 250,000 returned Peace Corps volunteers and former staff, many of them, like me, members of the National Peace Corps Association, acting in support of the organization and its work.

Another survey I conducted—this one of returned Peace Corps volunteers—probed their biggest concern upon coming back to the United States. These days, when I ask my current Georgetown students (some of whom are former volunteers) what they think returning volunteers' main concern was, they often guess it was about getting a job or fitting back into American society. But the biggest concern back then, and I feel certain it remains so today, was the fear that the sand would blow over their tracks and that all their hard work in the country where they had served would disappear. This fear was well founded, as I learned later in my work for CARE. But this concern doesn't just apply to developing countries. How do you sustain positive social change? It's a key question across all settings and issues today. Change is seldom permanent and can be reversed. New generations grow up, lessons are forgotten, program funds are diverted, different leaders take over, and technologies emerge.

One of the first things I did when I went to the Peace Corps was try to recruit Bob Druckenmiller, whom I had worked with when I was at Unilever and he was at J. Walter Thompson, a major New York ad agency. It took a while to entice Bob and his wife, Benne, a dedicated nurse, to Washington. I would call him at his New York office and say, "How's it going, Bob?" A positive guy, he would respond, "Things are going very well. I'm mostly working on the Scott paper account." That gave me my edge. In future calls I'd say, "Hey, Bob, we're down here making a huge social difference. But tell me, how's the toilet paper business?" After a while Bob got the message, which he was partial to anyway, and he and Benne joined us in DC.

Joe Blatchford was then the head of the Peace Corps, and Richard Nixon was president. The Vietnam War was still going on, and the Peace Corps was one of America's few shining examples of good work abroad.

I took my first trip to Africa—to Kenya and Uganda—during my Peace Corps tenure. The volunteers were still mostly dedicated recent college graduates, but more technically trained people were moving into the ranks. I met a young Peace Corps couple at Lake Victoria, where the husband was doing scientific work with fish and other lake aquatic life and his wife was teaching art to local kids. I still have one of her prints of a Lake Victoria tilapia on my wall at home.

While we loved our Peace Corps work, Jack and I weren't especially enthusiastic about being in government, even though the Peace Corps was surely the least bureaucratic organization in town. We decided to go out on our own and start a company. The Peace Corps is dedicated to social change, to international development, and to international friendship. These are great objectives. But we wanted to run our own operation and to use our marketing and communication skills directly. And while I hadn't focused on entrepreneurship in college or in the big organizations I had been part of, both Jack and I had caught the bug. We had confidence in ourselves, we thought we had the skills to compete and make a difference, and we were excited to make it on our own.

But first, politics intervened. Dick O'Reilly, who had recruited me to Wells Rich Greene, told the White House about my marketing background, and I was invited to help start and manage the in-house advertising and promotion agency for the re-election of President Richard Nixon.

A Detour into Politics

I wasn't particularly political or ideological at that point in my life, but I thought it would be great experience to work on a political campaign. Marketing a national candidate, in this case an incumbent president, would be a test of my idea that marketing was marketing, and a robust discipline that had many applications.

So in January 1972 I moved to 1701 Pennsylvania Avenue, diagonally across from the White House, to work on setting up the November Group, the name we chose for our agency. We were housed in the same space as the Committee to Re-elect the President, which became known as CREEP. A lesson here: watch what names spell out in acronyms. Years later, the marketing conglomerate Omnicom named a division of the company DAG (Diversified Agency Group) until someone pointed out that in New Zealand or somewhere "dag" referred to the back end of a sheep. But CREEP it was, and there I was.

Meanwhile Jack had left the Peace Corps to go out on his own until I could join him after the presidential campaign. Mike Carberry, another refugee from New York advertising, who had moved to Washington to help market the US Postal Service, joined him. Since we had no capital with which to start a firm, Jack convinced a local advertising agency in Georgetown, Henry J. Kaufman, to provide office space in return for our professional services.

The November Group drew talent from across the country. It was headed by Pete Dailey, who had his own agency, Dailey and Associates, in Los Angeles. Phil Joanou, on leave from Doyle Dane Bernbach in Los Angeles, was our executive vice president. Bill Taylor, on leave from Ogilvy & Mather, was creative director; George Karalekas, on loan from Canada Dry, was media director; Mike Lesser from Marschalk was senior vice president account manager, New York operations; and I was senior vice president account manager, Washington operations. Because it wasn't feasible to move the New York people and their families to Washington for the 10-month campaign, we had two close-knit operations, one in DC and the other in Manhattan. I was responsible for supervising the advertising planning, copy, media, and promotional materials for all voter blocs (youth, African Americans, women, Hispanics, labor, veterans, and so on); for planning and analyzing polling and attitudinal research; and for being the liaison to our New York shop.

The November Group was a smart strategic decision; rather than retain an outside advertising and promotion agency for the presidential campaign, we created our own. Our entire focus was on one client: the president of the United States. As we stated it back then, "By forming our own advertising agency . . . [we] could . . . choose the best talent available and could assure loyalty, confidentiality, and greater control of [the] operation."

In our short existence we produced some 30 to 40 television commercials, two documentaries on the president, one documentary on Mrs. Nixon, and numerous radio commercials, newspaper ads, issue brochures, and other materials. After the Republican National Convention, a group known as Democrats for Nixon was formed and headed by John Connally, the former governor of Texas who had been Nixon's treasury secretary. We developed several strong commercials for that group.

We also said, perhaps in self-promotion:

In recent years, the "selling" of a political candidate has come under increasing fire—and justly so. A political candidate is not, in fact, a commodity to be wrapped in the American flag, force-fed popular rhetoric, and "sold" to the public. The American electorate demands that candidates for public office, most particularly the highest office of the land, exhibit a considerable amount of credibility. The American electorate also demands to know what the candidates have done and will do in public office and where they stand on the pertinent issues of the day.

The November Group was separately incorporated and not officially part of the Committee to Re-elect the President. Nonetheless we were housed in CREEP and, in reality, subject to CREEP and White House decision-making. We were proud of our standing and our work, but we were constantly straining for enough independence to be objective and do our jobs.

What we could not foresee, and what influenced our campaign plans and my thinking for decades afterward, was the Watergate scandal: how it changed us and America, and how it still reverberates today. Several powerful memories come to mind.

First, on a June day five months into the campaign, I went to New York to meet with our November Group team there. I hadn't seen the morning papers, and as we sat down my teammates dropped the *New York Times* on the table. The headline was about the Watergate break-in. It named G. Gordon Liddy, the general counsel for CREEP and for us, and Jim McCord, the chief security officer for both organizations. The question my colleagues asked was, "Do you think this is a rogue operation, or do you think somehow CREEP and the people we're working with are in on this?" I was from Washington, and I was supposed to know something about the world down there. I gave them my best answer: "There's no way this has anything to do with CREEP or the White House. We're so far ahead in the polls that you'd have to be crazy to orchestrate something like this." It seemed like a logical answer. Everyone agreed, and we went about our business.

Another recollection was an ethical lapse on my part. The finance people at CREEP held a major meeting of everyone but the top CREEP brass. They explained that the law limited the amount of money an individual could give to a political candidate but that a number of donors wanted to give more to the campaign. They asked each of us to sign several cards that would enable these donors to increase their gifts. I looked around the room. Everyone I could see was signing cards. I signed too.

It was wrong, and I've never forgotten it. Today I teach ethical leadership in Georgetown's MBA program. We discuss how pressure from the top is often a deciding factor in people's unethical behavior and how to resist that pressure. I was under pressure that day, and I did not resist; I gave in. I use this as an example in my class and in my life.

One afternoon, Alexander Haig, a retired general who was an assistant to national security advisor Henry Kissinger and later secretary of state under President Ronald Reagan, came to our offices to brief CREEP and the November Group on the war in Vietnam. He had statistics on enemy casualties and other specifics, and his message was a positive view of US progress in the war. The room was full of Republicans and Nixon loyalists, of course, but they weren't swallowing the Haig pitch. They asked a number of challenging questions that Haig hadn't expected, and he left abruptly with his papers and slides. Like the executives back at Unilever, they weren't buying this war.

The 1972 presidential election was a landslide. Nixon beat George McGovern in 49 of the 50 states. McGovern won only 17 electoral votes. A White House guy came around and asked people at CREEP and the November Group if we were interested in positions in the upcoming second Nixon administration. "No thanks," I said—I had other plans.

After the election, as Jack and I started planning and building Porter Novelli, most of our November Group team returned to their advertising and marketing careers. Pete Dailey was later made US ambassador to Ireland. Jeb Magruder, the deputy director of CREEP, went to prison for his role in the Watergate affair. So did Chuck Colson, among others. Colson, a White House operative who had given us a hard time during the campaign with his dirty tricks ideas, was known as "the evil genius" and one of the Watergate Seven. Several years later Phil Joanou called to ask me if I was interested in heading the in-house advertising and promotion agency they were setting up for the Ronald Reagan campaign against incumbent Jimmy Carter. I was building Porter Novelli and had had enough of candidates and campaigns. I again said, "No thanks."

One Sunday a few months after the election I got a call from Gordon Liddy's lawyer. His trial had begun, and his lawyer wanted me to testify two days later, on Tuesday. I said I knew absolutely nothing about Watergate or Gordon's involvement. That wasn't the point, he said. He wanted me to tell the court what Gordon did for the November Group, which was primarily to interpret the election spending laws. Trying to get out of it, I said I would be in New York on Tuesday and not available. He said, "Bill, I'll make it clear and easy for you; I'm giving you a subpoena."

Two days later I appeared outside Judge John Sirica's courtroom at the appointed time, just as the court broke for lunch. I was looking for someplace to hang out—to hide, actually—when Gordon spotted me. We shook hands in front of a large crowd, and he said jovially, "I'm going to beat this. Wait till you see the jury; they fall asleep right after lunch."

I spent the next hour in a waiting room with a nun who was there to testify about Gordon's moral character. When my turn came to take the stand, the defense attorney asked me what Gordon had done for the November Group, and I explained. He asked a follow-up question or two, and the prosecution had no questions. The whole thing took five minutes. I was dismissed and out the door. I knew Gordon was toast. The next day I bought all the newspapers and listened to the news. Relieved that my name didn't appear, I went about my new job. Gordon was found guilty and spent more than four years in federal prison.

A year or so later, Jeb Magruder came to see me at Porter Novelli. He said his book was selling well and being translated into Japanese. He was considering several job offers. Then he asked if Porter Novelli could do a glossy brochure for his prayer breakfast group, pro bono. I said, "Jeb, we're operating on a shoestring and struggling to get a start in this business, and you want free brochures?" Again, "No thanks."

CHAPTER TWO

PURPOSEFUL WORK

*Building a Purpose-Based Company
and Applying Social Impact
around the World*

We started Porter Novelli by applying our marketing and communications skills to what we thought Washington was all about: health and social issues. Today we all know Washington is essentially about power, politics, money, and sex. But we were naïve, and our approach paid off, both in the growth of the firm and in professional and personal satisfaction. We became involved in many social issues, including environmental protection, cancer prevention and treatment, high blood pressure control, and reproductive health and infant survival in developing countries.

As soon as we could afford it, Bob Druckenmiller came over from the Peace Corps to join us. We were applying our commercial marketing and communication skills, plus what we had learned at the Peace Corps and what Mike Carberry brought from the US Postal Service. I found academic thinkers working on theories and hypotheses about how to apply marketing practices to social issues and causes. It may have all begun with an article I dug up from the 1950s asking "Why can't we sell brotherhood like soap?" We thought maybe we could.

We consulted with Phil Kotler at Northwestern, who at one point had the best-selling marketing textbook and the best-selling social marketing book in the world. We brought Alan Andreasen at Georgetown into our orbit, as well as Paul Bloom at Maryland and Chris Lovelock at Harvard. As a result of all this, we pioneered social marketing to create a unique, successful position for the firm, essentially helping invent the field. We took academic theories of social marketing and put them into practice to demonstrate that not only would they work in the real world to make life better for people, but they were also powerful enough to build a business around.

Combating High Blood Pressure

Jack had secured a small purchase order to help plan a new government program in the National Heart, Lung, and Blood Institute (NHLBI) at the National Institutes of Health (NIH). It was 1973, and a young cardiologist, Ted Cooper, was in charge of the new venture. He formed three planning committees: patient education, public education, and physician education. Today we would call the third group "clinicians" instead of physicians, understanding that care delivery is performed by a team (doctors, nurses, social workers, chaplains). But back then the docs reigned supreme.

Planning was under way when the physician committee presented their recommendations. They said the evidence was now clear that treating hypertension (high blood pressure) offered clear benefits and that the means to do so—medications, exercise, and salt reduction—were available. They concluded that NHLBI should delay public and patient education for up to a decade while physicians were informed and supported in hypertension control. And then, they said, we could inform the lay population.

Cooper firmly rejected that recommendation and instead took another path. He told his physician colleagues that we were going to educate health providers, patients, and the public *all at the same time*. We would, as he put it, stress the system. It was a critical decision and a lesson I have applied ever since. Stress the system. Put public pressure on the decision-makers, whether they are physicians, politicians, or regulators. Public pressure can be a powerful force for change.

Cooper's decision made a big difference. Persuasive messages were delivered to all three audiences at the same time, and behaviors changed. Deaths and disabilities declined, and the National High Blood Pressure Education Program (NHBPEP) is still considered one of the most successful national health education initiatives in American history.

We identified a broad audience for our campaign, but we also zeroed in on high-risk populations, including young black men. I brought in Bert Neufeld, a talented creative director from my Wells Rich Greene days, to help out. He did a campaign for this audience based on the Broadway show *Ain't Misbehavin'*. It featured characters resembling the show's cast, including Miss Pills, Mr. Salt, and Mr. Weight.

We tested the concept and then the TV spots and other materials among the target audience, and it did well. That's when we ran into trouble. NHLBI had a minority advisory committee of medical and health professionals, and they didn't like what they saw. They said the campaign was demeaning to African Americans and that the Institute shouldn't go forward with it. We explained that it had been thoroughly tested and that young black men (and older men as well) liked the messages and responded to the appeal for blood pressure control. The committee's response was that while this may be true, *they* (the committee) found the campaign offensive. That was that. We should have brought them in at the beginning, involved them in the research, had them observe the focus groups, and given them ownership in the campaign. They were part of the client mix, and the client, like the customer, is (almost) always right.

Bill Matassoni, a newly minted Harvard MBA, was a young account guy with our fledgling firm. We had little office space, and Bill sat in a virtual cubbyhole, bumping knees and sharing a single phone with another Harvard MBA, Eve Bund. Nothing is too good for Harvard grads, I always say. Bill was working on the high blood pressure program, which he wrote about in his terrific book *Marketing Saves the World*, highlighting the strategy of focusing on patient compliance rather than just a broad education and detection message. In those days hypertension medication had serious side effects, including sexual performance dysfunction. You might think the risk of stroke from untreated high blood pressure would outweigh the side effects of the medication. But our research showed that many men preferred another outcome to both stroke and medication side effects—death. "I'd rather be dead than a vegetable in a wheelchair" was a comment we heard from our qualitative studies. How do we deal with that? It has taken decades for the treatment (now with fewer side effects) to catch up with consumer attitudes. Men are often a tough audience when it comes to health and health care behavior change.

Although the program was government led, a number of pharmaceutical companies joined in. The reason was obvious: the more detection and treatment increased, the bigger the market and the more medications they sold. It was a perfect example of self-interested social good. Another key player in the NHBPEP was the American Heart Association, a powerful and effective organization today led by Nancy Brown, their innovative CEO. I've been working with them ever since.

Improving Public Health

Our work with NHLBI helped us get involved with the National Cancer Institute (NCI), where we worked on patient education, including breast cancer, and smoking cessation. Back then, physicians and nurses actually smoked at higher levels than the general population. In the 1970s about half of all American adults smoked, and youth smoking was growing as well. The head of a major NCI division, with a cigarette in her hand (yes, people smoked in offices and other public places, including airplanes and restaurants), said to her senior team, "We've got to do something about smoking in this country."

Our clients, Paul Van Nevel, the head of NCI's communication office, Elaine Bratic Arkin, and others were good strategic thinkers and knew well that docs and nurses were exemplars. If they smoked, their patients and the rest of the country would think smoking was acceptable. As a smoker himself, Paul knew that smoking, though detrimental to health, was a powerful communal experience. He told a story about being part of a cancer control meeting in Moscow with NCI officials and their Soviet counterparts. When the Russians, who all smoked, saw Paul lighting up, they said, "You ride with us to the next meeting." So Paul was able to get chummy with the Russians, which he saw as a real benefit of his unfortunate habit.

Working with NCI was a great privilege. We were able to bring our marketing skills to bear on huge public health issues. Terry Baugh, who oversaw our breast cancer work, produced the *Breast Cancer Digest*, an important public and patient resource that was used far and wide by organizations throughout the country. Terry also started our first Porter Novelli office in New York City and later she and another Porter Novelli alumna, Randi Thompson, founded Kidsave, an important child-focused nonprofit that Fran and I enthusiastically support.

With NHLBI's and NCI's help, we started a health message testing service that government agencies and nonprofits could use. It helped them improve their messages and gave us a good database of broadcast and print communications to apply in our work. Murray Hysen, the research director at Wells Rich Greene, came up with the idea of the health message testing service and helped us set it up. Murray could communicate comfortably with anyone, from young Wells Rich Greene copywriters to government officials. He eventually came under pressure back at WRG to stop working on our health message testing because the firm had the Benson & Hedges cigarette account. But he was committed to health and stayed with us, although he made us promise to keep his name out of everything. A research firm we were dealing with had the same pressure. They were doing consumer studies for R. J. Reynolds and Philip Morris and had to bow out of our business. We presented our findings to conferences of the Association of American Medical Colleges, on whose board I served many years later; the American Cancer Society (where I am now a member of the board); and the American Marketing Association. It was a good way to promote our work.

Spreading the Word

Social marketing was a new discipline, and I wanted to teach it at the university level to spread the word and promote our firm by getting Porter Novelli's name and image into the marketplace. Paul Bloom, a marketing professor at the University of Maryland, and I approached his dean about teaching social marketing in the MBA program there. The dean was for it but said that students only had one required marketing course, called Marketing Management, in their MBA curriculum. He said there were three sections, and we could focus one of them on social marketing as long as we taught the basics of the marketing discipline. That was fine with Paul and me, and we team taught social marketing at Maryland for many years. Our young Porter Novelli people audited the course, and Bill Matassoni, Randi Thompson, and others on our staff guest lectured; it was an excellent way for them to practice their craft.

As the discipline of social marketing advanced, it was usually defined as a noncoercive approach to creating behavior change.

I came to reject that. Yes, most social marketing strategies are based on persuasion and voluntary behavior change, but many social issues require some sort of sanction to make them effective. An example is seat belts. Despite years of appeals, seat belt usage didn't increase appreciably. It wasn't until fines were levied for not buckling up that behaviors changed, and slowly positive attitudes followed. Today we have traffic cameras recording speeders. Like most drivers, I really dislike that—but I don't speed on Seven Locks Road going to work anymore.

We had an in-house shorthand name for Porter Novelli: Porno (from our two names). Randi, Terry, Jill Lucas, and some other female staff decided to run a DC women's race in Porno T-shirts. They got a lot of looks and some local publicity, but in hindsight, I wasn't so sure we wanted it. The old adage that any publicity is good publicity was not true and still isn't, even in today's much more permissive age.

Infant Survival and Reproductive Health

I wanted to do international social marketing work in addition to our domestic work. Thanks to Bill Smith, a senior executive at the Academy for Educational Development (now part of FHI 360), I began to consult with the US Agency for International Development. Bill and I served on some advisory groups, and I did a feasibility study on nutrition education via radio in Haiti with Tony Myer, a USAID official. All that led to Porter Novelli's working in infant survival and reproductive health assignments in Egypt, Haiti, and other countries. We became part of SoMarc (Social Marketing for Change), a contraceptive social marketing program, and our primary work was with Family of the Future (FOF) in Egypt.

When we started, there was a national public education campaign based on the slogan "Look around you. Egypt is crowded." I doubted such an impersonal idea could persuade couples to reduce their family size. Fortunately, the head of FOF was a smart businessman named Effat Ramadan, who had emigrated to the United States, learned English and marketing, and returned home to lead the program. We did some excellent work together, and as usual we learned as we went along.

We once did focus groups among Egyptian women, and our Porter Novelli research director, Sharyn Sutton, asked her Egyptian colleagues what size monetary incentive we should offer the group respondents. The advice was "not much." Sharyn decided on two Egyptian pounds (about three US dollars). In the United States it was typical to recruit perhaps 14 respondents to get 10 or 11 to show up. The night of the first session in Cairo, about 50 enthusiastic women tried to push into the room, and many stood outside the door and on the street. They clearly wanted their money. Sharyn had to pay them all, including those who didn't participate. Again, live and learn.

Effat wanted to select a new ad agency for FOF's work. He winnowed the field down to three for final presentations. I invited Jim Williams, who headed the Washington office of Needham Harper Worldwide, to come to Cairo and sit in on the agency selection. One agency called itself America and clearly had Madison Avenue pretensions. They took about two hours to set up, and when they invited us into the conference room, not a word was spoken. They gave us a fancy book to follow, and the entire presentation was given by a powerful, solemn recorded voice—like the voice of God in the nightly sound-and-light show at the pyramids in Giza. This went on for a solid hour. At the end America's executive asked if we had any questions. Jim said, "Well, it was very nice meeting your equipment." They did not get the business.

Rachel Greenberg, a good planner on our staff, came back home through Kennedy airport in New York after a couple of weeks working in Egypt with FOF. The customs agent asked her if she had been abroad on business or pleasure, and Rachel replied,

"Both." He asked her what was inside her valise. Rachel answered, "Condoms, vaginal foaming tablets, IUDs, and some other things." The agent said, "Miss Greenberg, does your mother know what you're doing?"

Expanding the Business

We did know what we were doing, and we were proud of our social and health accounts and our contribution to social impact. But we needed to grow. Every day Jack would wait for the mail to arrive and take any checks straight to the bank. I am a lifelong worrier, which I consider a positive trait. One night, Fran was startled when I sat up in bed in the middle of my sleep and called out, "Can we make payroll?"

Some of our other accounts included the Environmental Protection Agency's program on noise abatement, New York State's Office of Developmental Disabilities and Mental Health, the National Flood Insurance Program, and a cardiovascular risk reduction program with the State of Pennsylvania. We also had some trade associations: the Can Manufacturers Institute, the National Pool and Spa Institute, and the National Soft Drink Association. We didn't think of the latter as a threat to good health. Our position was that soft drinks in moderation are an acceptable part of daily living. I still feel that way, although soft drinks have come under attack as obesity has increased.

Merrill Rose, one of our top account people, and I focused on AARP, a client that was then called the American Association of Retired Persons. Our work was to help protect Medicare, educate people to be better consumers of health care, and promote wellness. I didn't know it then, but that was the beginning of a what would become a wonderful new adventure for me.

To build our revenues, we thought we'd better go back to the private sector, where we'd learned our trade. We hired Chet Berger, a well-known PR guru, to analyze our client mix and our people and make recommendations about how to use our social marketing positioning and our private sector antecedents to attract corporate clients. He presented his ideas, and we began to court companies that might be interested in what we had to offer.

A few months later Chet came back to say he was representing a large ad agency that might be interested in acquiring Porter Novelli. We had had other such inquiries, and we weren't interested. That's where we had come from, and we liked where we were. Maybe Chet's client thought we were playing hard to get. He came back after another week to say now they were *really* interested, and would we at least meet with them?

The agency was Needham Harper & Steers, a well-respected Chicago firm, and the meeting went well—too well, for our taste. There was no hard sell, no mention of money or acquisition or deals, just a discussion of values and clients and what we did. They said they were impressed with how we handled "sensitive, complex issues." Paul Harper, their CEO, led their team. His colleague Barry Biederman was creating a unit within Needham that would work on social issue campaigns. We talked about that, and about Porter Novelli's approach to social change and to marketing communication. They seemed impressed with our focus on building partnerships, on consumer research, and on the health and social issues and clients we represented. And we were impressed with their understanding that every marketing problem couldn't be solved with a 30-second TV spot. As we left, we said to each other, "Uh-oh, that went too well. These are good guys, and now we're going to have to think seriously about this."

We finally decided to join Needham Harper & Steers for three reasons: We had common values and liked and trusted each other. They had capital that we could use to build our agency and give ourselves, including our young stars, a bigger canvas on which to paint. And they had an impressive client list that we could tap for new business.

The night before the sale, I asked Bob Druckenmiller if he was totally on board. "I bought two new suits," he said. "Let's do it." And we did. Feeling cocky, we told our new ad agency friends that we were going to put them on the map, and we all had a good laugh.

After a few years of being part of Needham (whose name changed to Needham Harper Worldwide), we developed a growth plan for Porter Novelli which called for investing in people who had the skills that we lacked (such as tech and financial PR); acquiring several small firms to bolster our offices in Los Angeles and New York; making a major acquisition; opening a Chicago office (we bought a firm there instead); and developing relationships with Needham offices in Amsterdam, London, Milan, and possibly Japan.

Our expansion was underway. I was 42 years old. My personal goal was to invest another eight years in the firm and then become CEO of a major nonprofit or social organization. I've always been in a hurry.

Then, after a few years of expansion and success, the Big Bang—a major merger—happened. Two large ad agencies, BBDO and Doyle Dane Bernbach, merged with Needham Harper Worldwide (our parent) to form Omnicom, a holding company of marketing communications agencies. DDB Needham became one division, BBDO become the second division, and the third, called Diversified Agency Services, consisted of Porter Novelli, Tracy-Locke, Waring & LaRosa, and other smaller firms. We also completed the acquisition of a New York PR agency, Richard Weiner, that BBDO had been in the process of buying and that now became part of Porter Novelli.

Integrating all of these elements presented big challenges. There were discussions and disputes about combining Porter Novelli with other agencies, and for a while, we merged with Doremus, a firm that worked primarily on the tombstone print ads used to announce financial transactions—a practice now largely lost to online announcements. In all, we saw the Big Bang as a major opportunity. Just as we had gained clients to solicit when we joined Needham, we now had a whole new world of potential clients. The name of the game was "integrated marketing communications," in which Omnicom agencies could offer complete soup-to-nuts services to any client in the world.

BBDO introduced us to Gillette, and we won the competition to help them launch a new razor called Sensor. At the time, I wore a beard, and the Gillette marketing VP said, "Are you going to represent us looking like that?" I went home that night and shaved it off, but I kept the moustache for a while. Client service is my middle name.

It was a challenge to incorporate the Richard Weiner firm into ours. They were primarily focused on publicity, and they did work for Philip Morris, including promoting Marlboro and Virginia Slims tennis. Dick Weiner didn't see a problem. He argued that the agency wasn't promoting smoking, just publicizing the sports and philanthropic donations that Philip Morris made to arts and culture. That's how the tobacco companies bought respectability, I said, and I told him he was on the wrong side of history. I asked if his staff had any qualms about their tobacco work. Some did at first, he said, but they went to a religious leader in New York for advice. The rabbi's counsel was to take the tobacco business, because if they didn't someone with fewer scruples would. I'm still pondering that one. Eventually we got rid of the tobacco account, but never truly got Dick himself into the fold. I spent two tough years working to integrate our New York office and build our relationship with Omnicom and its many agencies.

The Next Challenge

Omnicom was a big player: top people, top accounts, and major growth opportunities. It was exhilarating, but I was planning my

exit. I wanted to focus entirely on public interest and public service work—in other words, where Porter Novelli began. My objective was to head a major nonprofit organization, based on my career
goal of making significant contributions to solving major social
problems.

I was on the board of CARE, the international relief and development NGO, and they wanted me to become their first chief operating officer. CARE was operating in some 40 developing countries, and, as part of the CARE International network, they needed
management. It wasn't the CEO position I was striving for, but it
would be a great start. Fran, as usual, was up for it. So I left Porter
Novelli, with my name on the door, and moved across Manhattan
to the East Side and a new adventure. As you can tell by now, I
believe in renewal.

It was December 1990. Porter Novelli held farewell parties for
me in several offices, and there were lots of laughs and tears. The
essence of my goodbye speech was this:

> We (Porter Novelli) have great people, wonderful opportunities,
> and terrific spirit. But now I'm changing careers. I've enjoyed our
> journey together, and each New Year's Eve I've been able to say,
> "Wow, what a year!" The way I feel can best be summed up by a
> letter I received from Leslie Curtin, one of our Porter Novelli team
> working on a research assignment in our Egypt program. Leslie
> ended her letter by saying, "I've only been sick once, I've adjusted
> to the noise and dirt, and I've become a real pro at bargaining and
> catching taxis. I am very grateful to have this opportunity . . . and
> I've enjoyed it immensely." That sums up 18 years at Porter Novelli
> for me. I've only been sick once, I've been very grateful for the
> opportunity, and I've enjoyed it immensely. Fran and I will always
> be part of Porter Novelli. In our P/N client work, we're always
> looking for the big idea. Well, CARE is a big idea. Alleviating
> poverty, the core of CARE's work, is a big idea. Henry David

Thoreau said, "Be sure you give the poor the aid they most need. If you give money . . . spend yourself with it." And that's just what I'm going to do.

Today, many years later, I am as fiercely proud of Porter Novelli as ever. Our ambitions for the agency have been realized, and it is a global organization with some 60 offices and over 1,000 employees across the world. Rosy McGillan is the head of their Purpose practice area, today's equivalent of what had been our social marketing and social impact positioning. Rosy comes to Georgetown to address our MBA class on corporate social responsibility and to talk about social impact platforms, strategic philanthropy, community relations, public-private partnerships, social innovation, employee engagement, and thought leadership. The Purpose unit is one of several practice areas at Porter Novelli, along with Technology, Health, Food, and Reputation. Cone Communications is now part of P/N's Purpose work. The agency's social impact clients range from big corporations to nonprofits to government agencies around the world. As more and more companies see the business value of positive social impact to bottom-line growth and incorporate it into their business strategies and practices, the Purpose practice area and the firm itself will do well and do good.

Not long ago I was in San Francisco for a Georgetown alumni event on impact investing, and Karen Ovseyevitz, the managing director of Porter Novelli San Francisco, invited me to speak to her staff. What a feeling of déjà vu. As I looked around the room, I could easily imagine myself in any of our offices decades ago—a roomful of smart, dedicated people with big smiles and tons of energy. A few years ago when I was in the Porter Novelli Chicago office, I heard one young account executive say to the woman next to her, "I thought he died." Nope, not by a long shot.

Applying Purpose around the World

And so I was off to CARE, which had a powerful mission and was full of grown-up Peace Corps volunteers. As a board member before joining the organization, I spent a couple of evenings a week working with the fundraising and communications staff on a new strategic plan. I hadn't told them I was joining CARE though, and when the announcement came, they were, fortunately, delighted.

CARE had outstanding and dedicated people, and I was able to recruit others. Jennifer Dunlap, the director of development—that is, fundraising—was a young pro on her way to an outstanding career. She later became COO at the American Red Cross and today has her own fundraising consulting firm in Washington. After reorganizing the Marketing Division, I recruited Kathy Bremer, an executive who had overseen about $100 million in P&G ad spending at N. W. Ayer, a major ad agency. She became our senior vice president for marketing. Kathy went on to become the general manager of Porter Novelli Atlanta years later and today oversees a search firm, Boardwalk, that recruits senior people to nonprofit management positions.

The people in CARE's Program Division posed a challenge for me. They knew of my background at Peace Corps and Porter Novelli, including our work with USAID in reproductive health and infant survival, but they didn't necessarily accept those as sufficient credentials to lead CARE. And that was my job—to lead. In time we brought in Marc Lindenberg to oversee the Program Division, and along with Kathy and a few other senior people, we had a strong executive team.

The president and CEO, Phil Johnston, was a big, affable man who had spent a good deal of his career in the field in developing countries. Every organization has its hierarchy. At Unilever, the marketing people are kings of the hill. At Georgetown and other universities, it's tenured professors. At CARE and other development NGOs, it is the country directors and their program colleagues in regional offices and at headquarters. Was I going to fit in?

Phil was a genuine international development expert. He dressed the part, talked the language, and believed deeply in the mission and the cause. He was a big, strong guy who claimed the record for most penalty minutes by a defenseman on the Northeastern University hockey team. Phil was a leader but not a particularly good manager—there is often a difference. As a result, the board had commissioned a study by Ernst & Young that recommended hiring a chief operating officer to whom every department would report and who would in turn report to Phil. That was my job. Would it work? I was determined that it would.

My immediate goals were to earn the respect of the program high priests, to visit CARE mission offices around the world to get to know the staff and their work, to support Phil and what he was doing (mostly fundraising, public speaking, and visiting country offices), and to solidify my position with my former colleagues on the board of directors.

The board had earlier decided that the headquarters office in New York was too expensive and that we should find cheaper space in New York or, more likely, move out of the city. We advertised our availability to a number of cities, and it finally came down to two contenders who really wanted us and would provide financial incentives: Baltimore and Atlanta.

We met with the colorful governor of Maryland, William Donald Schaefer (and his first lady, Hilda Mae Snoops) in the executive mansion. The meeting also included Baltimore mayor Kurt Schmoke and other local leaders. In Atlanta, we had breakfast with Georgia governor Zell Miller (who insisted I eat the grits) and with Mayor Maynard Jackson. But it was Pete McTier, head of Atlanta's Robert W. Woodruff Foundation, founded on Coca-Cola holdings, who came through with the incentives, including a no-cost five-story building that made Atlanta our choice. Later, when I met again with Mayor Jackson to tell him the news, he asked which building it was. When I told him it was next to a strip club, he said, "I know exactly which one you mean."

Once the move was complete and we were at work in Atlanta, the manager of the strip club came to Jack McBride, our VP of management services, to propose a deal. The club didn't have enough parking after 8 p.m., the manager said, while our lot was usually empty at that time, so he offered to pay us per car to use our lot in the evenings. Jack told me the arrangement could bring in as much as $650,000 a year in unrestricted money. That was big for any nonprofit back then and still would be today. But how would this look on the front page of the *Atlanta Journal-Constitution*? I asked Jack to do an informal poll of about 25 women around the building and get their opinions. He reported a mixed reaction. About half said they didn't like the idea—strip clubs were demeaning to women and we shouldn't do it. The other half said, essentially, "We don't care. We go over there at lunch for two-dollar sandwiches. Money is money."

I decided to turn down the offer. The potential bad publicity could be a huge negative. Months later I was in the airport in Lima, Peru, with some board members waiting for a flight. I told them the story to get their reaction. The two male board members said they couldn't believe I would even entertain such an idea. The two women said "What? You didn't take the money?" I've always been aggressive, but I'm glad I played that one safe.

Some years before CARE USA had started CARE International to strengthen and broaden its reach and its fundraising. CARE organizations, which served mostly as fundraising operations, were set up in Denmark, Germany, Great Britain, Italy, Norway, and several other countries. To be seen as legitimate, they needed to have staff and projects in our host countries (for example, Bangladesh,

Ecuador, Ethiopia, India, Kenya, and Peru), but their primary purpose was to work with the government and nonprofit funding agencies in their countries to support CARE USA's program work.

CARE Australia and CARE Canada were different. They were determined to be on the ground in developing countries, and in fact CARE Canada was the operating CARE organization for Angola, and CARE Australia was in charge of the network's activities in Bosnia.

The chairman of CARE Australia was Malcolm Fraser, the country's former prime minister. He was a big, tough guy who wanted to show that Australia was a world player. He would run over you if you let him, but when you stood your ground, he would give you what I called his SIN speech: "We're just a Small Island Nation." A world traveler, Malcolm had no regard for time zones. Once he called in the middle of the night, and Fran answered. Sleepily handing me the phone, she said, "It's an Englishman." It was Malcolm, who said, "No, it's an Australian!" To offset Malcolm's bluster, his chief of staff was a veteran politician named Tony Eggleton, who was understated, diplomatic, and effective. Tony's favorite saying was, "Softly, softly, catchee monkey." CARE Australia's CEO, Ian Harris, was as tough as Malcolm, but not nearly as eminent or well respected. In turn, Ian no doubt considered us Americans to be arrogant and overbearing.

This all came to a head when we learned that a large quantity of cooking oil had gone missing from a warehouse in Maputo, Mozambique, a CARE USA mission. The missing oil—apparently two large truckloads of Australian oil, worth about a million dollars—was taken from a warehouse one night, and a security guard was reportedly killed. Nobody discovered the theft until a staff member happened to stop by the warehouse some time later. Ian Harris immediately wanted to know what we were going to do about it.

I turned to Trish Shannon, who headed our internal audit unit, and we sent in a team, as did CARE Australia and the Australian government, to figure out what had happened and how to respond. Police reports were incomplete and inconsistent. The death notice claimed the guard had been killed by a pen driven into his ear. All the local documents had different dates and facts. No oil turned up in the local markets, and the warehouse and insurance policies had no protections for the parties involved. Trish went to Maputo herself. The best guess was that the oil had been sent to South Africa, Lesotho, or maybe Swaziland.

Meanwhile, Ian Harris kept up the pressure. What were we going to do about this? The donation was between the Australian government and CARE Australia, but it was CARE USA who ran the local operation and had therefore "lost" the oil. Without consulting us, Malcolm Fraser issued a media statement saying he blamed CARE USA and expected full restitution.

We had a real mess on our hands. Trish kept after it, and finally, after months of audits, reviews, and negotiations, we settled with the government of Australia, ate some crow with Ian and Malcolm, and made a vow not to let something like this happen again. Trish set up new controls with clear responsibilities and expectations for staff and others, made sure we understood local laws and legal contracts, and double-checked on partners.

In addition, my lesson was to improve our communications, including making clear what was being done to prevent this type of episode from happening again. I call these "turnaround" stories. Years later I was on a professional medical association board when the COO called to say that a mid-level accountant had embezzled nearly $5 million. How should we handle the communications on this? I asked if they had an internal auditing department. They didn't. "Establish one right now," I said, "and communicate that therefore this kind of theft is not going to be possible in the future." That's a turnaround story. Today Trish is the COO of the AARP Foundation, where she has all her policies and procedures firmly in place.

In 1992 Somalia erupted. It was a CARE USA country and a tough situation, as warlords and intense fighting made relief work there extremely precarious. We were handling food logistics but not end-point feeding programs. CARE Australia came in and helped us out with food distribution in two hot spots. It was dangerous work.

Phil Johnston offered himself to the United Nations to coordinate humanitarian relief in Somalia. Three months later he pulled out, saying nothing was working and there had to be protection for food distribution. We and others began to advocate for troop deployment, and in a dramatic move, President George H. W. Bush—a lame duck after losing to Bill Clinton in the 1992 presidential election—offered to send in the US military. Other countries made similar offers. UN secretary general Boutros Boutros-Ghali accepted, and Phil returned to the action for an additional three months.

I was acting CEO and coordinating things from headquarters. Phil and I had had numerous talks about his retirement and his interest in having me take his place. I had a few outside opportunities and a couple of offers, but I decided that becoming CEO of CARE was worth waiting for. My question to myself was, how long would I wait?

I loved CARE because the people—both the international and in-country staff—were so dedicated and hardworking. As I traveled around the world, I had the opportunity to see what life was really like in low-income countries and how resilient people were. In Kenya, our mission HR director, Joyce Nyamweya, told me how important it was to combine solid training for staff with a demanding attitude. "We don't have the money or time to babysit people," she said. A member of the Kisii tribe, she talked about the difficulties of modernizing her country. Her family's land had been handed down through her father-in-law, who had five wives and many children. This practice was a problem throughout Kenya, as land parcels began to shrink with the growing population.

CARE did a lot of work in microlending. A key strategy was to work with women's clubs, whose members engaged in a variety of moneymaking activities, supported each other, and almost always paid back the small loans from CARE. Kenya is a highly patriarchal society, and I asked one club member, through an interpreter, if her husband minded her doing business outside the home. "He did mind," she said, "until I bought him a bicycle."

My most searing experience was seeing the sprawling Benaco refugee camp in Tanzania. In April 1994 some 250,000 people, mostly Hutus fleeing the civil war in Rwanda, streamed into this camp across the border. The UN High Commissioner for Refugees (UNHCR) called it the biggest and fastest refugee movement he'd ever seen. CARE's job was to manage food supplies for other agencies to distribute and to coordinate with other NGOs and the UNHCR, which I helped to do. The camp eventually grew to 600,000 refugees. In flying over it, you could see the circle of trampled ground around the camp growing larger and larger as women and children foraged for firewood and anything else they could find.

When Phil returned, we resumed our partnership. Peter Bell, the head of the Edna McConnell Clark Foundation and a former official at the US Department of Health and Human Services, was CARE's board chair. He and Lydia Marshall, a key board member, told me they thought I should have more overseas experience to be considered for, and prepared for, the CEO job. I was constantly traveling to CARE missions and CARE International countries, but what else should I do? We came up with the idea of a tour of duty in a CARE mission, perhaps India.

Then Phil proposed an alternative. He wanted me to stay and have the top job, and he was willing to sacrifice to make it happen. His suggested that he become head of the CARE Foundation, opening the way for me to become CEO of CARE itself. The board liked the idea of Phil's moving to the Foundation and praised me for my good work. But they also hired a recruiting firm and began an international search for a new president. Yes, they valued my contribution and leadership, but now they wanted to see if they liked someone else better. Peter Bell named a search committee headed by Lydia Marshall and began to contact NGOs, UN agencies, USAID, and the rest of the world.

In the previous year, I had been to Bangladesh, Ethiopia, Haiti, Kenya, Mozambique, Tanzania, and Thailand, with a stopover visit in South Africa. I had been to London several times on CARE International business, as well as to Brussels, Copenhagen, Ontario, and Oslo. Combined with travel crisscrossing the United States, I told myself that I had the credentials and the experience the board was looking for. I believed that if I were selected, it would be to CARE's advantage as well as my own. If not, I would go someplace else where I could and would be appreciated as a leader and a CEO. But of course, I really, really wanted this job.

In March 1995 I had my initial interview with the search committee. I had given them a resume with my full experience, on which I had spent a great deal of time. In the meeting I focused on where CARE stood and where we could go, and why I was the best person to take us there. I was well rehearsed and confident. Two of their questions gave me pause. One was expected: Did I really have enough international experience? I explained that I did and that my CARE colleagues agreed. I knew most of them did, but of course there would be a few naysayers. I also knew I had many letters of support and recommendation from our people and from the NGO community. The second question was from Lydia Marshall, the chair of the search committee, which she stated more as an assertion than a question: we were not doing well enough at hiring for diversity. Of course, we could always do better.

Rumors abounded: they had three former congressmen as candidates; Andrew Young, the iconic civil rights advocate living in Atlanta, may be interested in the job. Peter Bell and the other two board officers joined the search committee. Phil was suffering from separation anxiety. I could sympathize with how he must feel.

A few weeks later, Lydia called to ask me to come to Washington to talk. I didn't like what I heard—she sounded quite matter-of-fact—but I flew to DC and went to her office. "You did not get the job," she said. I wondered which congressman they had selected. "It's Peter Bell," she went on. I was astonished. Peter, the chairman of the board, who had appointed the search committee and later joined it, had now been chosen by his own committee. Lydia went on to say that she hoped I would stay and work with Peter, and she asked that I attend the board meeting the following week for the sake of my executive team colleagues. She also asked me to be there the following Monday when Peter would be introduced to the staff. I left in a daze.

I had a couple of hours until my flight back to Atlanta, and I started walking, past the Lincoln Memorial and the Vietnam War Memorial, and thought about what had happened. Then I went to the airport, called to tell Fran the news, and flew home. Peter called twice over the weekend. He asked me to stay and work with him. He said the search committee had approached him several times about taking the job, and the last time he said yes.

Why did they choose Peter? They pointed to his 30 years of international experience and world view. Various board members now asked me to stay on. I decided to take the high road: I would go to the meeting to introduce Peter as the new president and attend the board meeting. I was going to support my colleagues and be a team player if it killed me. The board passed a resolution praising my work and asking me to stay. Humble, humble pie.

Lydia, Phil, Peter, and I stood in front of the Atlanta headquarters staff, with a video for CARE offices around the world. When it was my turn to speak, I said that the most important issue was whether CARE would have the leadership it needed for the challenging years ahead. With Peter as the CEO, Phil heading the Foundation, and the outstanding executive and senior management teams in place, it was clear that the leadership was there.

Afterward a board member said, "That sounded like a farewell address." It was. I submitted my resignation and began to look for a job. Headhunters called. People wanted to talk. Julia Taft, the executive director of InterAction, who had been my companion on a trip to Africa, advised me not to look too hard. "Let them come to you," she said. I went through the motions, but my heart wasn't in it. I had just lost the job I wanted at an organization with a great mission that I loved.

And it wasn't just that I had lost a job. I truly believed that I could have made a major difference in advancing CARE's mission, acquiring the resources, and developing the strategies and programs in agriculture, girl's and women's empowerment, economic development, and emergency relief. I believed all that and more.

There were farewell parties with laughs and tears. I was getting good at those. I received humorous going away presents and a plaque that hangs on my wall at Georgetown. It reads: "In gratitude for his dedicated service, CARE honors Bill Novelli, whose commitment to change has shaped our future and shall endure in the hearts of the people we serve." I like to believe that's true. I also treasure a picture, hanging near the plaque, of kids receiving CARE packages after World War II.

Fran's advice: "You did your best; get over it." Kathleen Jamieson, dean of the Annenberg School for Communication at Penn, and Bob Hornik, a professor there, invited me to spend a semester with them to teach and engage with students as a professional-in-residence. That was appealing. Fran and I could go back to Penn and enjoy the university life, and I could figure out what would come next.

CHAPTER THREE

FIGHTING THE TOBACCO WARS, THEN AND NOW

Dan Glickman, a friend and former secretary of agriculture and Kansas congressman, likes to say, "When one door closes, another one opens. But you need to be standing by the door." And that's just what happened to me.

On the day Fran and I planned to sign a lease on an apartment in Philadelphia, where I would spend a semester at Penn's Annenberg School, Nancy Kaufman at the Robert Wood Johnson Foundation (RWJF) called to ask if I would instead take on a six-month assignment to head a committee on the problem of tobacco and its appeal to kids.

She explained the situation and said this effort could potentially grow into a larger, permanent operation. I agreed to do it. Through my Porter Novelli work with the National Cancer Institute on smoking among physicians and nurses, I had learned what a major social problem this was. I was returning to the tobacco wars and back on track to tackle a major social problem.

This was 1995, and about a quarter of the US adult population smoked, down from about 43 percent in 1964, when the first surgeon general's report on tobacco and disease was released. But cigarette smoking among high school students was climbing to about a third of kids. (It reached 36.5 percent in 1997.) It was a national crisis, and a whole generation of kids was at risk.

At the World Conference on Tobacco and Health in Paris the previous year, several of the Americans who attended were pondering how to reverse this trend. They included Matt Myers, a lawyer in private practice and long-time advocate for tobacco control; Mike Pertschuk, who had headed the Federal Trade Commission (FTC) under President Jimmy Carter; and Nancy Kaufman.

The US tobacco industry had their own version of a trade association—the Tobacco Institute—that spoke on their behalf when the companies wanted a united front. Christopher Buckley, the political satirist, used it as a model for his character's employer in his book (and movie) *Thank You for Smoking.* Nancy, Matt, Mike, and others decided that what was needed to fight the industry was a Tobacco Institute for the good guys.

There was already an alliance at work, called the Coalition on Smoking OR Health (COSH), funded by the American Cancer Society, the American Heart Association, and the American Lung Association. It operated at a low funding level and didn't have the clout or support to mount a substantial resistance to the industry or to coordinate forces on a national basis.

This opportunity to fight back aggressively was made possible because Steve Schroeder, a physician and public health expert who was president of RWJF, saw the carnage from the tobacco epidemic and resolved to do something about it. A few years before the Paris conference, Steve had presented a proposal to his board to fund tobacco control in a big way. The board was composed largely of corporate executives, and many were dubious about Steve's recommendation. The meeting was contentious, and the board was divided. At a key moment the former chairman slipped Steve a note saying the board wasn't going to approve the proposal and that Steve should drop it. Instead, Steve tore up the note and kept arguing his cause. He finally carried the day, and the eventual result was a multi-million-dollar commitment and great leadership for national and state initiatives. It was a powerful turning point in American public health.

The time seemed right for a major, coordinated effort. Elaine Bratic Arkin, my client at the National Cancer Institute and now a consultant, wrote a report for RWJF recommending the creation of a new national center that would support tobacco control strategies and speak out with a strong public voice. Nancy and RWJF launched it with an existing grant they had with the American Medical Association. The new entity had the awkward name of the Coordinating Committee to Prevent Tobacco Use by Youth.

Part of the strategy was to support David Kessler, the administrator of the Food and Drug Administration (FDA), and the work of the FDA. Kessler had recently claimed regulatory oversight over the tobacco industry. His argument was that nicotine was a drug, and cigarettes are drug delivery devices. Since the FDA regulates drugs, it therefore regulates tobacco products and their manufacturers. Kessler called tobacco use a pediatric disease. At the time the tobacco industry, a powerful force in America, was essentially unregulated. President Bill Clinton and his administration were strong proponents of protecting kids from the tobacco epidemic, and he announced the FDA's proposed rule to protect children and adolescents from cigarettes and smokeless tobacco. The goal would be to reduce underage tobacco use by half over a seven-year period.

Building a Tobacco Institute for the Good Guys

I started with a small team paid for by RWJF grant money. We set up shop in the back room of Mike Pertschuk's Advocacy Institute and took steps to create a major operation called the Campaign for Tobacco-Free Kids. To secure some real operating money and attack the problem in a big way, I wanted to make a splash so that we looked formidable.

One of our first steps was to do some advertising to establish ourselves. I brought in Mike Carberry, my Porter Novelli buddy who was now at Henry J. Kaufman, the agency that Jack Porter had talked into giving us office space when we started Porter Novelli. But Mike backed out, saying he didn't want to get into difficulties with the media, since the FDA proposals threatened outdoor and print media. So we engaged individual freelancers, a media planner, a copywriter, and others, and retained two local PR firms. We were ready to go.

We publicly announced our official start-up and told the world how we were going to defend the FDA, attack the industry, and protect kids (and adults) from tobacco. We got excellent media coverage across the country, with lots of follow-up media inquiries as well as calls from people who wanted to help. Old comrades offered congratulations, job seekers reached out, and people sent bright ideas for the campaign. One suggestion was to erect a giant cigarette on the Mall near the Washington Monument to dramatize the problem. Another supporter suggested holding a Kick Butts Day. The name came from his son, he said, and he wasn't sure what it should be, but wasn't it a great name? We actually followed up on that one, launching Kick Butts Day in schools around the country. The kids came up with their own clever ideas, such as a mock trial with the Marlboro Man in the dock, and kids playing all the roles: judge, jury, defendant, prosecuting attorneys, and a courtroom full of students. Garry Trudeau, the creator of the Doonesbury comic strip, assigned us the use of his Mr. Butts character. Today, Kick Butts Day has grown into an international event, with thousands of participants.

My mother was pleased with the news coverage but unhappy about some of the details. A reporter from the *Pittsburgh Post-Gazette,* looking for a local angle, asked me what I thought about Burson-Marsteller doing tobacco work in their Pittsburgh office. I criticized the PR agency's efforts on behalf of Philip Morris and went on to say that the entire marketing communications industry needs to examine its conscience about promoting tobacco-related disease. In the story, the reporter said I was from Pittsburgh. Mom wanted a correction to say I was from Bridgeville.

Not long after we got started, I got a call from Rob Gould at Burson-Marsteller. He said, "Bill, the tobacco people are doing a dossier on you." A little nervous, I asked him what kind of information they were collecting. He said, "They want to know everything, but especially, are you competent, can you hurt them?" Then he added, "I told them you were totally incompetent. You don't have to worry about a thing!"

In the first 60 days, we ran three tough newspaper ads, each aimed at policy makers, thought leaders, and the tobacco industry more than at the general public. The photos in these ads were of kids holding cigarettes, an arresting look. While we wanted to attack smoking broadly, including adult use and its effect on families, we had "kids" in our name, and we led with children as the most vulnerable victims of tobacco.

The first ad headline read "The Tobacco Industry Can't Be Trusted with America's Children." The second was "Can You Name America's Most Advertised Cigarette Brands? She Can" (referring to the girl in the ad). And the third was a clear message to Capitol Hill: "What Are Tobacco Lobbyists Trying to Buy from Congress?" The White House wasn't happy with the last one. They were concerned that it implicated Democrats in taking tobacco money as much as Republicans. Well, if the shoe fits. Through Matt Myers and others, we also began coordinating with the Clinton

White House and with health and human services secretary Donna Shalala's chief of staff, Kevin Thurm (now head of the Clinton Foundation). It was Kevin who suggested we call ourselves a "campaign" to signify action and immediacy.

We didn't have much money or size, but we were causing trouble and stirring the pot. Just what a Tobacco Institute for the good guys should be doing. We were on the map. But nobody said startups are easy, and tobacco was an especially nasty challenge.

The tobacco companies were (and still are) enormously wealthy and powerful. They employed a skilled army of lawyers, lobbyists, and PR and ad agencies. They sold an addictive product, were accepted as legitimate companies by corporate America, and had a heavy influence, including through financial contributions, on Congress and state politicians. In addition, they had smooth, well-honed public and policy messages that went like this:

- Tobacco use is an individual choice and a right. After all, it is a legal product.
- Tobacco-related disease is the user's responsibility. Caveat emptor.
- Government intrusion is bad and dangerous. Watch out, other companies and industries (e.g., fast food); if they come down on us, you could be next.
- The science about tobacco harm is in doubt. (It certainly was; the industry knew about the danger of their products and had been concealing it for years, as well as hiring "experts" to question legitimate research.)
- Kids will be kids. They might experiment with smoking and chewing, but we don't want kids to use our products, and we—the industry—will educate youth.

I once sat next to a research director for Leo Burnett, the ad agency for the Marlboro account. I asked him how he justified researching the best way to market cigarettes. He hesitated and then said, "Well, I just like to think that our advertising isn't too effective." Wow, what a way to make a living. But in reality, tobacco marketing *was* effective.

In fact, today it's hard to remember how sexy and alluring tobacco marketing was. The Marlboro Man was a handsome, rugged individualist. Joe Camel was super cool. The Salem couple was clearly having a world of fun. They flooded the world with what we called trinkets and trash, but in truth they had great merchandise like gym bags, clothing, and other goodies. Point-of-sale merchandising was powerful. They were terrific marketers. We had our work cut out for us.

The next challenge was to make our organization strong and financially sustainable. John Seffrin, CEO of the American Cancer Society, and I, along with several of John's staff, went to meet with Steve Schroeder, Nancy Kaufman, and their RWJF team. Steve's board was serious about providing major support but wanted other organizations involved. They didn't want to go it alone.

John stepped up. He said he would take the concept of the Campaign for Tobacco-Free Kids back to his board and do everything he could to get funding. And he did—a commitment of $2 million a year—based on a letter I was asked to write making the recommendation. With John's involvement, Steve could now ask his foundation board to make a major commitment. Then they turned to me. Was I going to commit to all this? Of course I was. I also said that we were going to be extremely aggressive in attacking the tobacco industry. Everyone was in.

The first thing I did back in Washington was to meet with Matt Myers in his law firm. A leader in the fight against tobacco for years, he was working informally with us as we put things into place. I asked Matt to join the campaign if the money materialized. He agreed, and we shook on the deal. He would be senior vice president and general counsel. It took him several months to extract himself from his firm and come on board full time, but he was a big contributor on a part-time basis.

The money came through. Two months later, in January 1996, the RWJF board approved an initial investment of $20 million in the campaign, plus $10 million more later if progress was made. The Annie E. Casey and Conrad N. Hilton Foundations came up with some funding at Steve's request. The American Heart Association also contributed and became an important partner. Peter Angelos (later the owner of the Baltimore Orioles), Dickie Scruggs, and some other trial lawyers contributed, and other money came our way.

We had solid governance from the earliest days, with a strong board of directors, including John Seffrin; Ernie Fleishman, a senior vice president at Scholastic, Inc.; Chris Conley, a financial services executive (who remains on the board today); and Diane Disney Miller, a philanthropist. Later, Lonnie Bristow of the American Medical Association and Dudley Hafner, CEO of the American Heart Association, joined our board. We were in business.

Criticizing ad and PR agencies wasn't going over well with that industry, which was fine with us. We wanted them to think about what they were doing by representing tobacco. As a result, there was a great deal of coverage in the trade media, including a positive editorial in *Advertising Age* calling for the reform of tobacco marketing.

The White House invited us to an event with President Clinton, where we would be invited to talk about our new campaign. RWJF didn't want us to go because they didn't want to be seen as too chummy with one political party over another or too tied to the administration. This was disappointing, because to make progress we did have to align with the president. We soon persuaded the foundation to let us call the shots. No micromanagement. President Clinton held the event with a group of kids, and he praised our new organization. With this and the media coverage of our launch, we were off to a good start.

Later in the year we held our first event, with Secretary Shalala (now a member of Congress), Steve Schroeder, and George Dessart, the chairman of the American Cancer Society board and a former CBS executive who taught the TV Lab at Annenberg, a favorite class and where I courted Fran back in college. We gave our first award, the Youth Advocate of the Year, to Anna Santiago, a poised eighth grader from Chicago. The idea of youth advocacy came from the American Heart Association; today our Youth Advocates of the Year Awards (YAYA) is a huge annual event, and the campaign supports thousands of youth advocates across the country.

President Clinton soon held another event, this time in the Rose Garden, to announce the FDA rule claiming regulatory jurisdiction over tobacco and restricting tobacco marketing and sales to kids. David Kessler, surgeon general C. Everett Koop, Secretary Shalala, and a number of our partners were there, including Lonnie Bristow, a campaign board member and president of the American Medical Association. We attended and supplied the kids who appeared on stage with the president, including our youth advocate, Anna Santiago.

The tobacco industry countered aggressively, and over the coming months things heated up. We took advantage of every opportunity to make news and criticize Big Tobacco. We held press conferences based on surveys about how kids thought tobacco marketing was aimed at them, tobacco companies' political contributions, the Virginia Slims "Woman Thing Music" promotion, a tobacco industry junket for members of Congress, and a media event with African American groups angry about a new Camel menthol product they said was targeted to black youth and adult smokers. We tackled what we thought would draw media attention, and we were good at it.

In addition to working the media and putting pressure on policy makers, we took care to stay in good contact with our funders and partners. Once Steve Schroeder got RWJF involved, that foundation invested more than $700 million through 2009, according to a report called *The Tobacco Campaigns* summarizing their efforts. Through 2010, they spent about $90 million of that money on our campaign, and Steve's successor, Risa Lavizzo-Mourey, continued to invest, although at a lower level.

RWJF had another smart strategy: its SmokeLess States program, a network of state-level coalitions that undertook public education, community and state-based increases in excise taxes, tobacco marketing restrictions, and other tactics. The tobacco industry fought back hard at the state level, pouring money and lobbyists into the battle, but the public health community more than held its own. We supported state and local coalitions through information and data sharing, model legislation, advertising and other media support, and our voice at the national level. Pete Fisher, our state coordinator, knew more about state-by-state activities than anyone else in the country.

Danny McGoldrick, Patricia Sosa, and Anne Ford joined us. They turned out to be stars and are still on the campaign team today.

Support for the FDA was a top priority, and Anne, Matt, and others worked the Hill hard, urging members of Congress and their staffs to get behind the FDA. We backed up this lobbying with aggressive communications and engaged state allies. We ran a TV spot with voiceover saying: "Tobacco companies say they don't target kids, but the facts tell a different story." Our print ads zeroed in on specific Senate candidates: "When it comes to tobacco, will South Dakota's Senate candidates stand with America's kids?" The ad went on to name Larry Pressler (R-SD) and Tim Johnson (D-SD) along with their office phone numbers. We didn't have the money the tobacco industry did, but when our efforts were combined with news placements (often built around polling showing strong public support for the FDA to limit youth access to tobacco) and other media relations, we made a difference.

Sabrina Corlette of Senator Tom Harkin's (D-IA) staff said that the FDA had us to thank for the funding to enforce their rule. She credited us, working with the public health community in key states, with turning the votes around. Our partners were pleased as well. "If there were no Campaign, we'd have to invent one. No one else is out there with the same goals," said Susan Hildebrandt of the American Association of Family Physicians. John Seffrin told his American Cancer Society board and staff that the campaign's ability to make tobacco policy a front-burner issue was a watershed change.

We developed other strategies: to try to exert pressure on stockholders in tobacco companies, we put together a "Tobacco Road" initiative in the tobacco states, where tobacco growers were hostile to tobacco control efforts and, as we saw it, were being used as pawns by the tobacco companies.

One strategy that didn't work was to attack tobacco executives directly. "Does Your Mother Know What You're Doing?" was a test campaign to shame senior tobacco company employees and build on public dislike for the industry. But when we tested the concepts, we found that although people might revile tobacco companies, they didn't like direct criticism of individuals.

We kept after the marketing communications industry, from which I had come. But our Madison Avenue initiative soon stalled out. The American Association of Advertising Agencies and the National Advertising Review Council debated and then rejected age-sensitive guidelines for tobacco, alcohol, and other products. Then they announced that they were seriously considering a public service campaign to persuade kids not to smoke. This was a red herring, and not even a good one. To add to the insult, they said they were looking for a nonprofit client to pay for the campaign.

I said we would, just to call their bluff. We needed to keep the pressure on.

At that point we had an annual budget of $9.2 million and were gaining momentum. But we didn't have the money for a major national youth campaign against smoking and spit tobacco (our icky term for chewing tobacco). It wasn't until some years later, when the American Legacy Foundation (now the Truth Initiative) was created with tobacco settlement money, that this effort became possible.

We also had our detractors, even within the community of anti-tobacco organizations. Some state groups that had been working on the issue for years felt we were taking over and trying to lead the parade. Several prominent academics and advocates questioned why we had been anointed the chosen ones and had all this money. Several minority groups asked the same questions, including the Rev. Jesse Brown and the National Association of African Americans for Positive Imagery. Even the ever-popular Joe Garagiola, who had been my boyhood favorite when he played for the Pittsburgh Pirates before he became a household name as a broadcaster on the *Today* show, was piqued. He had been visiting major league clubhouses to warn against the dangers of chewing tobacco, and he was annoyed that we were now soaking up resources. I saw him at a White House event, and Joe said, "Where's *my* money?"

The American Lung Association (ALA) was smaller than the American Heart Association and the American Cancer Society, and the ALA didn't contribute funding to our campaign. They had been part of the earlier Coalition on Smoking OR Health, and they worked hard to be major players in the tobacco wars. At one point, their Washington office thought we had not adequately cooperated with them and sent a directive to their field offices saying we had not been sufficiently candid and that they did not support our state ads. We patched things up, but never completely.

This competition for money and leadership is common in every issue I've ever worked on. Some of it is the struggle for scarce resources. Part of it stems from the conviction and passion people bring to fighting for important causes. And part of it may be me. I've never been as good as I should be at placating the many diverse players among the social organizations. As long as the tobacco industry was the common enemy and the strategy was attack, attack, attack, there was virtual unanimity. But as soon as things got more complicated, disagreements emerged. These issues later came to a head in a major, painful way during our negotiations with the tobacco industry.

Negotiating with the Tobacco Industry

As a result of the surge in youth smoking and chewing tobacco use in the 1990s, the United States was in turmoil over tobacco: leaked documents, whistleblowers, lawsuits, congressional action, and above all, a mounting concern for bringing some level of accountability to the tobacco industry. When Philip Morris chairman Geoffrey Bible was asked in a 1998 *Wall Street Journal* article if anyone had died from smoking cigarettes, he replied, "I don't know if anyone dies from smoking tobacco, I just don't know."

State attorneys general (AGs), with their lawsuits against the industry started by Mississippi's Mike Moore, were ramping up the pressure. Led by Bible, the industry reportedly wanted to cool down the furor and achieve legislative, legal, and marketplace certainty in which to conduct their business. In early April 1997 the industry entered into secret negotiations with the state AGs to try to reach a settlement. Three former Senate majority leaders—George Mitchell (D-ME), Bob Dole (R-KS), and Howard Baker (R-TN)—represented the industry and opened the initial sessions. The White House, through Vice President Al Gore, got our Campaign for Tobacco-Free Kids into the talks, and Matt Myers, our general counsel (and himself a trial lawyer), was our representative.

Anne Ford, our chief lobbyist, sometimes sat in, and as the Campaign's CEO, I also attended some of the sessions. In late April, the negotiations were leaked to the *Wall Street Journal,* and a firestorm erupted.

Some members of the public health community, legislators, and others were outraged. How dare you sit down with the enemy? Who appointed you to speak for us? Why didn't we know about this? We issued this public statement:

> Our objective in participating has been to ensure that the views of the public health community are expressed. . . . [These views] have been critical to these discussions. Our goal has been to ensure that the opportunity for fundamental change not be lost or compromised away, that nothing be done to weaken the FDA rule to protect children from the marketing and sale of tobacco products or to weaken FDA authority to oversee the tobacco industry. We have consulted with the leadership of the American Cancer Society, the American Heart Association, the American Academy of Pediatrics, the American Medical Association, and the American Lung Association in formulating viewpoints for these discussions.

This didn't quiet things down in the least. The surgeon general, C. Everett Koop, attacked the "deal," as did a number of prominent tobacco control advocates around the country. But we kept at it. Each evening after the talks, we would go over the day's negotiations on the phone with our leadership group—Dudley Hafner, CEO of the American Heart Association; Lonnie Bristow, a member of our board and president of the American Medical Association; Richard Heyman of the American Academy of Pediatrics; and John Seffrin, CEO of the American Cancer Society.

There was nonstop drama. Bennett LeBow, the CEO of the Brooke Group, the parent of the tobacco company Liggett, settled a case by admitting that tobacco causes disease, that nicotine is addictive, and that tobacco companies target kids. He released a trove of documents and agreed to make his company executives available for testimony. Several individual cases involving tobacco-related deaths were in the news. In the midst of all this, we were scrambling to get our allies to support the negotiations and us. The media were reporting dissension among the anti-tobacco forces. They were right.

Matt and I went to see Congressman Henry Waxman (D-CA), who had been a strong voice against tobacco for years. In 1994 he had held a famous hearing with the CEOs of all the major American tobacco companies. A widely published photo showed each of them, hands raised in solemn oath, declaring that tobacco does not cause disease and is not addictive. It was a powerful reminder of the industry's arrogance and lack of accountability.

Waxman was furious—at us. He said there was nothing the tobacco industry could give us that we couldn't get another way, that they were on the ropes, and that we could finish them off without negotiations. He was the negotiator and legislator, he said, and we were the advocates—so go out and advocate, and stop interfering.

I was amazed. One of the strongest, richest industries in the world, with huge clout in Congress, was on the ropes? Years later Henry Waxman used that same argument with me with regard to Medicare and prescription drugs. I'm the legislator; you're just the advocate. I didn't buy it in 1997 with tobacco, and I didn't buy it later when I was at AARP fighting to get prescription drugs covered under Medicare (see chapter 4). That time he called me to say he understood what I was doing and he ultimately agreed with it. But not this time, not with tobacco. And Waxman was a force.

He held a press conference and invited many of our partners, plus David Kessler. Our partners told us they knew Waxman was working to split us apart but believed they had to attend. He spoke against what he called "immunity" for the tobacco companies but stopped short of calling for the negotiations to be halted.

We asked the American Cancer Society to hold a conference where we hoped to convince all the players to wait and see what negotiations with the industry would yield. Nearly all the interested parties came, including a number of tobacco researchers and policy experts. Congressman Waxman and two of his aides showed up, and he was invited to speak. He said the talks were a mistake, that we were advocates for a deal, that whatever went to Congress would be changed, and that he himself would bring amendments. He called for a halt to the negotiations. Mike Moore spoke and was effective in explaining what the state AGs were negotiating and that the conclusions would be debated in the full light of day.

Then all the organizations went to a separate room to discuss the situation. They decided to support continuing the negotiations via our Campaign, to add Lonnie Bristow to our negotiating team, to give the American Cancer Society the option of adding another negotiator, to run a national ad espousing our collective core principles, and to form an executive committee of all the organizations and a technical committee of research and policy experts. All the groups except the American Lung Association agreed. We thought we had achieved a measure of unity, but in fact the strife continued.

We were constantly attacked, and it became clear that there were dissenters within the ranks of our allies, even within our own Campaign. Everybody had an opinion. It got silly at times. A relative of Ralph Nader (the well-known social advocate who had taken on automobile safety and other issues) picketed our offices. Fringe groups were accusing us of selling out public health.

Matt and I went to a status meeting at the White House with Bruce Lindsey, the Clinton aide who was overseeing the administration's monitoring of the situation. Bruce Reed and Elena Kagan (now a Supreme Court justice) sat in. The discussion centered on achieving full FDA jurisdiction over tobacco while allaying the companies' fear that this was an open door to banning nicotine or cigarettes themselves. The industry wanted some legal protections, such as a cap on punitive damages. Was that possible? And how could we get the public health community on board with a good agreement and steer it through Congress? As we were leaving, we bumped into Rahm Emanuel (then a White House staffer), who said, "I'm of two minds: go for a fair deal with the industry, or kill it and go for what we already have in FDA authority." Everybody had an opinion.

The negotiations with the tobacco industry continued. In May 1997 I sat in on a day and a half of discussions. The state AGs were represented by Chris Gregoire of Washington State (later Washington's governor) and Tom Green, assistant to AG Scott Harshbarger of Massachusetts. The industry had a team of outside lawyers and company representatives. Chris was known for lightening things up with stories about her mother, a smoker who just couldn't quit. But the talks were anything but light. The sticking points remained the same: how to assign the FDA full authority over tobacco without enabling a ban on cigarettes, and whether and how to achieve some civil liability protection for the companies.

The AGs told the tobacco group that their proposed legal protections were too much and weren't acceptable. The response was a major pushback. The industry representatives said their CEOs were angry that the AGs kept pulling agreed-upon elements off the table, and they weren't sure they wanted to continue the discussions. Later they called to say they wanted a firm written proposal from the AGs. Matt and the AGs spent the next day working on it.

The AMA called another big meeting to give public health organizations an opportunity to be heard on the issue. Those opposed to the talks in any form were making a lot of noise, and the media were covering the food fight.

The next day David Kessler and I made speeches at the World No Tobacco Day event at the Pan American Health Organization.

Afterward Kessler told the media the negotiators were trying to do too much and "the deal wouldn't fly in its current form." He said the agreement had to be about public health and not about lawyers or money. I asked him exactly what he meant, and David said, "This is positioned wrong. You're an expert on positioning. Go reposition it."

He and C. Everett Koop set up a committee to bring public health groups together to discuss the situation, but it turned out to be a strategy to oppose the potential agreement. Jeff Nesbitt, who staffed the Koop-Kessler Committee, told me that Kessler was neutral but that he was not a fan of a liability shield for the industry. However, if there were a game plan for the eventual demise of the industry, even in 20 years, then he'd be willing to give them immunity. Later Kessler and Matt had a phone discussion, and Matt reported that Kessler opposed the deal. Matt asked him what we could do to make it more acceptable, and he said, "Think." So all we had to do was "reposition" and "think."

The coming weeks were a frenzy of activity: dueling press conferences, a Koop-Kessler Committee meeting, leaks to the media, constant discussions, a lobby day on the Hill, and our scramble to persuade individuals and organizations to hold their opinions in check until a final agreement was available for analysis and comment.

We talked to David Adelman, a stock analyst at Morgan Stanley who followed the tobacco industry. I asked him how he saw the future of tobacco in the United States if the settlement, as laid out at that moment, went forward. He said he would anticipate an immediate reduction in smoking and then a long-term decline. He drew an analogy to the market in the United Kingdom, where companies raised cigarette prices and cut costs every year. He noted that cigarettes then cost about $5 a pack and that the smoking trend was curving downward. In that situation, the long-term trend would be a decline in smoking while the industry would still make money. That might be a good scenario for us, given our smoking and disease epidemic, with more than 400,000 Americans a year dying from tobacco use.

There were constant last-minute snags in the negotiations. We wanted more document disclosure from the industry in the final agreement. The AGs wanted the tobacco company Brown & Williamson to drop its suit against Jeffrey Wigand, a whistleblower. B&W refused, and Mike Moore said, "We're not going to leave any prisoners on the beach." B&W finally gave in. The last negotiation session went on until 3 a.m., but on June 20, 1997, we emerged with an agreement.

We prepared our statements and went to the hotel for the big press conference. The AGs were all there, and the media were swarming. During the wait, Ralph Nader strolled up to the open microphones and cameras and gave an impromptu press conference of his own, in which he denounced the settlement. CNN carried him live.

This was perhaps the biggest press conference I've ever been part of. Eight attorneys general spoke. Bob Butterworth, the Florida AG, painted a vivid picture of the impact of the agreement, saying, "The Marlboro Man will now be going off into the sunset, riding Joe Camel." I spoke briefly about the importance of the settlement and how we would work to inform our members and the public. Lonnie Bristow stepped up to the mics and did the same, and then Matt talked about how this agreement brought true, fundamental change after years of working on the margins for tobacco control. After a long period of questions, a hard-nosed newspaperman from the *Los Angeles Times* said as I walked past, "Mazel tov."

The media coverage was national and enormous. The *New York Times*, where we had conducted what I thought was a positive briefing, editorialized against the settlement agreement. The *Washington Post*, where I believed our editorial board meeting had gone badly, came out with a well-balanced editorial. So much for my knowledge of positioning.

Selling the Deal

The summer of 1997 was a blur of activity. Every organization and individual who had a stake in the outcome, and many others who did not, worked to promote their viewpoint. For us, the key questions were: How could we rally the public behind a settlement agreement that would reduce tobacco use, give the FDA authority, and at the same time—the big sticking point—offer the industry some limited liability? How could we bring the public health community to a unified stance on all this? And how could we lobby members of Congress as they were considering their interests and angling for jurisdiction in the legislative action to come? Meanwhile, the Clinton White House and the Department of Health and Human Services (HHS) were working on their analysis of the situation from a policy, and certainly from a political, standpoint.

Koop and Kessler held another committee meeting on what they saw as the flaws in the AG agreement. Although Matt and I had agreed to keep a low profile there, I finally had to speak up. I said that the war against tobacco was not being won, that the industry could carry on its business, and that we needed the resources and interventions in the agreement to reduce tobacco use among children and adults. The debate continued, and the media reported it as an outcome hostile to the settlement agreement.

We met periodically at a law firm with various players, including representatives of the tobacco industry, to share information, although not much was being shared. Among the industry people, Steve Parrish, senior vice president for corporate affairs at Philip Morris, stood out as a spokesperson, partly thanks to his cool demeanor and partly because Philip Morris was the dominant company in Big Tobacco.

We worked the media hard and gave speeches all over the country to present our case in support of the settlement agreement. Often we would debate opponents of the agreement, or at least critics—including members of Congress. One of my more challenging outings was at the Cato Institute, a libertarian think tank that enjoyed sticking needles in both Democratic and Republican policies. Bill Pryor, attorney general of Alabama, and Bob Levy of Cato squared off against Dennis Vacco, attorney general of New York, and me. It was a full house, with lots of journalists attending. I think we won, primarily because libertarians seem to have a tough time applying their free choice and personal responsibility arguments to kids, who aren't old enough to think for themselves. At one point Levy said he'd grant me the kids issue if I would say that they could all quit smoking, as they wished, at age 18. The libertarians didn't want to accept nicotine addiction as a reason people don't quit. It interferes with their philosophy.

The White House continued to play an active role. In July we discussed the situation with White House aides to the president, including Bruce Lindsey, Bruce Reed, and Elena Kagan. We came away thinking it had been a productive discussion. They said they would further sound out the industry and Congress. They seemed to lean toward having the president announce his position before he left for vacation in mid-August.

Our partners were dealing with their boards and management, who all wanted to weigh in. The American Cancer Society held a press conference and issued a statement with so many ifs, ands, and buts that it was almost ambiguous, although they stayed with us. Much more positive, the American Heart Association and American Academy of Pediatrics called the agreement a major opportunity and added that improvements were needed. The American Medical Association was also leaning to the positive side.

Mike Moore and his AG colleagues and their own lawyers (yes, lawyers have lawyers) met on the Hill and heard just about every opinion, including complaints about how high lawyers' fees were in all this. Alan Kaplan, an analyst with Merrill Lynch, told us we were never going to reduce kid smoking and that the lawyers were getting filthy rich. It's always good to have encouragement like that.

Later, when Senator John McCain took on the Senate leadership of the settlement legislation as chairman of the Finance Committee, he would say, "Remember, it's always darkest before . . . things turn completely black." We weren't there yet; we still saw glimmers of light.

The industry signaled that they were willing to give in on several issues: elements of FDA authority and the so-called look-back penalties (how much tobacco companies would have to pay if smoking among kids did not decline to specified levels). Congressman Tom Bliley (R-VA), known as the congressman from Philip Morris, had House jurisdiction over the impending legislation. He and other Republicans in both Houses were said to be waiting for Clinton to pronounce on the settlement before taking action. Many of our partners said they were waiting for the same thing. Along with our allies, we drafted a letter calling for the president to lead in creating a national tobacco control policy based on comprehensive legislation that would result in a national, sustainable program to reduce tobacco use in America.

In the midst of all this, a Fourth Circuit Court of Appeals hearing was held in Roanoke in which the tobacco industry appealed a lower-court decision giving the FDA jurisdiction over tobacco. Several of us attended; it was a lesson in legal maneuvering and oratory. Acting solicitor general Walter Dellinger argued for the government. He didn't fare well. The tobacco industry's top lawyer in the hearing was superb, although one of his arguments was Kafkaesque. He said tobacco is a harmful and dangerous product, and if the FDA were granted jurisdiction it would have no choice but to ban the substance. He went on to say that the FDA should not have this authority; only Congress should. In other words, tobacco is too dangerous to be regulated. For his part, Dellinger had to argue that the FDA wouldn't ban tobacco. The judges asked why Congress shouldn't be responsible for all this. Everyone present knew the answer, as far as I was concerned. Congress was under the influence of the tobacco industry. Money and nicotine are both addictive.

After the hearing, the media asked my opinion of the proceedings. Not being a lawyer, and of the opinion that the tobacco industry had won the day, I gamely answered that judges often act as the devil's advocate and that they would determine that the FDA had a strong case. The media weren't so equivocal. They reported that the industry had bested the government that day, and Gary Black, a Wall Street analyst, said the government "got creamed."

The AGs told us that behind the scenes the White House was asking for more from the industry and that it looked like we would have to go back to the negotiating table. Koop told me we were taking the wrong tack and that you have to demand a lot more in negotiations to get what you really want. He didn't realize how tough the negotiations were, with lawyers battling lawyers and no quarter given.

Things were getting personal. Stan Glantz, a professor at the University of California, San Francisco, and a tobacco control proponent, continued to attack the deal, and us in particular. He sent out a broadside saying several lawyers had told him that I called Koop and Kessler "extremists." I refuted it on the grounds that it wasn't true. Besides, I couldn't imagine any lawyers who would talk to Glantz. But he and his allies kept stirring the pot. They argued that an agreement would give "immunity" to the industry, that Big Tobacco should never be trusted or negotiated with, and that the rest of the world would suffer if the agreement went through because it would free up Philip Morris and other companies to train their firepower and seductive marketing on markets outside the United States. The latter argument was their main refrain at an international tobacco control conference we attended in Beijing that year (1997). It echoed a concern raised by some tobacco control advocates from other countries, who were worried that the United States would solve its problem at the expense of the rest of the world. In truth, though, the tobacco industry was already effectively plying its trade across the globe.

The White House Weighs In

Rather than announce his position on the settlement and his administration's role, President Clinton went on vacation to Martha's Vineyard, not to return until mid-September. There was lots of time for squabbling while he was gone. Finally, in mid-September, the president held a session in the Oval Office with nearly all the factions. He said he was building on the attorneys' general settlement and called for an increase of $1.50 a pack if youth smoking didn't decline. But he said this price hike could be phased in over 10 years. Beyond that, he didn't call for a specific course of action. He talked about making the deal better and said his administration would provide the leadership that was needed. He said nothing about liability protection for the industry and then avoided the subject in later questions. HHS secretary Donna Shalala commented that the objective was to get all the public health provisions in place and then focus on liability, which was not a deal breaker.

The AGs weren't happy, and we and our partners weren't either, but Koop and Kessler seemed supportive of Clinton's comments. As soon as the session ended, Minnesota AG Skip Humphrey, who was preparing to run for governor, hustled outside to the waiting media and declared that the "tobacco bailout is dead."

Republicans were caustic. While House speaker Newt Gingrich was uncharacteristically silent, Congressman Tom ("the Hammer") DeLay (R-TX) made a scathing comment about Clinton and his buddies the trial lawyers. Congressman Bliley said he was disappointed that Clinton had taken so long only to bring forth generalities. Bliley said he cared about youth smoking and would hold hearings. He was also reported to be angry with the tobacco industry, normally his allies, for not letting him know they had been in negotiations with the AGs and us. Later in the fall, at his first hearing, Bliley showed his irritation by demanding some 800 Liggett documents that were supposedly not covered by attorney-client privilege and said he would issue a subpoena if they were not handed over.

The Battle Rages On

Now it was back to the battleground. Our coalition, which we had named ENACT, now counted 11 members, including our stalwarts—the American Heart Association, the American Cancer Society, and the American Medical Association. Others were the Association of State and Territorial Health Officials, the National Association of County and City Health Officials, the Partnership for Prevention, and a number of medical specialty groups (American Academies of Pediatrics and Family Physicians, American College of Chest Physicians, and American College of Preventive Medicine). Later the American Psychological Association came on board.

We were opposed by a rival public health coalition (Save Lives, Not Tobacco) overseen by Tom Downey, a lobbyist and former congressman, and reportedly funded by Mike Ciresi, a lawyer and colleague of Skip Humphrey, and supported by Henry Waxman. The overall result was an alphabet soup of organizations putting out media releases and looking for an edge. Senator Dick Durbin (D-IL) implored the public health community to come together. Fat chance.

At a conference in Houston, I realized how many people in the field believed that the American Lung Association, Skip Humphrey, and our other opponents were right in fighting a deal with Big Tobacco. They seemed to think that Congress could pass legislation imposing a big tax on tobacco and other favorable provisions without Republicans and the industry going along.

I told Steve Schroeder, president of the Robert Wood Johnson Foundation and our financial benefactor, that we may need more money to win the battle for public opinion, to generate broader support from the public health community, and to achieve favorable legislation. Later we agreed to add $6 million to our spending for the coming year, and we selected districts and states for targeted advertising, media, and events. It wasn't nearly enough. Failing to aggressively follow up on this was a major mistake on my part (more on that later).

The personal attacks continued. A big, well-attended event at the National Press Club with Knight Ridder editorial staff included a panel session sponsored by Bloomberg, with Bruce Reed of the White House, Mike Moore, Phil Carlton representing the tobacco industry, and me. When it was time for questions, the usual opposition in the audience attacked the settlement. Then a relative of Ralph Nader went after me. He said I was a former PR executive who cut deals with the pesticide industry and was therefore the last person who should be representing public health. I had no idea what he was talking about. Afterward even our opponents came up to say, Don't take this stuff personally. OK, I won't.

At another meeting with Congressman Waxman, he was even more negative about the settlement and our role in it. He reiterated his previous argument that he, not us, would decide whether to compromise with the industry, that he didn't want us to enter further negotiations, and that we should join with the opposing coalition, which he was supporting. Then he asked where our money came from and whom we had hired as lobbyists. We were politely nonresponsive.

One of our lobbyists was Vin Weber, a good strategist and a former Republican congressman from Minnesota. He and our team met with the staff of the House Republican leadership, who were gearing up for the tobacco legislation fight.

There was also a flurry of legal activity. A class action suit in Pennsylvania against tobacco companies was dismissed, a state suit in Texas was delayed, and a suit brought by flight attendants was settled, apparently with big money for the lawyers and virtually nothing for the flight attendants. The media interpreted these results as signs of the continuing legal strength of the industry and the need for some sort of settlement.

There were lots of dueling poll numbers. In October 1997 the *Wall Street Journal* reported that Congressman Bliley had survey data showing that the more the public knew about the settlement, the less they liked it. That's not what our research showed. The day before, the *Wall Street Journal* had reported that momentum was swinging toward settlement legislation.

The AGs and the industry, with Matt's involvement from our coalition, continued to work on settlement language, incorporating Clinton's stipulations and adding stronger FDA language. The tobacco companies were unhappy because more and more demands were being piled on them. They weren't naïve about Washington, but they complained that they thought they had had a deal.

On New Year's Day 1998 the *Washington Post* published a lucid, comprehensive, and positive editorial. It captured the situation we faced as a country with a youth tobacco epidemic. It said, in part,

> The principal test the president and Congress will face [this] year . . . is literally a matter of life and death. . . . The demands are not just political but moral. . . . The question . . . is whether they can set aside normal politics long enough to pass decent, comprehensive tobacco legislation. . . . The outlines of the possible bill are

familiar. . . . The companies want relief from future liability from further lawsuits . . . for the insidious health effects of the addictive product they have sold with a full understanding of those effects for years. . . . In return for the limited liability, they would pay a sum of money . . . about a third of a trillion dollars over 25 years—and submit to various kinds of regulations, including advertising and other marketing restrictions. . . . Not a bad framework if the details are right—but those of course are the hard part. . . . The last thing this bill should contain is a retreat from current regulatory authority. . . . This is an issue on which the politicians can't afford to play the usual games.

The state of play was this: we were in the midst of a youth to-bacco epidemic, the AGs took on the industry, and now Congress and the Clinton administration had to work through the complexities and deal with proposed major legislation that had a million moving parts. The public health community was split, and the battle was fierce.

We learned that the tobacco industry had considered a major ad campaign in support of the settlement but backed off because they thought it might backfire. Frank Raines, President Clinton's director of the Office of Management and Budget, said on TV that the administration projected billions in settlement money in the coming year's budget, that the legislation had widespread support, and that they expected it to pass. We got calls from government officials and others saying that there were lots of important uses for the settlement money. Everyone saw dollar signs dancing in front of them.

Along with the White House aides, we continued to talk to the industry and various trial lawyers. These talks didn't reveal much, but we had the impression that Big Tobacco had lost influence on the Hill, although we couldn't gauge how much. But this shift played into the hands of Congressman Waxman and others who claimed that the tobacco companies were vulnerable and that we didn't need to negotiate with them to control tobacco use in America.

Around this time the Justice Department took criminal action against a small biotech firm and named Brown & Williamson as an unindicted co-conspirator, charging that they had illegally imported high-nicotine tobacco leaf. This revelation led legislators and our opposition to say that these people couldn't be trusted and certainly did not merit "immunity."

In late January 1998 Congressman Bliley and his House Commerce Committee held a hearing with the heads of the five major US tobacco companies. The company officials acted contrite, saying they would reform their industry and turn over non-privileged documents from Skip Humphrey's Minnesota trial, which was now underway.

We held a media briefing with excellent attendance and good questions from reporters. The very next day the opposing coalition, Save Lives, Not Tobacco, held its own media event to denounce "immunity." John Garrison of the American Lung Association was their featured speaker. This infighting continued for months.

In his 1998 State of the Union address, President Clinton called for national comprehensive tobacco control legislation to protect kids from smoking. I went to a White House event where Vice President Gore and HHS Secretary Shalala presented huge increases in the National Institutes of Health budget for cancer research. What they didn't say was that this was essentially money they were counting on from the settlement. I gave Secretary Shalala an article from *Roll Call* saying that GOP leadership was ready to pull the plug on comprehensive tobacco control legislation and looking at a much smaller bill as a way out of the dilemma. That way they could say in the upcoming midterm elections that they had done something about the problem. I told her that we needed more push and more leadership from the administration. "We're providing the leadership," she said as she took the article.

We met with Congressman Bliley and his staff. Bliley was a tall, courtly man with a sharp edge. He was angry at the White House because he said Clinton was talking about principles, not specifics. This seemed disingenuous because Congress was supposed to be drafting the legislation. He criticized the president for his budget, which projected billions in tobacco settlement money. If the money materializes, said Bliley, we'll give it back to the people who earned it. I wasn't sure who that was supposed to be. His main gripe was that the White House wasn't being specific on industry liability protection, the biggest sticking point in the whole package. A White House official told him it wasn't a deal breaker. "Good," said Bliley sarcastically. "Now what does that mean?"

As an aside, I saw Tom Bliley a few years after all this. Fran and I were at the wedding of the granddaughter of my uncle, Dan Dorchak, who had been president of the Bliley Co. Funeral Home, Congressman Bliley's family business. When we bumped into each other outside the church, Bliley said with a small smile, "You aren't going to cause trouble today, are you, Bill?" No Congressman, no trouble—not today.

But it was then back to the White House for another strategy session. Administration officials said collaboration with Congressional Republicans wasn't working. Thus their strategy was to find or concoct a bipartisan bill and try to rally enough support to move it forward. I sat there thinking that this whole thing was precarious, and maybe falling apart. The White House was not the juggernaut I expected. Clinton was in the middle of the Monica Lewinsky scandal; could that have something to do with it? We were losing momentum and at risk of losing national comprehensive settlement legislation.

Throughout February 1998 the infighting within the public health community continued. The media thrived on the controversy. Koop and Kessler pounded on the theme of "no immunity" for the tobacco industry. They got several of our ENACT members to sign on to a letter they handed out at a press conference the same day as their *Journal of the American Medical Association* article to the same effect. The American Medical Association fired a number of staff who were working with us after the AMA pulled back from an ill-conceived plan to endorse Sunbeam products. As a result, they became less effective, and tobacco seemed to drop off their priority list. When the AMA's House of Delegates voted to oppose any immunity for the industry, they essentially defected. We had lost one of the core members of our ENACT coalition.

We were scrambling to recover and regain momentum. In March 1998 we held a media conference to introduce clear and concise position papers detailing where we stood. I also argued that we badly needed marketing curbs on the industry, and such curbs were part of the settlement agreement. I showed the current swimsuit issue of *Sports Illustrated*, which featured a sexy swimsuit model on one page and on the facing page an equally sexy model in a Camel ad with a camel tattoo on her arm. I wasn't at a loss for examples.

For a survey we conducted of registered voters, we asked Republican staff on the Hill to help shape the questionnaire. The results were mixed. Respondents had positive attitudes toward FDA regulation and protecting kids from tobacco, but a large percentage of Republican voters were concerned about federal government involvement.

Our ENACT coalition participated in a media conference with Senators Tom Harkin (D-IA), John Chafee (R-RI), and Bob Graham (D-FL) as they introduced their bill. It had all the public health provisions we wanted, without the extra money the Clinton administration was calling for. It also contained an $8 billion liability cap for the industry but no other liability protection. Our spokespersons were John Seffrin (American Cancer Society), Cass

Wheeler (who had taken over as CEO of the American Heart Association), and Bill Roper of Partnership for Prevention (and later head of the Centers for Disease Control in the George W. Bush administration).

Senator McCain, as chairman of the Senate Finance Committee, was given the leadership role in the tobacco legislation. He and Senator Orrin Hatch (R-UT) were working on a bill, and their staff asked us to help draft language. McCain was a good choice for us. Even though his committee had members favorable to the industry, John McCain was not afraid of crossing GOP leadership in the Senate. The Harkin-Chafee-Graham bill was introduced, and we hoped it might influence what McCain would produce. Congressman Bliley, supposedly still annoyed at the industry, was keeping his own counsel. There was little action in the House, although Bliley and McCain were said to be talking. President Clinton picked up the pace and was pushing harder for legislation in his speeches.

Through the rest of March, McCain's staff and the Finance Committee worked on a comprehensive bill, but they didn't seem to be consulting with or involving Big Tobacco. Everyone was posturing about loading up the settlement agreement with more money, more restrictions, and less legal protection. The state attorneys general were busy promoting the agreement they had negotiated. There was a fervor to see who was toughest on tobacco.

In the midst of all this, I went to Florida to review and assist with the state's new tobacco control program, to be paid for with settlement money (Democratic governor Lawton Chiles had settled with the industry). It proved to be a preview of what grew into the Truth campaign, which later played a significant national role in persuading kids to reject tobacco. The ad agency, Crispin Porter Bogusky, and the PR agency, Porter Novelli (yes, my alma mater) developed a program around youth advocacy that they tentatively called RAGE. The idea was not to communicate how harmful tobacco was but instead to turn kids' natural tendencies to rebel against the right target. That target was the bad guys in suits—the tobacco industry executives—who were marketing to kids as the replacement smokers for the adults who would die from addiction. This evolved into one of the greatest public health campaigns of all time. A year later the pro-tobacco forces in the Florida legislature tried to eliminate the program because it was working so well.

McCain's bill was voted out of the Commerce Committee, 19 to 1, and would cost the industry about $506 billion over 25 years, compared with $368.5 billion in the original AG settlement. The Centers for Disease Control and Prevention published new data showing that tobacco use among kids had risen again, with past-month tobacco use among boys (cigarettes, cigars, smokeless tobacco) above 50 percent.

Winning a Battle Does Not Mean Winning the War

Now things took a dramatic turn. Steven Goldstone, the CEO of RJR Nabisco (the parent company of Reynolds), took the stage at the National Press Club in Washington and defiantly announced that the settlement was dead. The industry had entered into negotiations in good faith with the state AGs, he said, and it had made every effort to craft an agreement that would be in the interest of public health and provide reasonable protections to the industry. Now, Goldstone said, Washington—in its zeal to cash in—had piled on to the extent that the tobacco companies would no longer participate. He claimed that the industry would protect its interests and oppose any legislation.

This was where I compounded the mistake I had been making for the past nine months. I sat there in the Press Club and told myself that although the tobacco companies had plenty of clout and resources, there was no way they could win this new fight. With the Clinton administration and McCain and all of us, divided as we were, and with youth tobacco use climbing and the public concerned, we would win this legislative battle. Matt and I told the media just that as we exited the Press Club and all through the next day. We were wrong.

I should have gone back to Steve Schroeder months before and asked for enough money to mount a major national campaign to promote the settlement. I had requested an incremental amount, but it was not enough. And now was an even more important moment to go big. How much? Maybe $50 million for a national media and grassroots effort. Would the Robert Wood Johnson Foundation have given us the war chest that would fund all this? I've thought about it many times, and I don't know. Years later I asked Steve what the foundation would have done. He thought about it and said he didn't really know either.

We kept up the drumbeat with media conferences and interviews, strategy sessions with our partners, visits to the Hill and the White House, and presentations around the country, and we constantly worked the phones. Some Senate Democrats, including Kent Conrad (D-ND), Ted Kennedy (D-MA), Frank Lautenberg (D-NJ), and Ron Wyden (D-OR)—all strong advocates for tobacco control—held a hearing in late April to criticize the McCain bill and urge that it be toughened. Koop testified at great length about how weak the bill was. Congressman Bliley released the 39 documents he had demanded from the industry, which Minnesota AG Skip Humphrey had been calling "smoking howitzers."

Everyone was anti-industry, which was where the sentiment and the headlines lay. We were too. But we also wanted national comprehensive tobacco control legislation. There is a lesson here that has been repeated many, many times: there is no such thing as a perfect bill.

The *New York Times* and *Washington Post* both reported that House Republicans would craft a much narrower bill than McCain's Senate version. We and the American Cancer Society agreed to share the cost of ads aimed at House Republican leaders. One example: "Congresswoman Pryce [D-OH], are you going to stand with the tobacco industry or America's kids?" Matt and I had an op-ed in the *Washington Post* arguing that the McCain bill was a major opportunity that should be improved and supported. Newt Gingrich declared that Joe Camel had nothing to do with kids smoking. At the White House Correspondents' Dinner, President Clinton joked that Newt had just announced that Tony the Tiger has nothing to do with kids eating Frosted Flakes. Tobacco was everywhere in the media and in the political and policy spheres.

The president held another big White House event to keep the pressure on. Newly appointed surgeon general David Satcher released a report on tobacco and minorities showing that cigarette smoking was a major cause of disease and death among African Americans, Native Americans, Asian Americans and Pacific Islanders, and Hispanics. We were front and center at the event with colleagues from our ENACT coalition. A number of our youth advocates were on risers behind President Clinton and Vice President Gore, and Senator Bill Frist (R-TN) was prominent. He continued to try to build bridges.

We held strategy meetings with White House officials as well as with McCain, who was his usual darkly humorous self. He was almost proud of the attacks he was sustaining back in Arizona for his support of tobacco legislation. One ad read "What's happened to John McCain?" His fellow Republican senator Don Nickles (R-OK) said McCain's bill would come in at $890 billion over 25 years, not the $516 billion contained in the draft bill. Nichols said the numbers came from his staff. McCain said, "You've got a very creative staff; we had to get ours from the Treasury Department."

Then the real legislative battle began. The Senate started its tobacco debate in June 1998, and it went on all week. Our coalition set up a war room at the foot of Capitol Hill and worked every angle we could. At one point a coalition member came back to report that she had heard a member of Congress say, "Who are these public health people? They can't help us, and they can't hurt us." Several early amendments were defeated, and then the senators accepted an amendment from Senator Judd Gregg (R-NH) to strip away the liability cap and other legal protections for the industry. Both liberal and conservative members went for it. The liberals didn't want the industry to have any liability protections, and the conservatives wanted to gut the bill so it would fail. The Senate went into a recess; we tried to catch our breath and rally our troops. Then it began again.

I had a bad feeling when a cab driver told me he didn't like what was going on with the smoking stuff because there was too much big government at work. When the Senate resumed, more amendments flew; some of them were creatively designed to throw things off track. Phil Gramm (R-TX) proposed that the tobacco settlement money be used to end the marriage penalty tax. The Republican strategy was to load up the bill to make it too big and too much "tax and spend." McCain worked hard to keep things going. On June 17, after a long debate and intense media coverage, Senate majority leader Trent Lott (R-MS) held a GOP caucus meeting to decide what to do. The Republicans came back determined to defeat a cloture vote, which they did. We needed 60 votes and got 57. Then Senator Ted Stevens (R-AK) called for a budget point of order, which carried and meant the bill was removed from the floor of the Senate and sent back to the Commerce Committee. The bill was dead.

Picking Up the Pieces

As the legislation died, so did our opportunity for national tobacco control legislation to give the FDA authority over tobacco, to curb tobacco marketing, to require the industry to pay if youth smoking didn't decrease, and to enact a number of other important provisions. It was an enormous defeat. The administration and the

Democrats had added on too much money, and the Republicans didn't want the legislation in the first place. The industry players had walked away and succeeded in defeating the legislation they had come to abhor.

We were beaten up, devastated, and angry. Now what? Our reaction was to hold Congress accountable for kowtowing to the industry, to attack the tobacco companies even more vigorously, to try to bring the advocacy community together as best we could, and to redouble our efforts in the states, where we saw opportunities for progress even without national legislation. And that's essentially what we did.

The state attorneys general were furious. As Mike Moore said in reflection, "Washington can't get anything done." He and his fellow AGs decided to go back to the negotiating table with the industry and reach a deal that would not require congressional ratification.

John McCain said he didn't know what he could have done differently on the tobacco bill, and he was angry about the industry's attacks on him. He was as depressed as we were. He guessed I was despondent too. I said that we would continue the fight and that we wanted him to be energized. "OK," he responded, "I'm reenergized!" If it were only that easy.

We knew we couldn't get back to productive legislation without industry agreement. The tobacco companies were too strong and had too much influence in Congress. At a meeting of the National Conference of State Legislators, I sat on a panel with Mike Moore and Phil Carlton, a key representative for the tobacco companies. Mike was critical of the White House and Congress for not getting the job done after the AGs had negotiated a feasible agreement with Big Tobacco. Carlton attacked me and our Campaign, along with Koop and Kessler and the overreaching and unrealistic public health community at large. He was brazen, aggressive, and confident. And why not? They had dodged a bullet (the McCain bill), they were holding their own in the courts (a judge had just dismissed Indiana's case against the industry), and they were renegotiating with the AGs to settle the remainder of the state suits in a way that would avoid Washington interference. Beyond that, they continued their disingenuous ad campaign about wanting kids not to use tobacco. It was infuriating—even worse, a lot of the state legislators in the audience were nodding in agreement with him.

We went back to the White House to see if they could broker something to break the logjam. We wanted to salvage FDA oversight, some lesser look-back penalties (if youth smoking didn't decrease), public health provisions, and maybe some lesser liability protections, like a cap on past wrongdoing and some protection for companies' non-tobacco subsidiaries. Bruce Reed said they would discuss it, and later Phil Carlton said the industry would consider it, although he predicted there would be no legislation that year. That much we could all agree on. The White House was in the middle of the Lewinsky scandal, Congress was past thinking about tobacco, and the public health community was as raw as could be.

To make the situation more poignant, John Pierce, a professor at the University of California San Diego, did an analysis showing that over the preceding decade 34 percent of all underage smokers had taken up the habit as a result of industry advertising and promotion. Of this population, some 400,000 people who were attracted to smoking by the Joe Camel campaign would eventually die prematurely, and so would another 200,000 who were attracted by Marlboro marketing.

None of this made any difference to our opponents. The Capital Research Center, an organization favorable to the industry, issued a report saying we had misused our nonprofit status to lobby and called us a powerhouse advocacy organization. And the National Smokers Alliance ran an ad headlined: "There are lies, damned lies, and Campaign for Tobacco-Free Kids lies." They challenged our claims about the number of youth smokers. Kathleen Jamieson at the Annenberg School at Penn responded with justification for our statistics.

The biggest blow in the aftermath of the legislative defeat came in August 1998, when the Fourth Circuit Court of Appeals handed down its decision that the FDA did not have jurisdiction over tobacco. The White House said it would appeal. The saga went on and on. If the AG industry settlement agreement had been shaped into legislation and passed, we'd have had FDA jurisdiction over tobacco then, instead of a decade later.

The AGs and the industry went back to the negotiating table. We set up a briefing for the public health community by Chris Gregoire, the Democratic attorney general of Washington state, who was involved in the negotiations. She briefed us on a confidential basis and gave us a list of those groups she didn't want invited. Chris presented a general sense of where the discussions were going, accepted questions and suggestions, and made a key point: this new settlement was now only a step along the way, and there had to be a new partnership between the state AGs and the public health crowd. Meanwhile, her own state suit with the industry was underway, and she had her hands full.

In November the new settlement was completed, crafted in a way that would not require congressional approval. The AGs had a media conference at the National Press Club, and we had ours there as well. We said that the new agreement was a step forward but no substitute for comprehensive legislation, and we called for earmarking a substantial portion of the money to the states for public health and tobacco control. (The latter point proved to be wishful thinking; the states later used the money for every possible budget need, and not many seriously tackled critical health issues, including tobacco.) Afterward, we all gathered at the White House, where the president praised the AGs, called for comprehensive legislation, and again promised to lead.

A month later we met with Chris Gregoire again to talk about what was ahead. She said she and her AG colleagues would try to help move legislation. Based on her negotiations with the industry, she thought there might be a chance for FDA jurisdiction and maybe more money for education. But the look-back penalties were dead; the industry would no longer consider them, unless they got something really significant in return, which she and the other AGS didn't want to be part of. Chris went on to say that no one now trusted the public health people; the only way to regain trust would be to formulate an agenda and stick to it. "Not like last time," she said.

Like the original settlement proposal, the new settlement included provisions for a foundation to be funded by industry money to do research and counter-marketing to persuade kids not to smoke. There was a lot of money involved: $25 million a year for research and another $300 million a year for education. We promised to provide ideas for moving it forward. This body later became the American Legacy Foundation and eventually the Truth Initiative, today headed by an outstanding advertising executive from Madison Avenue, Robin Koval.

A group of Republican consultants came to us with an idea. Their party was strongly opposed to illicit drugs, especially as used by youth, while the Democrats were vigorously opposed to kids smoking. Why not close the political divide by creating a movement against drugs, tobacco, and alcohol and make the enemy youth addiction? It seemed worthy of consideration, but the more we thought about it the more unwieldy and unworkable it seemed, and in any case we had our hands full. In hindsight, maybe we should have researched their idea and seen what we could create.

Joe Marx at the Robert Wood Johnson Foundation was steering our new grant request through the organization's process. It was for $50 million over five years—the largest grant proposal ever brought before their board—and Steve Schroeder was again our champion. After all that had happened, I was nervous. Would they continue to stand with us? But I was also optimistic. We received another three years of money from the Annie E. Casey Foundation—only $150,000 a year, but it was a good sign. In late January 1999 the RWJF board passed our grant request, apparently with hardly a murmur and some praise. So we would fight the tobacco wars for another five years.

Vin Weber and his team at Clark & Weinstock were taking political soundings on the Hill for us. There was lots of posturing, but nothing significant was in the works. White House leadership wasn't clear. In his February 1999 State of the Union address, President Clinton announced that the Justice Department was preparing to sue the tobacco industry to recover Medicare costs. This was a new attack, since the AG suits were based on *Medicaid* costs to the states from tobacco disease. The administration wanted a 55-cents-a-pack federal tax increase in cigarettes. And the industry agreed to a $5.15 billion fund for US tobacco growers.

To take advantage of the settlement money that would go to the states, we held a conference for state advocates called "Show Me the Money" on how they could advocate effectively for state health spending. Our state coordinators, Pete Fisher and Danny McGoldrick, did a great job making it work, and Len Fishman, the New Jersey health commissioner, also worked with us on this. It was a way to patch up some animosity as well. Christine Todd Whitman, the Republican governor of New Jersey, proposed to spend some 20 percent of her state's settlement money on tobacco control. That was in line with our recommendations and all the more useful because Whitman was a Republican.

We got a call from Steve Parrish of Philip Morris, who wanted to discuss the company's youth anti-smoking campaign. We were leery of having the industry take on the role of health educator: first, we didn't believe they would do a good job, and second, we didn't want them to gain any respectability out of it. Parrish, a top executive at Philip Morris and its chief strategist in the company's foray into FDA regulation, was the public face of the company's legal, stakeholder, and communications work.

We agreed to meet, both to hear what he had to say and to learn what we could about Philip Morris's current thinking. Steve introduced Carolyn Levy, the Philip Morris executive for youth tobacco prevention. It sounded like an oxymoron, but I didn't say so. Philip Morris was launching a $100 million-a-year campaign to convince kids that smoking isn't cool and they don't need to smoke to define themselves. Levy showed us a small portion of the consumer research on their TV commercials—just the data on message comprehension—and admitted it was a narrow strategy. It contained nothing about the immediate or long-term consequences of smoking and certainly nothing on industry manipulation. The Marlboro Man was nowhere to be seen. Levy argued that because their strategy was unlike all the current anti-smoking messages, the company was "doing something valuable . . . adding to the mix."

Matt and I asked how they could not address the reality that Philip Morris was "the kid smoking company" (some 60 percent of youth smokers were smoking Marlboro). Her response was that they were doing something, and that they had an obligation to do all they could, within reason, to reduce youth smoking. Then she said something I just couldn't leave alone. She remarked that she had seen no evidence that cigarette advertising causes kids to smoke or that lack of cigarette advertising would reduce youth smoking. If that was her point of view, I asked, why didn't she conduct the research to test her hypothesis? Her answer: "I'm thinking about it." Actually, she could have saved herself time and money. There was plenty of research, including John Pierce's, showing the connection between the Marlboro Man, Joe Camel, and the other seductive campaigns and youth tobacco use.

As Levy got up to leave, she said to Parrish, "Well, your campaign to fight hunger started well." He said, "Yeah, until I saw today's *USA Today*." He turned to me. "You were quoted in it." I asked what the quote was, and Parrish said, "You said Philip Morris was a bunch of assholes." No matter what we did, he said, he and his company would continue to fight hunger and domestic violence (which he said he and his CEO had both experienced) and work to prevent kids from smoking. I was surprised at the outburst. Genuinely aggrieved, he went on to say we were clearly out to sabotage their youth anti-smoking program.

He related a story that Colin Powell had told Philip Morris executives at a company conference. When Powell and then secretary of state George Shultz met with Soviet president Mikhail Gorbachev, Gorbachev had screamed at the two Americans, "Don't you understand that every time you attack me, you are making it easier for those who want to get rid of me and go backward?" Steve said, "That's just what you are doing to me and my company and our industry. Your criticism is killing opportunities for dialogue. Animosity and mistrust are at an all-time high."

We responded that we weren't backing down, that youth tobacco use was an epidemic, that tobacco killed hundreds of thousands of people every year, and that we were going to do everything we could to change the status quo. Then we offered an olive branch: how about a top-level discussion on this stalemate with Parrish and his senior management, and us and a few of our trusted partners? He said he'd think about it. We all walked away with chips on our shoulders.

After the meeting, I looked up my quote in *USA Today* about Philip Morris's program to combat hunger. I had said, "They're giving this money to a worthy cause. They're doing it to look like a normal, responsible company, which they are not." As I thought more about the encounter, I told myself maybe I should have majored in psychology. Parrish was a complicated man—a senior tobacco executive presiding over an empire of tobacco disease. At the same time he clearly cared about youth smoking and about the

Philip Morris philanthropies he considered socially responsible. I would encounter Steve Parrish in later years, and our conversations were always memorable.

The rest of the year was more of the same: working hard to make something happen. There were meetings with the AGs, White House staff, and members of Congress, as well as intense efforts to get the states to commit to spending settlement money on health and tobacco control. The industry was making inroads in buying respectability; the state of West Virginia and the city of Louisville took tobacco company grants to create school lifestyle programs. The National 4-H Council accepted tobacco money. Philip Morris was visiting school districts and state school boards across the country to offer support. And to my great consternation, the School of Social Work at Penn, my alma mater, was partnering with Big Tobacco. We joined with the American Cancer Society and the American Heart Association on an accountability project, to combat the industry's quest for partners and to attack its legitimacy.

One step forward was our progress with the faith community. Working in social movements throughout my career, I learned that the faith community is powerful at the grass roots. In many places, faith groups are the real, and perhaps only, community infrastructure. Earlier I had tried to interest evangelical leadership in tobacco control but didn't get far. Now Patricia Sosa, who did a lot of our outreach work, organized a two-day meeting of Christian denominations: Presbyterians, African American and Southern Baptists, Catholics, Episcopalians, and evangelicals. They were involved and moving forward.

A few big events kept things churning. First, Skip Humphrey, who had opposed the AGs' broad settlement and lined up with Koop, Kessler, and others and who had settled Minnesota's suit separately with the industry, lost his race for governor. He came in third, behind the winner—Jesse "The Body" Ventura, a pro wrestler—and the Republican candidate. Now Skip, seeking to work with us on getting states to commit tobacco money to public health, wanted to put together a legislative leadership group at the state level. OK, we could do that.

The Supreme Court agreed to hear the case on whether the FDA has jurisdiction over tobacco. That idea had failed as part of the McCain bill, but this was another chance. Meanwhile, the Justice Department announced its lawsuit against the industry, and the media covered it extensively. The tobacco companies had two swift reactions: the suit had no merit, and it was politically motivated.

There was also some bad boy humor to appreciate—and to overcome. At our Youth Advocates of the Year Awards gala, we gave our champion's award to Senators Harkin and Chafee and to trial lawyers Dickie Scruggs and Ron Motley. Scruggs brought his brother-in-law, Senate majority leader Trent Lott. Our two celebrity speakers, Al Franken (later a US senator representing Minnesota) and Rob Reiner, the TV star who became a strong public health advocate in California, took umbrage at Lott's presence. Taking aim at Lott, Reiner said, "What store did he go to, to get the balls to show up here tonight after killing the McCain bill?" Franken said, "Cojones El Grande, the store on Capitol Hill, has Lott's order ready." We didn't need that. The next day a reporter for "Heard on the Hill," a gossip column for *Roll Call*, called me to verify Reiner's comment about Lott. The reporter's quote read, "He's got the biggest balls in the world to come here tonight." I said it wasn't accurate (which, technically, it wasn't) and that his comments didn't represent our Campaign or the event to honor youth advocates. He wrote the story anyway. Lott's spokesperson claimed the senator had left before Reiner's statement and went on to say, "If Meathead [Reiner's nickname on *All in the Family*] has anything to say to Senator Lott, he should put it in writing." What fun the tobacco war had become.

I went to a speech in Baltimore by Governor George W. Bush of Texas, who was the clear front-runner for the Republican nomination for the 2000 presidential election. He said we had to protect America's children from alcohol and drugs. Afterward I introduced myself and told him it would be very productive if he could say we need to protect kids from alcohol, drugs, *and tobacco*. He said, "I'll try to work that in." We were working with a Republican consulting firm, the American Continental Group, to get tobacco-control language into Bush's campaign speeches. At this point, he was well ahead of other GOP candidates in the polls and in money raised and seemingly ahead of Vice President Gore and former senator Bill Bradley, the two Democratic front-runners.

Internationally, the World Health Organization (WHO) began work in 1999 on a novel treaty against tobacco, the WHO Framework Convention on Tobacco Control. The objective was to "protect present and future generations from the devastating health, social, environmental and economic consequences of tobacco consumption and exposure to tobacco smoke" through standards across countries to limit the use of tobacco worldwide. We worked on this initiative and helped found the Framework Convention Alliance. The treaty eventually came into effect in 2005 after being signed in 168 countries and ratified in 181 countries. The United States has never signed. This was the first of a number of effective international initiatives by the Campaign for Tobacco-Free Kids to combat tobacco and the tobacco industry worldwide.

Taking On a New Role

In the middle of all this, AARP, which had been a client in my Porter Novelli days, came calling. They wanted me to come on board in a senior role, and I knew that Horace Deets, their executive director, was planning to retire. I kept thinking about this possibility as the stalemate in tobacco control went on. AARP was attractive for many reasons. I liked their mission: to enhance the quality of life for all (not just older people) as we age—in other words, to think across generations. Also, it didn't take a demographer to see that the baby boomers were aging right into AARP's sweet spot (50 and older). And finally, I thought I could be the inside candidate to succeed Horace. I had lunch with Steve Schroeder to get his reaction. Steve was critical of the idea. He pointed to my belief in social change and said that AARP was just about marketing to greedy geezers. I told him I disagreed because I had worked with them and that, if I did take the position there, I would prove him wrong. Kathleen Jamieson said essentially the same thing as Steve. She thought that AARP was so big that it tilted public discourse away from children and youth and gave too much clout and public funding to older people.

I was also mildly interested in heading the new American Legacy Foundation, the entity born of the second settlement between the AGs and the tobacco industry. I considered my options. I was ready for some new horizons beyond tobacco control, although I remained fiercely committed to working on tobacco issues. The question was: could I have everything I wanted?

In November 1999, at our Campaign for Tobacco-Free Kids board meeting, I announced my resignation as president. I had told John Seffrin and several other board members in advance. They thanked me for my work and asked me to join the board, which I did (I still serve on that board, for the past decade as chairman). They also asked if I thought we needed to conduct a search for my replacement. Absolutely not, I said. We have our guy right here. Matt Myers was not just a powerful tobacco-control advocate and expert but also a deeply principled man who could lead us into the future.

What Did We Win?

When we began the Campaign, we wanted to challenge Big Tobacco, protect the FDA and its assertion of jurisdiction, support state efforts to control tobacco use, rally the many involved organizations, and work for policy change, especially at the national level. The recipe for tobacco control—five essential strategies— came into focus over time:

- increase taxes on tobacco products to reduce youth and adult consumption;
- persuade kids not to experiment and become addicted (most smokers began before age 18);
- provide help for adults who wanted to quit;
- eliminate smoking in public places; and
- curb tobacco marketing.

This was all condensed into a strong mission: "We work to save lives by advocating for public policies that prevent kids from smoking, help smokers quit, and protect everyone from secondhand smoke."

So while the Campaign had a broad mandate and supported tobacco-control efforts across the country and the globe, our primary focus became public policies—legislative, regulatory, and judicial—especially at the federal level. In virtually every social movement I've ever been involved with, advocating for policy change has been a critical lever to change social norms and expectations as well as individual and group behaviors.

Public policy advocacy in tobacco control required four supporting pillars:

- Communications: keep the tobacco issue in front of the public and decision-makers, and continue to expose Big Tobacco;
- Research: use it to reinforce advocacy and communications;
- Coalitions and grassroots initiatives: mobilize organizations and individuals to join the movement and provide support; and
- Legal assistance: analyze legislation and regulations, offer model legislation to states and others, and provide direct support in litigation (this eventually became a key

strategy in our international work as well as in the United States).

The Campaign's vision—its aspirational goal—morphed into "A future free of the death and disease caused by tobacco." Short, powerful, and to the point.

We employed the five key strategies to help drive down tobacco use. Increases in federal and state taxes put substantial downward pressure on consumption. In 1996 the federal tax per pack of cigarettes was 24 cents, and the average state tax was 33 cents, totaling 57 cents a pack. By 2001 the federal tax was at 34 cents, and the average state tax per pack was up to 43 cents, or 77 cents for a pack of cigarettes. By 2017 the federal rate was at $1.01 and the state average had reached $1.70, for an average tax per pack of $2.71.

State legislators and members of Congress took a while to accept tobacco tax increases. At first there was doubt that tax increases could actually reduce consumption of an additive product. Some argued that this was not a reliable, long-term revenue source; if consumption went down, the taxes would bring in less money over time. Finally, there was concern that voters would rebel. But after a lot of work by the Campaign and many others, tax increases came to be seen as a win for everybody: smoking decreased and lives were saved, government budgets benefited from the increased tax money, and politicians discovered that tobacco taxes were actually popular with most voters.

As the *Washington Post* editorialized in 2007,

For every 10 percent increase in tobacco prices, the number of adult smokers drops by 1.5 percent and overall consumption drops 2 percent. Young smokers are much more responsive to price increases than adults, so higher tobacco taxes are particularly effective in preventing youth from moving beyond experimentation to habitual smoking. Pregnant women are similarly affected: a 10 percent price increase produces a 5 to 7 percent reduction in smoking. . . . The Campaign for Tobacco-Free Kids estimates that a 61-cents-a pack increase would result in a 9.2 percent decline in youth smoking. Some 1.9 million children alive today would not become smokers, and 1.2 million adult smokers would quit.

By 2019 the Task Force on Fiscal Policy for Health (co-chaired by Michael Bloomberg and Larry Summers, former president of Harvard University, with representatives from 12 countries) reported that "a steep increase in tobacco taxes alone could do more to reduce deaths from non-communicable diseases worldwide than any other single health policy, averting more than 27 million deaths tied to tobacco use over the next 50 years."

Some states were devoting some of the settlement money to tobacco control. Only Arizona, California, and Massachusetts had budgeted money to combat tobacco before the 1999 settlement between the AGs and the industry, but after the settlement money came in, states stepped up, although not as much as they could have. Starting in 2000 all the states combined devoted more than $500 million a year to combating tobacco, with spending particularly high during the first three years of settlement money (2000 to 2003) and in 2008 and 2009. This spending made a huge difference in prevention and cessation.

State coalitions, advocacy groups, and our Campaign worked hard to get smoking banned in public places. Today we seldom think of the time when smokers lit up in offices, conference rooms, teachers' lounges, airplanes, restaurants and bars, and just about anywhere people gathered for business and pleasure. Physicians smoked in meetings at the National Cancer Institute. Back in 1996 there had been comprehensive smoke-free laws in just seven communities in the entire country. Late in 2002 Delaware became the first state to go smoke-free in all workplaces, restaurants, and bars. Thanks to a lot of lobbying and public support, by mid-2017 25 states and hundreds of communities had made the change.

The Aftermath: Carrying on the Fight

The effectiveness of the Campaign for Tobacco-Free Kids as a co-ordinating organization and policy force in the United States opened a whole new chapter in 2006, when Michael Bloomberg and his Bloomberg Philanthropies began to focus on international tobacco control. The worldwide tobacco epidemic is enormous: nearly a billion men and perhaps 250 million women are daily smokers, and tobacco use is estimated to cause some 6 million deaths annually across the globe. Fighting Big Tobacco country by country is difficult. The industry has a similar playbook in every country, depending on each country's tobacco culture and laws. It makes good sense to attack Big Tobacco broadly and to share techniques across countries.

By 2007 Bloomberg had launched a major initiative (over $125 million) to combat tobacco use in low- and middle-income countries, and it added more funding over time. The Bill and Melinda Gates Foundation invested another $125 million in the effort. Fifteen priority countries were identified, including huge population centers: Bangladesh, Brazil, China, India, Indonesia, Pakistan, and Russia. The strategy was to promote advocacy for effective policies and laws to curb tobacco-related deaths, an approach that fit well with the WHO Framework Convention on Tobacco Control. The Campaign for Tobacco-Free Kids is an ideal partner for Bloomberg and Gates. Our role was not to advocate directly in these low- and middle-income countries but rather to use the Campaign's expertise to select, support, and nurture local advocacy organizations in each country. It made sense to take the fight to a global level and use our experience from the home front, adapted to country conditions and opportunities.

We had to gear up to move to the international stage without losing momentum at home. Yolonda Richardson leads the international team, and Patricia Sosa moved from her work on US stakeholder relations to focus on Latin America. An international structure was established, with communications, legal, operations, and research units for geographic teams, which work directly with the in-country policy advocacy organizations. The Campaign provides strategic counseling, information and policy research, communications, legal assistance, and grant money.

It took a while to gear up, but the results are impressive. Within a few years of launching indigenous advocacy supported by our Campaign, Russia issued regulations for graphic health warnings on cigarette packs, Brazil established a national smoke-free law for public places, 17 of 28 Indian states increased tobacco taxes, Ukraine issued a law banning tobacco ads and a smoke-free law, and Vietnam succeeded in passing national comprehensive anti-tobacco legislation. Recently, Brazil became the first South American country to sue the major tobacco companies, with the same goals laid out by Mississippi AG Mike Moore over 20 years ago. And successes are occurring in other countries as well.

The industry is fighting back. They lobby hard, donate to politicians, and apply the marketing tactics that had been common in the United States in earlier decades (free samples, sponsorship of concerts, free gear, alluring advertising). And they actually brought legal action against an entire country: tiny Uruguay. The Campaign, with a Bloomberg grant, provided legal assistance to help Uruguay win the case.

By 2015, 44 countries had enacted policies mandating that indoor spaces be 100 percent smoke free. Some 85 countries required pictorial warnings covering more that 30 percent of the cigarette pack. And about 30 countries prohibited tobacco advertising, promotion, and sponsorships. World per capita cigarette volume declined and is continuing on a downward trend. This wasn't all attributed to the Campaign and its international work, of course. The WHO initiative and other factors also made a difference.

The international work has been so successful that Matt, his management team, and Bloomberg Philanthropies, with our Campaign board's strong approval, decided to apply the model to additional risk factors besides tobacco, including road accidents, obesity, and drowning. While we had some concern that this expansion could dilute our tobacco focus, we believed it was the smart, strategic thing to do. So in 2014 the Global Health Advocacy Incubator, under Danny McGoldrick's leadership, was born.

By 2009 it had been a decade since our loss of comprehensive tobacco control legislation in the Senate (which would have given the FDA jurisdiction over tobacco products) and the Supreme Court in *FDA v. Brown & Williamson* ruled that Congress had not given the FDA that authority. But with the intervening years of hard work, it finally happened. On June 11, 2009, the Senate voted, 79 to 17, to approve the Family Smoking Prevention and Tobacco Control Act, and the next day the House voted, 307 to 97, to approve the same bill. The sponsors were Senator Ted Kennedy (D-MA) in the Senate and Representatives Henry Waxman (D-CA) and Todd Platts (R-PA) in the House. Soon after, President Obama signed the bill in a joyful White House ceremony.

Many organizations had advocated to get this done, and the Campaign celebrated what we called "a common-sense law to protect kids and save lives. . . . Until the law was enacted, tobacco products had escaped regulation despite their devastating toll in health, lives and dollars. They were exempt from basic consumer protections, such as ingredient disclosure, product testing and restrictions on marketing to children."

This landmark legislation contained much, but not all, of what we and the attorneys general had negotiated over a decade earlier. It substantially restricted tobacco marketing and sales to kids; required disclosure of ingredients, nicotine, and harmful smoke; permitted the FDA to require changes to tobacco products to protect public health; regulated inaccurate and misleading claims (including claims of "reduced harm" such as "light," "mild," and "low") on labels and ads; required bigger and bolder health warnings on packages; and funded FDA regulation through a user fee on companies, cigarettes, and smokeless tobacco. Importantly, the new law did not preempt state and local governments, leaving them free to enact taxes, smoke-free laws, and other restrictions. Although the legislation gave the FDA the authority to reduce nicotine, Congress retained for itself the power to actually ban it. There is an old saying in the tobacco fight: whoever controls nicotine will win the war.

Later that year, Congress approved an increase in the federal excise tax on cigarettes from $0.39 to $1.01 per pack. A year later, regulations kicked in that required health insurance plans to cover "proven" tobacco cessation treatments and expanded Medicaid coverage for those treatments. Since many adults try numerous times before succeeding in quitting smoking, this was an important step.

The second attorneys general settlement with the industry in 1999—the one that did not require congressional approval—set up an organization to "create a culture where youth and young adults reject tobacco." First called the American Legacy Foundation, it has had, as mentioned, a major effect on tobacco prevention among kids. Since most smokers begin as teenagers, persuading youth not to start smoking is an essential strategy in preventing lifelong addition.

Kids have a natural tendency to rebel against authority, and the American Legacy Foundation built upon the campaign begun in Florida to encourage youth to go ahead—stage a rebellion—but aim it at Big Tobacco. It was a brilliant behavior-change strategy. Tell kids about the industry's lies and deceptions, turn them away from the allure of tobacco advertising, and help them focus on the bad guys in suits who are seducing and manipulating them into smoking.

The Legacy Foundation's Truth campaign used media effectively and staged youth advocacy events and other rebellious activities. One TV message showed kids stacking body bags outside a tobacco company's building—1,200 bags to indicate the number of people who died from tobacco disease every day in the United States. This was real life, and the kids expanded on it in their own creative ways. When Philip Morris USA changed its parent company name to Altria, youth advocates put two piles of manure in front of a hotel where a tobacco-control event was being held. In one pile was a sign that said "Altria." In the other pile was another sign: "Same old shit." The Legacy Foundation took the Truth campaign national, and it made a huge difference in youth tobacco use.

By 2014 kids were smoking and using smokeless tobacco (what advocates called "spit tobacco") far less, but the Truth campaign had begun to falter. Youth advocacy continued to be a major initiative at the Campaign and the Legacy Foundation, but a new strategy was called for. A new generation of kids were smoking much less but facing other issues: bullying, LGBT rights, gun violence, and more. Social media were more powerful and ubiquitous, filling kids' online feeds with glamorous imagery of smoking and making smoking seem cool again. The Legacy Foundation (now called the Truth Initiative) made the decision to engage the 91 percent of kids who didn't use tobacco to rally the 9 percent who still did. The battle cry became "Let's rid the world of smoking for good. A new generation of kids could do it; be the Generation to End Smoking. #FinishIT."

One of their cleverest appeals was to tie smoking to pets. Yes, cats and dogs get cancer from secondhand smoke, so the Truth Initiative told kids about it. Imagine a world with no cats, because of tobacco disease. A hugely popular cat video—Catmageddon—got the word out. How about dating? Using the online dating culture on Tinder, Truth put out the news that teens who smoked were twice as likely to get left-swiped (in other words, rejected). The message was "Left Swipe Dat."

The Truth Initiative has been instrumental in persuading kids not to start smoking. It is led today by Robin Koval, who left her successful position as CEO of the New York advertising agency Publicis Kaplan Thaler to become president and CEO of the Initiative. The organization's research shows that their efforts have prevented more than 3 million kids and young adults from smoking, and it's still working. This is one of the most successful health education efforts in American history.

The government—not always the best communicator in public health—also weighed in on tobacco prevention and cessation. In 2014 the FDA launched a media campaign, "The Real Cost," to tell teens about the dangers of e-cigarettes and to reach rural boys about the harm of smokeless tobacco. Their research also showed an impact on prevention.

In 2012 the Centers for Disease Control and Prevention (CDC) also began a controversial media effort to encourage adults to quit smoking. For everyone who dies from tobacco-related disease, another 30 people live with serious smoking-related consequences. So the CDC began to show—graphically—what those individuals looked like, including victims of secondhand smoke. The TV messages were gruesome. One featured a man shaving, with the message "Be careful not to cut your stoma." Another showed a tracheotomy. A third featured a woman putting in false teeth and donning a wig. I was sure these ads wouldn't work. Research had showed that fear-arousal messages would fail because the target audience would rather turn off the message than change behavior. But the CDC messages did work. Their research found that from 2012 to 2015 CDC's scare tactics (my description) caused more than 9 million smokers to attempt to quit; a half million succeeded. I thought of the research we had done at Porter Novelli for the National High Blood Pressure Education Program. We found that many people feared living with a hypertension-related stroke more than dying from one. Living with a disease or deformity is indeed a scary prospect.

More recently, the Truth Initiative has been applying its experience and creativity with youth and young adults to address the dangers of opioid use, with a focus on what kids need to know—such as that opioid dependence can happen in just five days. Like their tobacco messages, these are bold, edgy, and willing to make the audience uncomfortable to drive home an emotional response. They include depictions of a young man who broke his own arm to obtain an opioid prescription, an on-the-street view of a young woman's detox, and a how a star athlete can quickly become entirely different when opioids enter the picture. Their research shows the messages are having a positive effect, but the opioid epidemic may be an even tougher challenge than tobacco. Time will tell.

Several years ago I ran into Steve Parrish, who had retired as senior vice president of corporate affairs of Philip Morris/Altria Group. I had been invited to speak at a conference at the Yale School of Management on social responsibility in the beer industry, sponsored by the corporate giant AB InBev. One conference topic was how to avoid the mistakes and pitfalls that had befallen the tobacco industry, and I had been asked to talk about tobacco control. As the conference began, I looked across the room and there was Steve.

He spoke after me, and he didn't pull any punches. The title of his talk was "Lessons Learned: Altria and the US Tobacco Wars." His opening slide said, "Cigarette smoking causes many deadly diseases, including lung cancer, heart disease, and emphysema; cigarette smoking is addictive; and cigarette smoking has no proven health benefits." He went through a timeline of trouble—from 1953 studies linking smoking and lung cancer, to the FDA's attempt to gain jurisdiction, to class-action and state lawsuits, to whistleblowers and David Kessler's famous quote that smoking is a "pediatric disease." The audience was riveted.

Steve told them his corporation thought it had a "lawsuit problem," but what it really had was a "society problem." So, he said, the company set out to align itself with society and better meet society's expectations. He set forth a number of lessons learned: listen to the outside world, engage critics by seeking common ground, consider other companies in one's industry as key stakeholders with important views, and recognize the social, political and legal differences between the United States and the rest of the world.

At the conference lunch Steve and I talked. At this point the FDA had attained oversight over tobacco and smoking had dropped significantly in the United States. He had never stopped advocating for FDA regulation and his industry's protections, but there was a certain truce in our conversation.

Steve reminded me that back in 2003 (four years after the comprehensive tobacco control legislation had failed in the Senate and six years before Congress voted to give the FDA tobacco oversight), he had written an article in the *Yale Journal of Health Policy, Law, and Ethics* admitting essentially what he had just presented in the conference that morning. He had said that the industry had played a major role in creating the anger directed against it and that its cigarette marketing was too aggressive and didn't account for the unique dangers of tobacco. The article quoted several tobacco control advocates, including me ("If we can keep them perceived as pariahs in America, then we've got a much better chance of forcing them into reform") from a *Wall Street Journal* article. His article repeated his call for regulation and ended with a powerful statement:

Today, nearly six years later [that is, after the first tobacco settlement ended in legislative failure], there is still no FDA authority to regulate tobacco products. According to tobacco control advocates, each day of each of those years, thousands of kids have started to smoke, and hundreds of thousands of adults have died from smoking-related diseases. My company wants very much to resolve the impasse, and we are convinced that the remaining policy differences can be resolved through mutually respectful discussions that seek resolution rather than vilification. I hope very much that, together, we can bridge the divide and achieve our common goal.

Following that 2003 journal article, Steve had made a number of speeches to business clubs and other business audiences around the country. As in his Yale journal article, he admitted the dangers of smoking and called for reasonable dialogue, and he quoted Mike Pertschuk, who had written a book about the tobacco wars. Mike said, "It is never easy for . . . warriors to transform themselves into peacemakers, to shift from the comfort of combatting a . . . demonized enemy to the moral ambiguity involved in acknowledging an enemy as simultaneously a bargaining partner. . . . Many . . . were [not] capable of stepping back and asking themselves whether a time had indeed come to suspend the fighting . . . and negotiate." In those business speeches, Steve would end by saying that his company, "after having played a role in creating a polarized environment, [wanted] very much to do our part to suspend the fighting and help bring about a national tobacco policy that is good for our consumers, our shareholders, and our country."

Steve and I have kept in touch. Recently I asked him his views on the e-cigarette surge and on the tobacco industry technology called "heat don't burn." He responded,

I guess I am hopeful, if you take the long view. I used to compare the tobacco industry and the smoking cessation industry (in a very simplistic way). The tobacco industry had been very good at the "pleasure" part of the equation, but it had failed miserably at the "safety" part of the equation. The pharma industry (i.e., smoking cessation products) had done a good job with the "safety" part of the product equation, but it had failed with respect to the "pleasure" part of the equation. The thinking behind the FDA tobacco regulatory approach was to provide a framework for a new industry, one in which companies would be incented to address both sides of the equation, with the appropriate balance being struck on the side of public health. The hope was that a comprehensive regulatory approach, overseen by a single agency with appropriate resources and expertise, would be able to lead, or at least enable, that transformation. I think (hope) we are in the early stages of the transformation. Predictably, in the absence of serious oversight, many companies are behaving irresponsibly. My belief/hope is that as FDA ramps up and provides science-based policies, rules, and regulations, the industry will indeed be transformed.

A very thoughtful comment by a thoughtful man. But reasoning and dialogue weren't really enough back in the earlier days of the US tobacco wars, and they still aren't enough today throughout the world. The industry lied for decades while people died. They concealed research, bought support in Congress, paid scientists to endorse their claims, and addicted millions in the United States and across the globe. They never apologized for any of this. Instead, they reached a point where the pressure was too great to sustain their business and therefore came to the negotiating table.

Mike Pertschuk was right. It's hard, very hard, to shift from being enemies to bargaining partners, or to being both at the same time—to talk and fight. But that's essentially what it took to make much of the progress we have today.

As I look back, I know we did the right thing in working with the attorneys general to negotiate with the tobacco industry and then in fighting to pass the ensuing legislation. We incurred the wrath of those who saw this as treason, as capitulation, as social injustice. And we angered those who mistakenly thought that Big Tobacco was on the ropes and virtually defeated. In fighting for fundamental social change, when the enemy can't be conquered or eradicated—as, for instance, polio or cervical cancer could be—we need everyone at the table, adversaries included. And that's what we did.

Tobacco Control Today

Where are we today? Youth smoking in the United States has fallen dramatically, from 28 percent of high school kids in 2000 to 6 percent in 2019. In some states (California, Florida, New York, Rhode Island), it's even lower. These declines have had a remarkable effect on America's health. Millions of kids will not become addicted smokers, and many millions of adults will not die prematurely from tobacco-caused disease. Smoking declines have contributed significantly to declines in cancer, coronary heart disease, chronic obstructive pulmonary disease (COPD), and other illnesses. And maternal and child health has improved, since smoking by pregnant women greatly increases preterm delivery.

Just as the Truth Initiative is calling for kids to End Smoking (#FinishIT), the American Cancer Society, the American Heart Association, and the Campaign for Tobacco-Free Kids are working to drive the levels of "combustible" cigarettes down lower than ever thought possible. But as cigarette smoking declines, it becomes more difficult to target and reach current smokers. Who are they? Increasingly, it is the poor and less educated who smoke, although in states with strong tobacco control policies, there are fewer low-income smokers than in other states.

In addition, smoking rates are high in the lesbian, gay, bisexual, and transgender (LGBT) community. About 21 percent of LGBT adults, including nearly 36 percent of transgender adults, smoke cigarettes, compared with about 15 percent of straight adults. Part of this is due to targeted marketing by tobacco companies. Back in the early 1990s they started advertising in gay publications, often showing tobacco use as a normal part of gay life.

While this goes on, the tobacco industry is moving beyond just combustible cigarettes. They call their new technologies "reduced-risk" or "heat-not-burn" products (brands include IQOS and Eclipse)—"non-combustible alternatives to cigarettes with the potential to reduce individual risk and population harm." Philip Morris International has an array of these offerings in the pipeline and in the marketplace. They say they are developing "four product platforms—two with tobacco and two without [but with nicotine]—which produce aerosol that significantly reduces or eliminates the formation of [harmful by-products] when compared with cigarette smoke." Why are they doing this? The company says,

> We recognize that cigarettes are a dangerous product, and it is well known that the best way to avoid the harms of smoking is never to start, or to quit. Nevertheless, based on the World Health Organization's own predictions, there will be more than one billion smokers by the year 2025. Therefore, alternative products that significantly reduce the risk of disease compared with cigarette smoking are a fundamental complement to the regulatory efforts aimed at reducing smoking prevalence.

A billion smokers by 2025! And so the industry is working on alternatives "while continuing to deliver a satisfying experience." This is the "pleasure side" of the equation that Steve Parrish referenced. They say they want to encourage smokers to switch. As part of this, Philip Morris established a Foundation for a Smoke-Free World and funded it with some $80 million a year for 12 years. Derek Yach, who helped create the World Health Organization's Framework Convention on Tobacco Control back in 2003, switched over to the Philip Morris camp to head their new foundation.

Matt Myers and Robin Koval, commenting in *Fortune* magazine, called it the "height of hypocrisy" for Philip Morris to claim that it is helping to solve the tobacco problem while continuing to aggressively market cigarettes around the world—especially in low- and middle-income countries—and fighting legislation and regulations to curtail cigarette use. Matt and Robin said, "Philip Morris says it wants to quit cigarettes, but it's just blowing smoke." The World Health Organization said that it "will not engage with this new Foundation."

Philip Morris's parent, Altria, is betting on other technologies as well. The company recently acquired a Swiss maker of smokeless tobacco products that contain nicotine but are considered less harmful than cigarettes.

And Reynolds American is similarly diversifying. Natasha Webster of Reynolds told Fox Business, "We are excited about the future of the tobacco industry. At Reynolds American, we are pleased to provide adult tobacco consumers with a variety of options that meet evolving preferences and reflect dynamic consumer trends." The tobacco industry *never* gives up.

In the meantime, another menace has hit—e-cigarettes. E-cigarette use among kids has surged, with recent reports showing that 27.5 percent of high school students had vaped in the previous 30 days and 21 percent vape daily. These figures represent a doubling of vaping in just one year. So while the use of combustible cigarettes among youth is in steep decline, thanks to decades of hard work, this new epidemic has appeared. Is it dangerous? Yes, because e-cigarettes contain nicotine, the addictive substance in cigarettes, and because nicotine—besides causing addiction—is harmful to the adolescent brain and affects attention and learning. There may be other dangers as well. Research into vaping is ongoing.

Where did this e-cigarette epidemic come from? Unlike tobacco wars, which were fought against many companies, this time there was one prime culprit—Juul Labs. This is another story of brilliant marketing. A company spokeswoman, Christine Castro, said in a Bloomberg article in 2018 that Juul does little marketing and further commented, "I know we appear on social media quite a bit; that is completely separate from us." But the Campaign for Tobacco-Free Kids tracked the Juul buildup and showed that it launched its product with images right out of the old tobacco marketing playbook. They used a paid social media campaign via Twitter, Instagram, and YouTube and had "sponsored ambassadors" (young spokespersons) supplemented by social media promoted by Juul vendors. They featured cool, sexy young people at launch parties ("Having way too much fun at the #JUUL launch party #LightsCameraVapor #NYC"), magazine ads with attractive young people, YouTube videos, and discussions on Reddit, among other tactics. Their campaign had lifestyle appeal, portrayed images of social success and fashion, and promoted tasty flavors. The Juul campaign began in 2015 and continued for at least two years.

A team of researchers at Stanford concluded that "Juul's marketing was patently youth oriented." The *New York Times* reported that despite Juul's statements to the contrary,

> In reality the company was never just about helping adult smokers [to quit], according to interviews with former executives, employees and investors, along with reviews of legal filings and social media archives. . . . Juul's remarkable rise . . . came after it began targeting consumers in their 20s and early 30s, a generation with historically low smoking rates, in a furious effort to reward investors and capture market share before the government tightened regulations on vaping.

By mid-2018 the FDA had caught on to all this and challenged the company. Juul's response was that it didn't really target kids and would stop using models in social media to promote its product. Other vaping companies saw Juul's success and jumped in, but by the end of 2018 Juul had more than 70 percent of e-cigarette sales.

The *New York Times* commented,

> Juul Labs, the company behind the insanely popular vaping device, has a message for the nation's estimated 37.8 million adult smokers. It really, really, really cares about them. . . . "For Smokers. By design," blares the company's website. A new $10 million TV ad campaign, called "Make the Switch," echoes that theme, featuring testimonials from ex-smokers, all comfortably above the legal smoking age, who have swapped their cigarettes for a Juul. This benevolent-sounding mission—helping nicotine-addicted adult smokers switch to something far less likely to kill them—is Juul's new pitch, and the way it hopes to rehabilitate its image as one of Silicon Valley's most problematic start-ups.

Juul ran full-page newspaper ads saying adults are "making the switch from cigarettes to Juul" and displaying a warning: "This product contains nicotine. Nicotine is an addictive chemical." Other ads proclaimed that "Youth Vaping Is a Serious Problem" and therefore Juul was dropping some flavors, penalizing retailers who sold to youth, exiting Facebook and Instagram, and developing new restrictions on youth access. Juul Labs also sold 35 percent of its company to Altria, the parent of Philip Morris.

The FDA began cracking down and accused Juul and Altria of reneging on promises to keep e-cigarettes, especially flavored products, away from youth. The two companies had pledged to remove nicotine flavor pods from store shelves, but the FDA said they weren't doing so. It was further concerned that Altria's acquisition of part of Juul Labs would give Juul access to shelf space in some 230,000 retail outlets where Marlboro and other Altria products are sold—a major retail expansion for Juul. In the fall of 2019,

President Trump said he intended to ban all liquid vaping flavors except tobacco. But after intense pushback from the industry, the administration announced it would keep both menthol and tobacco-flavored pods on the market and permit vape shops to continue selling tank-based e-cigarettes in any flavor. This was criticized by many as a major loophole. Didn't I say the tobacco—now the nicotine—industry never gives up?

Things got even worse when a mysterious epidemic of lung disease related to vaping and e-cigarettes broke out across the country. Hundreds of people were made ill, and several have died. Health officials are investigating, including tracking illicit brands bought on the street. A CDC official said that given the large array of products, ingredients, packaging, and supply chains, consumers have no way of knowing what is in the liquids they are vaping. There is also the risk of secondhand vapor, similar to the danger of secondhand smoke.

In response to all this, a coalition consisting of the American Cancer Society, the American Heart Association, the Truth Initiative, the Campaign for Tobacco-Free Kids, and other public health groups, supported by CVS Health and the Bloomberg Foundation, has launched a sweeping public program against youth vaping, with media, grassroots, legislative, and regulatory policy initiatives, youth advocacy, and other tactics. Part of this effort is to pressure the FDA to take all non-tobacco-flavored e-cigarettes off the market, to push the agency to implement a public health review of e-cigarettes, and to move forward with reducing nicotine levels in traditional tobacco products.

On the other side of the vaping issue is the "harm reduction" faction—those who believe that e-cigarettes are a boon to adult cigarette smokers who want to switch to less dangerous vaping and that this benefit must be balanced against the potential harm to children. Tom Miller, the Democratic attorney general of Iowa, is one of the leaders of this contingent. Tom was one of the original

AGs who entered into the settlement agreements with the tobacco industry with Mike Moore and more than 40 of their peers. He cites a study showing that most kids who vape use e-cigarettes fewer than 10 days a month, so "if there is an epidemic, it is an epidemic of casual use. There is no fear of addicting a generation." The way he applies this study has been called into question by several authorities.

The message is that adults can use e-cigarettes (to switch from smoking if they can't quit), but kids should not. But it isn't all that easy to drive home this bifurcated message, and e-cigarettes are oh so cool.

I'm in full support of aggressively attacking youth vaping. We have to keep another generation of kids from addiction and harm. As the board chairman of the Campaign for Tobacco-Free Kids, a board member of the American Cancer Society, and a strong advocate for health promotion and disease prevention, I'm all in.

Join the Fight

As we move into the 2020s, where are we in the tobacco wars? We drove down adult and youth cigarette smoking in the United States, we're fighting tobacco use on a world stage, and we face new technologies ("heat not burn") and a huge new menace in e-cigarettes. Millions of lives have been saved, and millions more across the globe will be lost to tobacco-caused disease. We have FDA oversight over tobacco, including nicotine, but the FDA isn't moving as fast as most of us would like. Mike Moore, the attorney general who brought the original state lawsuit against the tobacco industry, looks at the landscape today and says, "You can't count on government alone to solve these problems. It's up to all of us." (Now Mike is working with state AGs on many opioid suits being brought against pharmaceutical companies and suppliers.)

In February 2020 the US House passed Reversing the Youth Tobacco Epidemic Act (the Pallone bill), which bans all flavored e-cigarettes. While the Senate is unlikely to take it up, it may help by boosting state and local efforts. And the FDA issued its final rule requiring graphic warnings on 50 percent of the front and back of all cigarette packs, with new warning statements and color graphics, to take effect by June 2021.

Influencing public and private policies at national, state, and community levels is the fastest and surest way to revamp broad societal norms and expectations. It also has a major effect on individual and group behaviors. It took me a while to learn and apply this. In my earlier social marketing days at Porter Novelli, we tended to adapt commercial marketing principles: we used the marketing mix—product, price, place (that is, distribution channels), and promotion—to focus on and alter specific target audience (that is, individual) behaviors. But lesson learned: policy change is powerful.

As individuals and in our roles in corporations, nonprofit organizations, and government, we can all play a role: influencing public and private policies at national, state, and community levels to get vaping out of our schools and communities; letting policy makers know where we stand on the tobacco companies' ceaseless peddling of harmful products; helping a family member or friend quit smoking; avoiding stock purchases in irresponsible companies; and supporting cessation programs at work. There are lots of ways to make a positive difference. Georgetown is only now becoming a smoke-free campus. I'm going to work on that.

And now, with the Covid-19 crisis in the United States and across the world, we can't foresee how this new reality will impact vaping and other nicotine and tobacco-related behaviors and illnesses. But one thing seems sure. When we get past this coronavirus pandemic, the cigarette and vaping industries will still be there, plying their trade.

CHAPTER FOUR

AARP AND THE BRAWL TO GET PRESCRIPTION DRUGS INTO MEDICARE

On November 14, 2002, I was invited to address a meeting of the board of directors of the Pharmaceutical Research and Manufacturers Association (PhRMA). PhRMA, representing the big drug companies, was a major adversary in the prescription drug battle, so going to speak to their board was like entering the lion's den. Although PhRMA viewed us as the opposition, I jumped at the chance to talk to them. It was an important tactic in our talk-fight-win strategy. We shared the common goal of prescription drug coverage for older Americans, but we had differing views on the best way to achieve it. I knew I could never win them over, but I thought that if I could at least establish some common ground for discussion, it would keep the lines of communication open and benefit us down the road.

I told them that prescription drug coverage in Medicare was inevitable and that it was in the best interest of both PhRMA and AARP to work together to get the best drug bill possible for the people who needed it most. I assured them that our opponent was not the drug industry; it was the high cost of drugs for our members, and it was our hope that we could work together wherever possible. I also said we were pragmatic and looking for a bipartisan, workable solution for the policy makers, the industry, the states, and America's health care consumers, including our own 35+ million members. I let them know that without a benefit, our members would continue to insist that we find more effective ways to constrain costs. And without an adequately funded benefit, pressures for cost controls would continue to increase.

I can't say that session was a meeting of the minds. The board members were polite, but there was a fundamental difference between us: they wanted to protect drug prices, and we wanted to reduce them. But I do think it helped convince the pharmaceutical industry that we could find areas of agreement and didn't have to oppose each other at every turn. Our chief lobbyist, Chris Hansen, checked the reactions of some of the companies present that evening and reported back that at least there was clear understanding about where we stood. This was a fight I was ready for, but first I'd had to win the battle to get the top job at AARP.

Joining AARP

In early 2000 I set off on a whole new adventure—striving to become CEO of AARP. I remained actively on the board, eventually as chairman, of the Campaign for Tobacco-Free Kids (where I continue to serve today). Now things were very different, with completely new challenges. The Campaign had been a start-up operation. AARP was nearly 50 years old and had a reputation as an 800-pound gorilla on Capitol Hill. The Campaign was focused on a single critical issue. AARP dealt with a multitude of issues related to the aging of society, ranging from economic security (pensions, Social Security, saving for retirement, financial fraud), health care, transportation, livable communities, work and jobs, age discrimination, and a whole range of consumer issues. AARP was a membership organization. The Campaign was not. AARP had a national headquarters in Washington and offices in every state.

I had never been afraid of risks and renewal, and now I was stepping into an opportunity to lead perhaps the largest, most important social advocacy group in America. The *Washington Post* reported that, for the third year in a row, *Forbes* magazine was about to name AARP the most powerful lobbying group in the country. As usual, Fran cheered me on.

As the year 2000 dawned, I had about a hundred pounds of reading material on AARP, and even though I had worked with them at Porter Novelli some years before, I began to realize how complicated the organization actually was. Too complicated, I thought. My initial assignment was to oversee public policy (legislative and regulatory), communications, publications (the largest-circulation magazine in the world), international affairs, and organizational relations (which needed definition). I added another task: to master the organization and prepare for the upcoming board selection of a new CEO (hopefully me). The last thing I wanted was the disappointment I had experienced at CARE in the competition to lead the organization.

I figured I had about a year at AARP to demonstrate top-tier leadership and management before the board chose a new CEO— in other words, move fast and effectively. I told the *Washington Post*, which called AARP the most powerful of the Washington power brokers, that older people were playing a bigger and bigger role in public life and that I saw AARP being a huge force for social change.

Before I arrived the overriding theme at the organization was, "The boomers are coming." But now the boomers were here. Baby boomers, those born between 1946 and 1964, were the largest population segment in the nation, some 78 million strong, and the media and academic literature painted them as unique in many ways. They were catered to at each stage of life, from infancy on, because of the size of the cohort. They were more "lifestyle" oriented than their predecessor segments, and they were said to be looking for something new, something novel in life. We called them feisty. They were an important target market not just for AARP, but for just about every marketer in the country. Peter Drucker, the management guru said, "It's an old rule that the population group that is both the biggest and growing the fastest determines the mood." That was the boomers. And Yogi Berra also had some advice: "The future ain't what it used to be."

AARP management was wrestling with whether the boomers could be incorporated into a membership organization known for "older" people. Would they join? Or should AARP consider splitting into two organizations—one for the boomer segment and one for older generations? I didn't like that idea. One AARP—with the appeals and flexibility for everyone over 50—was how I thought about it.

This organization was a complex enterprise that needed streamlining, but we had the tools and the talent. Horace Deets, then head of the organization, knew of my goal to succeed him, and he said, "Pay special attention to the business [the for-profit subsidiary called AARP Services, Inc., or ASI], our volunteers, public policy, and communications. Those are the keys to the organization." That was good advice.

AARP had a powerful genesis story that helped bring our employees and volunteers together. Back in the 1950s Ethel Percy Andrus had been the first female high school principal in the state of California. After a successful career as an educator, she retired to take care of her aging mother. In those days retired teachers had meager pensions and no health insurance. As the story goes, Ethel (we all called her that, though few current employees had ever met her) went off one day to visit a retired teacher she knew. She found the woman destitute, living in an old chicken coop.

Ethel got mad; she also got organized. She began a personal campaign to provide affordable health insurance for retired educators. It took her eight years, but her perseverance paid off. She was able to offer the first-ever group health insurance coverage to retired teachers throughout the country. On that basis, she started the National Retired Teachers Association. And then she founded AARP. She saw her new organization as an "army of useful citizens" who had the ability, the experience, and the desire to promote and enhance the public good. She created the motto that still reverberated around the halls when I arrived: "To serve; not to be served."

I loved that story, and I really believed in Ethel's message that AARP had and could make a huge difference in making things better, not just for older people, but for all generations. It was built into the mission of the organization: enhance the quality of life for *all* as we age. I dug into the research and saw how connected the generations of Americans are to each other. What do older people care about? Their children and their grandchildren, and leaving things better than they found them (a powerful legacy theme). And what do younger Americans care about? Their parents and grandparents. We think and act *across* generations.

When I arrived, AARP's management was in the final stages of choosing a public relations agency. I made the decision to award our account to FleishmanHillard. Porter Novelli wasn't in the finals, so I didn't have a conflict there. And although Fleishman was part of Omnicom (which was also the parent of Porter Novelli), I informed Horace of that to be clear about any hidden interests. FleishmanHillard turned out to be a good choice.

I set out to relaunch the AARP brand (restage it, as we said back at Unilever) to be clear about what we stood for and what defined us, and to enhance how we appealed to all segments of our members and prospective members. Second, I wanted to set clear boundaries between the various AARP operations, especially in attracting and working with outside partners, and between AARP the parent and ASI. And finally, even though I wasn't yet fully conversant with the complex policy issues we were dealing with, I wanted us to take stronger public leadership positions, especially in driving for a prescription drug benefit in Medicare and reforming Social Security.

I began to think of the parent organization as having two primary pillars. One was social impact, with an emphasis on financial security for older people, health and health care, and independent living (that is, living independently as well as possible for as long as possible). The other pillar was essentially marketing: winning and keeping members. This pillar required effective recruitment and retention strategies as well as the benefits (insurance, discounts, other offerings) offered by ASI.

The ASI business model came directly from Ethel's early work to provide health insurance to retired educators. Essentially, ASI—a tax-paying subsidiary—manages the organization's business activities, including the royalties paid to AARP for endorsing products. These endorsements are based on careful vetting of each offering and then constant monitoring to be sure that the customers (AARP's members) are satisfied. It's AARP's reputation that is behind the products, like a Good Housekeeping seal of approval. In turn, the revenues from these products are reinvested in social impact and member development, including keeping membership dues low. A key principle is that policy trumps marketing—always. Any potential offering from ASI goes through a policy screening to be vetted and to ensure it is consistent and compliant with AARP's policies and practices.

AARP attracts plenty of criticism. Some charge that it is just a marketing factory (ASI) disguised as a nonprofit. Some claim it is too partisan and political (usually that it leans left). Some say it is too cautious and afraid to take tough positions. And then there's the opposite charge—AARP is too strong and has too much power.

But the criticism that always concerned me most was that "children don't vote." This was about the clout that older people have in our society in comparison with the money and effort we spend on our kids. One estimate claims that government spending on older and retired Americans is already nearly half the federal budget and perhaps six times as high as spending on children. In effect, the criticism goes, this is because kids don't vote. A persistent, thoughtful critic along these lines is the economist Robert Samuelson, who has written columns for *Newsweek* and the *Washington Post*. Samuelson believes that US spending on "entitlements" (Social Security, Medicare, and Medicaid) will not be sustainable as the nation ages. These are all criticisms to be heeded, some more than others. But the need to be intergenerational in our programs and our advocacy never left my mind.

We had a set of tools to create social impact and member value: our policy advocacy, information and education channels, our volunteers, products and services, our philanthropy (via our foundation, which we later revamped), and strong partnerships.

A reporter called from *PR Week* and asked me what a PR guy— me—was doing in my new role at AARP. I said I was pursuing social relevance and solving social problems. I may have a PR background, but I think of my discipline as marketing and my career as social problem solving. Soon after, *Inside PR* called me a "PR legend." Not really, but what the hell.

As Horace said, I needed to pay attention to our volunteers, so I hit the road. One stop was an AARP grassroots event in Iowa with presidential candidate Bill Bradley. About 200 AARP members were there, asking Bradley a lot of good questions. He was thoughtful, farsighted, and—I thought—flat. He had a kind of serene, zen approach to campaigning. I thought that maybe, if it were a 10-year primary season, he might have a chance of catching Al Gore.

I also reconnected with Vice President Gore at an AARP board and management function. He had been and still was strong on tobacco control, but his message to AARP was about the risk involved in George W. Bush's call for letting people invest part of their Social Security savings in the stock market. Not long after this, Gore beat Bradley in the New Hampshire Democratic primary, but only by 4 points, and surprisingly, John McCain clobbered Bush by 19 on the Republican side.

During the South Carolina Republican primary campaign we did an "AARP Meet the Candidate" forum with Senator McCain. He congratulated me on my Campaign for Tobacco-Free Kids work, and I thanked him for his leadership in the tobacco fight. He had Senator Lindsey Graham with him, and we had some 600 AARP members there. I was surprised how thin and tired McCain looked, but he connected with our audience, and he was covered well in the media.

As for learning the policy issues, Horace and I and several of our staff met with House Speaker Dennis Hastert. It was a wide-ranging discussion, with emphasis on Medicare and Social Security. Horace really knew his policy stuff after 25 years at AARP.

The rebranding program, based on solid consumer research, was going well. We called it Project Fast Forward, and it created a lot of energy within AARP. Horace said it was the most employee spirit he'd seen in 25 years, and he approved additional spending on the program. Our internal challenge was to get everyone to understand that this wasn't just an advertising campaign. It was a total, integrated program in which all parts of AARP contributed to our brand image and objectives.

We decided to take our magazine, *Modern Maturity*, which was showing its age, and turn it into two magazines: one aimed at boomers, to be called *My Generation*, and the other to be a fresh, more interesting remake of *Modern Maturity*. We derived a lot of advertising revenue from our publications, and we wanted to do this right. Over time, we found that the two magazines didn't work well. But we learned a lot about communicating to boomers, and we incorporated those lessons into a revitalized new magazine with the name *AARP the Magazine*. It blossomed into a beautiful lifestyle publication that was published in three versions: one for 50- to 60-year-old members, one for 60- to 70-year-olds, and one for 70 and older. Hugh Delehanty, our veteran magazine guru, and Jim Fishman, our publisher, made it all work. I always use *My Generation* as an example of how to fail forward—to fail successfully.

I was out in the field a lot, engaging with volunteers (working retail, as David Ogilvy had advised) and pushing hard, giving speeches, and working the media.

We attended both the Republican and the Democratic national conventions and watched as George W. Bush and Al Gore were nominated as their parties' presidential candidates. We worked the two conventions, but they are such circuses that it's almost better to just enjoy the antics and get your political work done elsewhere. These were the first conventions I had been to since the Republicans nominated Richard Nixon back in 1972, and it was interesting to see how they had literally written Nixon out of their party's history.

Getting the Top Job

Later that fall, George W. Bush became president of the United States in a close, controversial election against Al Gore, and I was closing in on a full and intense year at AARP. Almost before I knew it, Horace and the board of directors announced his upcoming retirement. The competition for CEO was on. A board search committee was appointed, but at first little seemed to be happening. Then I discovered that they had hired a search firm (Korn Ferry) as friends began to call me to say the word was out far and wide to find candidates for the job. Another intergalactic search—it was unnerving.

Horace and I went to Zurich and Paris for a series of meetings. When I called my mother from Paris to wish her a happy birthday, she asked me what time it was "over there." I said it was 12:30 a.m.—tomorrow. Mom said, "That's nice. What's tomorrow like?" Good question.

Rumors were flying about how many high-level outside candidates there were for the CEO position. I learned that Vin Weber, the Republican congressman turned lobbyist with whom we had worked on tobacco, recommended me for the CEO job. An article appeared in *Roll Call* and was picked up by the *Washington Post* about a breakfast meeting among GOP senators and lobbyists at which Senator Rick Santorum asked how they could get a Republican into the AARP CEO job. The *New York Times* carried a piece saying AARP had lost its edge and identified me as a possible successor to Horace. I knew that annoyed the board, since they thought they were calling the shots. I was trying hard to lie low.

Cass Wheeler, the CEO of the American Heart Association, called to wish me luck and offer advice: to interview for his CEO job, he made a list of 120 possible questions and rehearsed his answers repeatedly on video, while wearing the same suit and tie he planned to wear to the interviews. I said thanks, but I don't think I can do all that. It's like leaving your fight in the gym.

For my interviews with the search committee, I wrote a one-pager on the challenges and opportunities facing AARP and another page on my vision and plan for making AARP truly great. That was it: two pages. Dawn Sweeney and a few other trusted AARP colleagues looked it over and made some comments. I was ready for action. In the meantime, I was making regular presentations to the board on policy, marketing, and other issues as though nothing else was going on.

Finally, my first interview with the board search committee arrived. As they and the search firm people were taking their seats, one of the committee members leaned over to me and said, "I understand you're not warm and fuzzy." I smiled at her and lamely responded, "I'm pretty warm." It was a fairly standard interview: 10 minutes of talking about myself, 45 minutes of competency questions (What's your management style? Your leadership style? What tough situations have you handled? What professional and personal accomplishments are you proud of? What's your perspective on diversity?). Then came the questions I was geared for: If you had this job, what would you do in the first six months? How about longer term? Where would you take AARP? I took out my two pages and made my pitch.

Among other things, I said we needed less complacency and more urgency; we needed to be leaner and redirect more spending to mission priorities. We needed more talent in key positions. I was specific and direct. Too direct? I wasn't sure. Then I went back to work.

I recruited an outstanding person to oversee our international operations: Nancy LeaMond, former chief of staff to US trade representative Charlene Barshefsky. Nancy asked if I would stay at AARP if I didn't get the CEO job. Probably not, I answered. Today Nancy oversees a huge part of the organization, including policy advocacy and state operations. In terms of placing more talent in key positions, she was exhibit A.

Then I got a call from Korn Ferry asking for references, followed by a letter asking for more specifics on where I would take AARP in the next five years and how I would lead us there. I got out my trusty two pages and expanded them into a short deck. Another search committee interview followed, and committee members began to offer me soto voce comments. Horace was on my side.

I later learned that Korn Ferry spoke to each of my references, plus all my direct reports and others inside AARP. Then at a special board meeting, each of the search committee members spoke on my behalf to the full board. I was invited in to give my pitch. I told them what we could achieve together, how committed I was, and that we would have a great partnership. Then I went out and paced the hall. It didn't take long. I was the new CEO of AARP. They invited Horace to join us for pictures and a toast. I was in.

The next day was gratifying. Fran was happy, and the senior staff gave me a big round of applause. I was stoked, but I took a minute that night to ask myself one of my favorite questions: What's next? How can I truly make the most of this opportunity?

I answered with action. Here was the chance of a lifetime to lead a large, powerful organization with a great mission and the resources to vigorously pursue it. I had told the board what I wanted to do, and I was ready to do it. The plan was this: eliminate low-level activities that weren't advancing AARP's priorities; redirect the resources into key program areas; be more aggressive, especially in public policy advocacy; and build revenues, especially in our for-profit subsidiary (ASI), where there were big opportunities to offer more products and services to our members. I was determined to make AARP the top organization in the country for positive, sustained social impact.

I went to my first ASI board meeting, and to my surprise there was little focus on revenues. Instead, there were a lot of soft, unquantified estimates and discussions of new product potential. We had a lot of work to do here.

We released a first-of-its-kind report on Fifty Plus America. It was well done and well received and got a lot of media attention. We decided to issue this report annually, before each presidential State of the Union address.

Now that I was the CEO, policy makers began to call me directly. Senator Jay Rockefeller wanted to meet to ask for our support for a prescription drug benefit in Medicare. His focus was on getting the lowest premium possible for his low-income constituents in West Virginia. Treasury secretary Paul O'Neill invited me to sit down and discuss Social Security. John Rother and I listened to his ideas for partially converting Social Security into private accounts, which would cost a huge amount of money during the transition phase. We asked him where the money would come from, and O'Neill said from general revenues. Later he told me he was going to join AARP so he could "keep an eye on" us. I said I would provide a complimentary membership, and O'Neill replied, "It's OK—I can afford it."

I wanted to get a fix on just how AARP was regarded among Republicans and Democrats in Congress. To find out, I hired two research consultants, one a Democrat and the other a Republican, to query members of Congress and their staffs. The answers were jolting. Both parties were well aware of and wary about the size of our membership, our access to the media, and our resources. But beyond that, the differences were stark. Democrats were essentially simpatico with AARP's policy positions, but they said we favored expediency above principles. We were too eager to scrape and bow to the Republicans, who were, they said, scornful of us for doing so. And what did the Republicans think? By and large, they thought we were a bunch of Democrats! As a result, we knew had to make our positions clear and strong, and advocate for our constituents, not for political constituencies or political parties. It was not an easy road to travel.

To keep abreast of the two parties and assess our positions, we used expert advisors. We retained Chris Jennings, a Democratic consultant who had been in the Clinton White House during my tobacco-control days, and Linda Tarplin, a Republican policy consultant. Both had excellent contacts within their parties and good instincts about our issues. Every Friday our policy team and I met with Chris and Linda for breakfast in the AARP cafeteria. They gave us straight talk, respected each other's positions, and helped us navigate the shoals.

As I prepared to make my inaugural speech to the entire organization, I took pains to listen: to our volunteers, to our staff, and especially to our second level of management. I called my top team the Executive Team, and the next layer (some 50 senior people) our Leadership Team. I met with each of those 50 and asked them what they were doing, how it fit into our mission and our priorities, and what they thought we could do to drive AARP forward. The responses were thoughtful and enlightening and helped me work through our options and our needs. At the end of our conversation, one woman jumped up, gave me a hug, and said, "You're not as stiff as you look!" Hey, maybe I was warm and fuzzy after all.

Early one morning I was walking through the underground passageway from my side of the building to our small gym. An employee stepped out of the mail room and said, without fanfare, "They say you're a millionaire. Are you a millionaire?" I came up with a lame answer: "I'm not sure—I'll have to check." We both smiled, and I walked on. So now my reputation was growing: I was warm, fuzzy, and rich.

I kicked off my tenure as CEO with an all-staff meeting in Washington in mid-2001 and began by thanking the board for appointing me and thanking Horace Deets for his leadership at the helm over 13 years. My comments came straight out of my two-page presentation to the board, plus ideas that had surfaced in my listening sessions with our management. I pointed out that we were operating from a strong base: a powerful mission, talented managers and staff, a large cadre of committed volunteers across the country (Ethel's army of useful citizens), and financial strength.

I then laid out my overarching priorities, which I called Three Great Goals that were worthy of our mission:

Goal One: AARP will be the most successful and acknowledged organization in America for positive social change. We will focus foremost on our members, but the benefits will ripple out to all older people, including the less well off, and ultimately will impact *all* generations.

Goal Two: We will deliver on our promise to each member: to help them make their own choices, reach their goals and dreams, and make the most of life after 50. This is the very essence of AARP member service. This is how we connect with people. It's what we want them to believe when they see the AARP logo and read and hear our name.

Goal Three: AARP will be a world leader in global aging. Working internationally is not new to us. But now we need to think more globally than ever before.

From that moment on, those goals served as our North Star. The first goal consisted of social impact—making a positive difference in people's lives, as I told Steve Schroeder we could do. The second was a marketing goal—winning and keeping members, the core of our strength. And the third was a reach—expanding our scope by going beyond our shores and influencing the world's rapidly aging societies. This third goal never resonated with some of the board and staff. Their attitude was that there were plenty of problems to solve at home. My point was that globalism was here, and we needed to lead. Later I retained a firm to assign a value to AARP's brand. They placed it at something like $7 billion. "Why not higher?" I asked. Their reply: "Because you're not global." I was determined that we would play on the world stage.

I continued the speech to say that, to achieve the Three Great Goals, we would need to beef up our results orientation, focus more tightly on our priorities, strengthen key operations, and improve the use of our resources. And I stressed our policy advocacy at state and national levels. As strong as we were, we could be stronger and better.

Building a Great Team

There's only one way I know to do great work, and that's to have a great team. Ours was taking shape. Dawn Sweeney took over as president of ASI and immediately began to raise revenues and staff morale (she later went on to become the CEO of the National Restaurant Association.) Tom Nelson became our chief operating officer and finished the job of opening an office in every state plus the District of Columbia, Puerto Rico, and the US Virgin Islands (Tom is now the CEO of Share Our Strength/No Kid Hungry). The three of us were a kind of team within a team.

Ellie Hollander, who was superb at talent management, became our chief people officer (she is now the CEO of Meals on Wheels America). John Rother, our policy guru, was top-notch at policy formulation and political thinking. While John wasn't a strong manager, Kevin Donnellan was, and he oversaw our advocacy operations while John focused on policy (Kevin is now chief of staff to AARP CEO Jo Ann Jenkins). One of my best moves was to move John to an office next to mine so we could have quiet policy discussions at any time of day (John now leads the National Coalition on Health Care). Nancy LeaMond began to lead our global aging work, and we recruited Chris Hansen, a government affairs expert from Boeing, to lead our team on the Hill and with the administration (see chapter 8 about Chris's later accomplishments).

Although he wasn't a member of the Executive Team, one of my most valuable teammates was Boe Workman (the editor of this book). He was my speechwriter, but I called him my "speech thinker" because he helped form and fashion ideas into effective communication. I gave Boe carte blanche to sit in on any meeting, in any AARP office, so he could be conversant with all that was going on. He helped craft policy speeches and everything else I wanted to say. I could get on a plane with a speech from Boe and know I might make some editorial changes but would virtually never have to rewrite.

Every day at AARP there were probably a hundred decisions being made that had important consequences for the organization, and I was making maybe five of them. That's the reason you can't overcentralize decision-making in a large organization. The leadership challenge is to provide values and goals and then give your executives the opportunity to lead their operations, and for them to cascade that leadership to the next level down.

One issue was effective strategic planning. AARP didn't have a standard planning format—a house style—and as a result it was difficult to work through and across planning exercises among various units. Fortunately, we had Lucy Theilheimer, who was tasked with putting an enterprise-wide dashboard into place to assess AARP's performance and progress. Lucy took on the job of setting up a standard planning approach, and this task dovetailed with the dashboard work.

The Battle to Get Prescription Drugs into Medicare

A reporter called to ask me, "Are you going to go after the pharmaceutical industry the way you went after the tobacco industry?" I said, "Absolutely not. The tobacco industry destroys lives; the drug industry saves lives. We need the life-saving drugs the pharmaceutical industry provides, but we also need to make them more affordable. As head of AARP, I'm going to work to make prescription drugs more affordable."

Several pharmaceutical companies approached me about working together on public education around risk factors like diabetes and high blood pressure. But they also made it clear that they wanted to discuss drug prices—and stave off legislation that would contain costs. Our strategy toward these companies was what I call "talk and fight": we would work with the industry where we could while also working against high drug prices. As I've said, to solve big social problems we need everybody at the table: friends, near-friends, and opponents. We need to talk as we search for possible agreements, but of course in this highly competitive world different companies, interests, and industries are going to fight it out as well. I've always found that the best strategy is to do both, to talk and fight. And often—though not always—that can lead to a win.

Later we launched a campaign about the wise use of prescription drugs. Many in the industry saw it as a thinly disguised advocacy campaign to attack drug prices. The media, most notably the *Wall Street Journal*'s Kelly Green, helped this notion along. The drug companies complained bitterly, and some pulled their advertising from our magazine and monthly newspaper, *AARP Bulletin*. When we joined three federal antitrust suits against industry pricing, things really heated up. As far as PhRMA and many of its members were concerned, we were doing more fighting than talking. But I was always able to communicate with several company CEOs and seek common ground.

The way we saw it, you can't practice modern medicine without prescription drugs. High blood pressure, congestive heart failure, arthritis, high cholesterol, and many other illnesses can all be treated and controlled with medication. Prescription drugs allow people to stay healthy, work, and avoid many hospitalizations and other forms of institutionalization.

In 2001 the seemingly out-of-control rise in the cost of prescription drugs was a major problem in this country, especially for older Americans, who are the highest users of prescription drugs. Because Medicare didn't cover prescription drugs, older people had to pay for them on their own. But too many older Americans and their families could not afford them. The marketplace was out of balance, and the cost of drugs that combat disease and ease suffering was simply too high.

Prescription drug costs were rising at an unsustainble rate. Between 1993 and 2001 spending on prescription drugs rose on average about 13 percent a year, and it was expected to climb about 12 percent a year for the next decade. The prices of brand-name prescription drugs had been rising at nearly four times the general rate of inflation. Nearly one in five American women between the ages of 50 and 64 did not fill a prescription because it was too expensive. Millions of seniors were skipping doses or splitting pills to save money. And prescription drugs were the fastest-growing item in many state health care budgets.

A study by Harris Interactive found that higher out-of-pocket costs were causing massive noncompliance in the use of prescription drugs. Millions of Americans did not ask their doctors for the prescriptions they needed, did not fill the prescriptions they were given, didn't take their full doses, or took their drugs less often than they should. The study also found that the higher people's out-of-pocket costs for drugs, the more likely they were to be noncompliant.

At AARP we were hearing from our members about this every day. It was a huge and persistent problem that would not go away by itself. It was affecting not just low-income seniors, but also middle-class people on fixed incomes. Businesses large and small were feeling the squeeze of high drug costs. Many were either dropping drug coverage from their health care plans or requiring employees and retirees to pay significantly more.

We were committed to helping our members and all older Americans and their families cope with this. Our goal was to get an affordable prescription drug benefit in Medicare, with some cost containment so that a Medicare benefit could be sustained. Older Americans and their families didn't expect first-dollar coverage, but they did want a benefit that was affordable and that they could depend on over time.

Medicare, the health insurance program for older Americans, is not just a government program; it's a cultural phenomenon and a battle cry for seniors, who claim it as their heritage. People pay into Medicare at work, and when they reach 65 they see claiming Medicare as a rite of passage and a benefit that they earned. Many people may not even realize it's a federal program. Signs always seem to crop up at rallies: "Keep government out of my Medicare."

Back in 1988, senior citizens started a near riot in defense of Medicare. Occupying a Chicago street, they began rocking the car of powerful Democratic congressman Dan Rostenkowski, chairman of the House Ways and Means Committee. He had led the passage of a change in Medicare limiting seniors' out-of-pocket costs and adding a first-ever drug benefit. Why were Medicare beneficiaries furious about these seeming improvements? Because they would have to pay a higher Medicare monthly premium.

Seniors across the country, a huge voting bloc, were angry and outspoken. Members of Congress, AARP management and board members, and anyone else who was involved in the changes were stunned, and abashed. The next year, Congress repealed the legislation by a substantial margin. Nobody—nobody—forgot this traumatic lesson.

While AARP had advocated for that legislation and had worked for years to get drug coverage into Medicare, the story in 2002–2004 was different. Now George W. Bush was president, and he and his administration and congressional allies decided that a drug benefit in Medicare was not only good policy but good politics as well. And this time AARP—and I as CEO—took a much more substantial leading role in the effort, as the GOP majority largely elbowed Democrats aside and revised Medicare, including a major drug benefit. It was widely agreed that AARP's support had pushed the Medicare Modernization Act over the top. And once again, all hell broke loose. Or as I like to say, no good deed goes unpunished. This is that story, as well as an account of where we stand today with senior health insurance in a country that can't get health care right.

Go Big or Go Home

When President Bush took on Medicare reform and prescription drugs, we decided to go all in. We calculated that if we didn't win this time, the opportunity might not come around again for years because of the expensive war in Iraq, the expanding budget deficit, and the coming presidential election. As a result of this calculation, we lobbied aggressively; incurred the wrath of many politicians, especially Democrats; helped author key provisions of the bill; fought for needed measures in the legislation; worked to inform our members and bring them along; and spent millions of dollars on advertising to promote the bill and then educate the public after its passage. Our strategy was simple to articulate—talk and fight every step of the way—but tricky to pull off.

The president and his advisors believed that traditional Medicare was inefficient because beneficiaries could go to any doctor or hospital they wanted, as long as those providers were in the program. The Republican answer was to push seniors into managed care plans that would be less expensive and potentially offer more comprehensive care. This was to be the trade-off for drug coverage. We disagreed and advocated for a drug benefit that would be universal under current Medicare.

We dramatized our position by delivering a Medicare birthday cake to all 100 US senators and 435 House members—with a slice of the cake missing. The missing piece represented the lack of drug coverage. Kevin Donnellan, then a senior legislative official at AARP and now chief of staff, came up with the idea and delivered many of the cakes himself along with our staff and a group of AARP volunteers. It was a great tactic and made for a compelling visual that gained a lot of media coverage.

Our legislative strategy was to focus on the Senate, which was a more favorable body for the legislation, and then work for a good compromise in the negotiating conference that would follow with the House. But we had to overcome some serious image problems. The Democrats were angry with us and called us "wishy-washy," unwilling to take a stand and back their legislative fight for what they saw as the right thing.

The Republicans, while respectful of our grassroots clout, believed that our members were older and had lower incomes than the general 50+ population. In fact, AARP is so large that it virtually mirrors the American demographic and political spectrum. Furthermore, Republicans considered us a "liberal" organization that sided with the Democrats. We ended up showing both parties that they were wrong about us.

I told the board and our management team that we had to be more aggressive and forceful in our advocacy; if we were going to succeed, we had to push the boulder up the hill. The board had awarded me the CEO job for just that reason, and the management and staff were yearning to flex our muscles. So we went on offense.

Each January we began the year with a media briefing on our annual legislative agenda. In January 2002 we included a letter I had sent to the president saying, "An affordable and meaningful prescription drug benefit in the Medicare program is a top priority for AARP, our members and the nation. We realize that budget constraints are greater than last year, but so is the need for a Medicare prescription drug benefit. We also know that providing our nation's older and disabled citizens with the choice of affordable drug coverage will not get easier. Therefore, we should not delay."

The administration offered a $190 billion package—not enough money for good coverage, but a start. I testified before the Senate Finance Committee and tried to up the ante. I said that seniors would assess any benefit via a "kitchen table" test, by figuring out how much they spent on drugs each month and how much help they needed. I quoted a poll we had conducted showing that the currently proposed plan would be viewed as inadequate. Our argument was that "everyone needs this as part of modern medicine."

Groups of senators began working on different approaches. We kept pushing, polling our members, speaking out, and lobbying behind the scenes. Finally, we decided that our best bet was a

$600 billion plan offered by Senator Bob Graham of Florida, a shrewd Democrat with a sense of what was possible for both parties.

Graham's plan was included in an amendment that was defeated 50–49, not really that close considering it took 60 votes to avoid a filibuster. According to senators in both parties—even those who wanted to pass a drug bill—it was just too expensive. The magic number seemed to be somewhere between $400 billion and Graham's $600 billion.

Senator Ted Kennedy, a leader among the Democrats, tried to broker a compromise, but it didn't go anywhere. And Republicans, who had a safe majority in the House, didn't want to make a deal with Democrats. Once again, as we assessed the situation, we doubled down on the Senate. And we made a mistake. We had run ads praising the Graham approach, leading other senators to say, "We thought you were working with us. Are you or aren't you?" There are some big egos on the Hill, especially in the Senate, and we didn't help ourselves with those ads. We weren't doing well enough with Senate Republicans. We signed on too early in support of the Graham approach. But we learned as we went along.

We ramped up our grassroots support for drug legislation and simultaneously worked the Congress harder and smarter. We generated some 200,000 contacts by our members with Congress, held "kitchen table" events across the country, and sponsored state-level meetings and rallies. Our Hill relationships had traditionally been better with Democrats, but Chris Hansen, a savvy lobbyist who had come to us from Boeing, and I were determined to change that. Chris, John Rother, and I became a strong team, with a great deal of support from David Certner, our director of federal affairs; our state offices; our policy research staff; and others. We were a good operation, and we learned from our mistakes.

We had to correct another weakness: we had not created alliances with the business community. In hindsight, this was a serious omission, and I of all people, who came from the private sector, should have done more to enlist corporate support or at the very least opened more of these channels. I was talking to pharmaceutical company CEOs, especially Ray Gilmartin at Merck and Pat Kelly at Pfizer North America, but that wasn't enough.

Then, in the midterm elections of 2002, the Republicans gained control of the Senate while keeping their majority in the House. As a result they held both houses of Congress and the presidency as well.

We had our policies straight, we had a good team, and we had public support. Now, could we get a drug benefit in Medicare or not? We caught a break when Senate majority leader Trent Lott of Mississippi resigned his leadership position after making controversial statements at a birthday party for Senator Strom Thurmond of South Carolina, who had run for president years before as a segregationist. Lott said the country would have been better off if Thurmond had won. Lott had never really cared about a drug benefit in Medicare and certainly wasn't fond of AARP. He had called us a wholly owned subsidiary of the Democratic party.

Lott was replaced by Bill Frist, a Republican from Tennessee who was a physician, a proponent of a Medicare drug benefit, and a reasonable legislator. On the House side, the Speaker was Dennis Hastert, who we believed wanted a drug benefit passed. We had two leaders we could work with.

During the last session of Congress in 2002, we were close to achieving drug coverage in Medicare. We believed the foundation for success had been laid. The House passed a bill, though in our view it needed improvements. Although the Senate failed to pass a drug bill, 99 senators had voted for some form of a prescription drug benefit for Medicare beneficiaries. The Senate had essentially reached an implicit bipartisan agreement on a number of key issues, including the need to contain the spiraling cost of drugs. But they could not reach agreement on two important issues:

whether to target the limited dollars to those most in need (people with low incomes or high drug expenses) and what the role of private insurers should be in delivering the benefit and controlling the cost. The differences between the two sides were substantial, but we didn't view them as insurmountable, and we were open to exploring compromises to achieve a drug benefit in Medicare. Nevertheless, it was clear that we would have to wait another year.

As 2002 came to a close, we had new research showing just what the public wanted and would support. Here again was a useful lesson. What the public wants and what we could reasonably achieve were not always the same. Our research showed that our members, and all seniors, hated the so-called donut hole that resulted from spending the drug benefit money primarily on people with the lowest incomes and on those with the highest drug costs. Everyone in the middle would face a gap—a "donut hole"—in payment where they would have to foot the bill until the benefit kicked in again. It was the best way to spread out the cost of drugs, but the average person didn't see it that way.

The lesson is to always understand what the public wants and to try to inform and educate people about what's possible and feasible. But at the end of the day, you have to make a decision that you think is best and deal with the consequences. In this case, we accepted the "donut hole" as a necessary concession to make the eventual bill affordable.

No Permanent Friends or Enemies, Just Permanent Issues and Principles

As 2003 began we worked to rally our troops—the board of directors, our advocacy team, and the whole of AARP. It was now or never—or at least not for years to come. The lesson I preached was one I had learned in the tobacco wars: get the best deal you can, and don't let the perfect be the enemy of the good. We kicked off the year with our regular January media conference covering our policy agenda, and I was as direct as I could be—a prescription drug benefit in Medicare was at the top of our agenda, and we were going all out to achieve it. The very next day the White House leaked its plan, which again called for beneficiaries to join managed-care plans to be eligible for a new drug benefit. We said no. The benefit had to cover everyone in Medicare.

I had been appointed to the President's Council on Service and Civic Participation and dutifully showed up at the White House with athletes, celebrities, civic leaders, and business executives, including Dick Parsons, CEO of AOL Time Warner; Bob Nardelli, CEO of Home Depot; and John Glenn, the former astronaut and senator from Ohio. Each of us had a separate photo op in the Oval Office with the president. As the picture was being taken, President Bush said to me, "Are you ready to talk about Medicare?" I said one word: "Yes." He said, "Something has got to be done." It was a personal moment that I read a lot into.

But we still had to deal with the Democrats, who were furious at us for talking to the Republicans in both houses and for not outright condemning their ideas. After all, Medicare had started as a Democratic program. What the hell were we doing?

Senator Kennedy complained that we were giving Bush too much room and said we needed to hit the Republicans hard. We did push back against some Republican proposals and even held a news conference to oppose their plan to revise Medicaid, the government program for the poor. But we never could satisfy the Democrats and appease their anger. A rock and a hard place.

A *Wall Street Journal* story said we were striving for balance between the two parties, and Newt Gingrich was quoted as saying that anyone who intended to get substantial changes in Medicare needed to understand the concerns of AARP and that we were trusted by millions of people.

Senator Frist was good at reaching out. In February 2003 he and Democratic senator John Breaux of Louisiana brought together all the interest groups: employers, including pharmaceutical companies; General Motors and other businesses; health systems; and others. John Rother and I were there, and John commented that the "donut hole" was a big problem. But we knew we might have to eat that donut to get the rest of what we wanted.

In a White House meeting Karl Rove, the president's chief political advisor, was playing hardball, as usual. Besides the change to Medicare, they wanted us to support other initiatives, including a tax proposal. We said we would call their Medicare framework a good first step and that we were glad the president was leading on this. The next day John Rother was quoted in the *New York Times* as being critical of the administration's Medicare approach. Rove was furious, having just told the president they had a good meeting with us. I was embarrassed at our media gaffe, and so was John. It wasn't our first media mistake, nor our last.

Later the White House offered up an olive branch by inviting us to a ceremony to mark the 38th anniversary of Medicare. They sat us up front, and the president said he was ready to sign a bill on Medicare reform with a drug benefit for seniors. Then he got a laugh by saying that a lot of boomers were thinking about retiring and "I might be one of 'em."

In March, House Democratic leaders invited us to a private meeting. Minority leader Nancy Pelosi, John Dingell of Michigan, John Spratt of South Carolina, Sherrod Brown of Ohio, and Henry Waxman, with whom I had had difficulties in the tobacco fights, were present. They started by heavily criticizing the Republican initiatives and told us we should endorse their Democratic bill, which cost some $800 billion. I tried to say it diplomatically, but the answer was "no."

I don't think they ever realized that we were 100 percent committed to getting a drug benefit, whatever it took. In hindsight, it is clear that I should have gone to each of them separately and tried to reason this out. I later had a contentious phone conversation with Nancy Pelosi that I don't think she ever forgot or forgave, although we have had a number of civil exchanges since.

The Republicans then stepped up to sweeten the pot. In a White House meeting they said that *all* Medicare beneficiaries would receive the new benefit once enacted and that $400 billion was a "plug" (that is, a marker) in the budget. Karl Rove implied there might be more money later.

One of our unlikeliest allies was former Republican Speaker of the House Newt Gingrich. A villain to Democrats and many AARP people, he was a hero to those on the right for leading the Republicans to a House majority during the Clinton administration, after years in the wilderness. What many people didn't know was that Gingrich had developed a healthy respect for AARP after working with my predecessor, Horace Deets, when Gingrich had been Speaker of the House.

Gingrich and I had several conversations about Congress and its workings, and about the opportunity for a drug benefit in Medicare. I wrote the foreword to his book *Saving Lives and Saving Money*, which contained a number of ideas about improving health care. Democrats later cited this as proof positive that I was a closet Republican. CNN quoted Nancy Pelosi: "I want you to know that Bill Novelli, the CEO of AARP, wrote the foreword to Newt Gingrich's book. . . . Did you know that?" Never mind that Hillary Clinton also had praise for Newt's book. Still, writing that foreword was not my best political decision.

Gingrich and Speaker Hastert were buddies who enjoyed sharing war stories. Hastert invited me to a dinner meeting with him and Gingrich in May. They spent a good bit of the evening reminiscing about their time together and the historic role of Speaker, and then we got down to business. Hastert said that they would make a drug benefit available to *all* Medicare beneficiaries, confirming what the White House had indicated. He said,

"I don't want to push 75-year-old grandmothers out of what they're used to."

Then he invited us to work with him and his caucus. "You need us to do this, and we need you," he said. It was an important moment for us and for getting the legislation we wanted. Handshakes all around. Then Hastert said, "How about if I pay for this dinner, and you can tell people you dined at the expense of not one, but two, House Speakers." I said, "Let me pay, and I'll tell people I took two Speakers to dinner." It was an AARP expense well worth making.

Despite the optimism of the evening, things began to drag. The political partisanship on the Hill was intense. No Democrat ever wanted to see President Bush proudly signing a big Medicare bill in the Rose Garden, and certainly not on the eve of a presidential election year.

The complexity of reforming Medicare and adding a prescription drug benefit was daunting, and things were tense. We tried to stay optimistic, but if we lost this opportunity and had to start over, it would be a disaster. As the baby boomers approached 65, the cost of the legislation would rise ever higher. I told the board we had to go all out, or we would end up looking like a paper tiger.

We tried to reach out to more players. I spoke to a breakfast meeting in South Carolina of the Congressional Black Caucus, hosted by senior House Democrat Jim Clyburn. The hope was that it could help us build African American alliances.

The Democrats tried again to bring us into their camp, and we attended a House meeting with their leadership. This time it was even more testy. I think they had planned a good cop, bad cop routine. Congressman Dingell said, "Tell us what you want in a bill, and we'll make it happen." And Congressman Waxman repeated what he had told me when I was at the Campaign for Tobacco-Free Kids, working with the state attorneys general in negotiations with the tobacco industry. He said, "We'll do the legislative work. Don't get in the way. We'll do the negotiating." They were angry and felt betrayed. And they clearly believed that the Republicans were out to destroy government-sponsored Medicare.

All this was a new, bold role for us—working with the Republicans on crafting a bill, laying out what we wanted, and negotiating our way along. We worked with House Ways and Means chairman Bill Thomas, House Energy and Commerce Committee chairman Billy Tauzin, Speaker Hastert, and House majority leader Tom DeLay (known as "The Hammer" for his take-no-prisoners approach to politics). At one point, Hastert asked me not to "blow up the bill." I didn't have anywhere near the clout to do that, but of course I agreed.

Probably my all-time least favorite politician was Bill Thomas. He loved to flaunt his intellect, and he is truly a smart man. He was also vain, insulting, and smug. Early in my AARP tenure, we invited him to address our board and management. He said he was going to reform Social Security by creating a generational war between young people and the older generation they had to support. He told our board, many of whom were of Social Security age, "Get out of the way; you're getting your checks in the mail." At one point in the Medicare negotiations, I thanked him for his "lecture" and walked out of his office.

On the Senate side, it was more cordial. Majority leader Bill Frist tried to reach across the aisle to bring in Democrats, including Senator Kennedy. He kept us involved and informed. We continued to believe that Frist would fashion a reasonable bill and then take it to a Senate-House compromise committee. But the House passed its bill first, largely along party lines, as expected. It had what we anticipated, including the donut hole, but it also contained elements we couldn't accept.

First, it had a so-called premium support, which encouraged people to leave traditional Medicare for managed-care plans.

Second, it had a means-testing provision, through which retirees with higher incomes would get a smaller benefit. To some this seemed reasonable, but to us it spelled trouble. It would erode Medicare as a universal social insurance program and eventually turn it into a welfare program. There was no way we could support it.

The Senate passed its bill without those objectionable provisions but with another poison pill for us. To try to save money, the Senate version required poor elders (called "dual eligibles" because they were eligible for both Medicare and Medicaid) to get their medication through Medicaid, the low-income program.

Now we had two bills, both with problems, going into conference negotiations. And nasty partisanship reared up again. House Ways and Means Committee chair Thomas decided to exclude House Democrats from the conference discussions. The only Senate Democrats allowed to attend were Max Baucus of Montana and John Breaux, both of whom raised suspicions among their colleagues on the sidelines.

We went back to our strength: our members. At a big event in Chicago, I called for demanding that Congress finish the job. Our president, Marie Smith, stoked people up and exhorted everyone to call their members of Congress and get their friends and neighbors to call as well. We held meetings all over the country calling for Congress to "fix and finish" the legislation. But back in Washington, it was dead time. Nothing was happening. In fact, the Senate Republican in charge of the conference negotiations, Chuck Grassley of Iowa, got so angry at Thomas, his fellow Republican, that he pulled out of the talks. To spark some action, the White House got involved, and Hastert pushed Thomas aside and worked with Frist directly.

At one point John Rother, Chris Hansen, and I were on the Hill four nights straight, meeting with Senator Frist on one side of the Capitol and separately with Speaker Hastert and Tom DeLay on the other side. DeLay said to us, "If we give you what you want, you'll still cut and run." How do you answer that? I simply said, "No, we're not running away from anything."

We spoke to every member we could, and often our lobbyists gave them (especially Democrats) information they didn't have. As we continued to negotiate provisions with the Republicans, the Democrats grew more and more angry at us and their Congressional opponents. We tried to get the Republicans to involve the Democrats, but they wouldn't hear of it. One Republican legislator told our lobbyist, "If you are telling us you will only support a bill if Teddy Kennedy agrees to it, you can forget it." Whichever way you sliced it, we were deeply involved in shaping the legislation.

In October Bill Frist said he was worried about how all this was playing out in the media. He asked us to help sell the pending legislation to the Congress and the public, and we asked him for more help with the provisions we disagreed with. I said that if the bill that came out of conference met our needs, we would take it to our board for approval and then launch a major member and media campaign to promote final passage. We walked out with some hope. But we had to push even harder for what we wanted.

A compromise was offered up on premium support—it would be a modest demonstration project. Kennedy hated even that. Bill Thomas hated it for another reason: because it was so watered down. He walked out of the conference and said he was going home. Time was running out.

Don't Let the Perfect Be the Enemy of the Good

In mid-November we reconvened our board for the fourth time on the legislation. There was still no deal in place, but we were on the goal line. I repeated my admonition that we could not let the perfect be the enemy of the good. Senator Frist and the White House had put several compromises in place, and things were tense but promising.

Our board hoped that Senator Kennedy would accept the revised bill, attracting broader Democratic buy-in. He didn't. During the course of the negotiations, he had advised me to "work the phones and talk to Democrats." But now, as Fran and I drove to a Penn homecoming football game in Philadelphia, he called to say that he was not going to endorse the bill. He told me, "You do what you need to do, and I'll do what I need to do."

Despite that setback, our board approved (although not unanimously) our support for the bill if there were two more changes, including reduced co-payments for low-income people receiving help with their drugs. We called Frist and Hastert with this news and got instant agreement. We were on board, and it was a done deal. The conference report—681 pages—was released on November 20, 2003.

The bill was not perfect. That only happens in Hollywood or Disney World. The $400 billion for prescription drug coverage was less than where we started, the donut hole was still in place, and there was no strong mechanism to put a lid on rising drug prices. But it did establish a prescription drug benefit in Medicare, gave solid help to low-income Americans and those with high drug costs, provided incentives to protect employer drug coverage for retirees, ensured that all Medicare beneficiaries would have access to drug coverage regardless of where they lived, and safeguarded the integrity of the Medicare system. All told, it was a victory for us, for our members, and for America's seniors. And it set off a firestorm.

With our strong support, the bill passed both the House and the Senate. Hastert and DeLay had to keep the House vote open for hours to arm-twist conservatives who hated an expansion of an entitlement program that would cost more as boomers reached Medicare age. Some other advocacy groups went along with us in supporting the legislation, but everyone on both sides of the political spectrum who didn't like the bill blamed it on AARP.

In fact, Democrats booed when Hastert praised us for supporting the bill in his final statement. Only 16 House Democrats voted for the final bill. We were attacked from many quarters. Thousands of complaints rolled in from members, and about 70,000 of them quit our organization. People burned their AARP cards to dramatize their objections. After it had passed, Democrats campaigned against the bill across the country and called us shills and stooges for the Republican Party.

Our board and staff were criticized as they explained what was in the final legislation. One mild-mannered board member went to a local meeting to discuss the legislation and was told, "Get stuffed, you son-of-a-bitch." When I addressed a meeting at the Harvard Club in New York, a woman raised her hand to say, "I have a Harvard MBA and I can't understand what's in this bill, and neither can my mother." In a moment of weakness, or just cheekiness, I said, "I come from Penn, and if you had a Wharton MBA and couldn't understand it, then I'd be worried." Fran and I got nasty calls in the middle of the night, and I received hate Christmas cards. "Merry Christmas, Bill, you blankety-blank-blank. May you go straight to hell!"

But we won. We played a major role in getting drug coverage into health insurance for older Americans. We were aggressive and played offense—talk and fight—all the way. *The Hill*, a newspaper covering Congress, reported that we had spent $20.9 million on lobbying in 2003, a $16 million increase over the prior year. The new legislation and drug benefits were confusing, and we mounted a multi-million-dollar advertising and education campaign to explain how it worked. In my column in the *AARP Bulletin*, AARP's monthly newspaper, I said we were going to invest in helping people prepare for the enrollment, and we would continue working with Congress to improve the legislation. And we did all that.

The program got off to a rocky start. Many beneficiaries weren't properly signed up. Within a few years, though, more than a million prescriptions were being filled every day, and people were realizing cost savings. More than 22 million Medicare beneficiaries were enrolled in the drug plans. The Kaiser Family Foundation did a study showing that about 80 percent of those enrolled were happy with the program. And a later Harvard study in the *Journal of the American Medical Association* (JAMA) reported that Medicare drug coverage was keeping seniors out of hospitals and nursing homes, helping them avoid medical treatment and enjoy a better quality of life.

The bill-signing ceremony was gratifying, to say the least. The event was too big for the White House Rose Garden, so it was held in the Daughters of the American Revolution Constitution Hall. President Bush called the legislation "the greatest advance in health care coverage for America's seniors since the founding of Medicare." I spotted Senator Frist's wife in the audience and told her what a champ her husband was. Even so, the controversy continued. CNN reported on the event by saying, "Backers say the $400 billion . . . Act will provide much-needed help for the nation's 40 million senior citizens to buy medications. Critics say it is a giveaway to drug makers and insurance companies and a prelude to the dismantling of the program."

Henry Waxman, who had twice told me to lay off being a legislator and leave that up to him, called to tell me that he knew why I had led the drug bill effort and that he respected me for it. I told him I felt the same way about him. Dennis Hastert fell into dark times. He was convicted of child molestation when he had been a high school coach many years before and went to prison. Tom DeLay was later indicted and convicted on charges of conspiracy to violate election laws but was acquitted. He founded a lobbying firm and wrote a book appropriately titled *No Retreat, No Surrender:*

One American's Fight. Bill Frist left the Senate and is now a successful businessman and health care advocate. Bill Thomas became a lobbyist and a fellow at a conservative think tank. Billy Tauzin became the CEO of PhRMA, the pharmaceutical trade association. Newt Gingrich is a political pundit and informal counsel to President Donald Trump. And Nancy Pelosi is back in the majority as Speaker of the House and battling President Donald Trump at every turn.

This landmark legislation was a major accomplishment for older America and for those who care for them and care about them. But we made a lot of mistakes along the way, and if I had it all to do over again, I could have done the job better. I wasn't always as diplomatic an advocate as I could have been. Our campaign to explain the legislation after it passed wasn't as well tested or clear as it should have been. We didn't engage enough opinion leaders and partners in this fight. Many would probably have not joined with us, but at least we could have done more to inform them.

The complexity of the issues and the legislation was a big challenge, and we could have done more research to learn how to explain it better. And my media performance was not as good as I could have made it. In fact, as I look back, public relations, one of my supposed strong suits, wasn't exactly a high point for us. Conservative media attacked AARP, including me personally. They asserted that we claimed to represent our members but really didn't, we refused to consider having private, competitive health plans in Medicare, and we were just too powerful. At the same time, we often took a drubbing in the mainstream media because of our seeming disregard for the traditional Democratic leadership role in Medicare. Even after the legislation passed, we were hit by many stories centered on the theme "AARP under attack." I didn't help matters by continually speaking out. I should have taken the advice I often gave clients in my Porter Novelli days—just be quiet for a while.

"It Isn't Easy Being Green"

I quoted Kermit the Frog from Sesame Street in a big staff meeting, as I talked about how lonely it can be in a legislative fight when you don't really fit in anyone's tribe: "It isn't easy being green." No, it isn't, and we took a lot of flak. But we won a great victory, perhaps the most extraordinary win in AARP history. We demonstrated that we could achieve our top national priority. And we showed that both political parties were wrong about us. We were in the pragmatic center of the spectrum, beholden to neither side. Within a year, our membership surpassed the level we had had before the big Medicare brawl, and three key measures of our organizational success—intent to renew membership, intent to join, and volunteer satisfaction and engagement—were close to our highest levels. I put a plaque on my office wall that I could see every morning as I arrived at work. It had two quotes. One was from Republican senator Trent Lott: "AARP is a wholly owned subsidiary of the Democratic party." The other was from liberal Democratic congressman Pete Stark of California: "What does AARP stand for? Always advocating for the Republican Party." That spelled it out for me. Seek the best path forward and call 'em as you see 'em.

Where is Medicare today? Virtually everything, including health policy, is on hold as the coronavirus sweeps the country and consumes government, the private sector, and civil society. Before that, however, there was the good news that the growth in overall health care spending had slowed. Catherine Rampell, a *Washington Post* opinion columnist, reported that this was true "whether we're talking about public- or private-sector health spending. Annual outlays have been lower than doomsday forecasters anticipated. And the sharpest slowdown has occurred with Medicare." She cited a study by Harvard economics professor David Cutler focused on medical spending for the elderly. It found that the categories with far and away the biggest drop in spending—and drops in elderly death rates—were related to heart health, including heart attacks, cardiac arrest, stroke, and other diseases. This finding was backed up by data from the Centers for Disease Control and Prevention. Cutler estimated that at least half of this welcome decline is the result of more people taking medications and taking them more regularly.

Why was this happening? Researchers don't know for sure, but there are several possibilities: more awareness of the need for treatment, existing drugs that went off patent and became less expensive, and the prescription drug benefit in Medicare, which reduced out-of-pocket costs for many seniors and seemingly led to more compliance. Here again, the Medicare drug benefit is paying off for the country.

In view of the pandemic, all bets and predictions are off. But as the nation recovers, the affordability of health coverage for seniors and the sustainability of the Medicare program will again be major issues. The Trump administration, Congress, many patient groups, and AARP—along with the public—are all conscious of this problem and calling for change. Not long before the coronavirus pandemic hit, the House passed a bill to contain the cost of prescription drugs, but it is vigorously opposed by the drug industry and seems to have little chance in the Republican-controlled Senate. The Senate has its own bill but has not taken action on it. In the absence of federal action to lower prescription drug costs, many states have passed legislation allowing for drug importation and other measures to bring down costs.

Medicare projections show that the program needs new attention and new strategies in the near future. If anything, the partisan bickering in the United States is actually getting worse. As the virus subsides and things, hopefully, return to a more normal state, health care is almost sure to return as a top issue among many voters, and there is a significant opportunity here to make a difference—to do well by doing good.

CHAPTER FIVE

THE BEST OFFENSE IS A GOOD DEFENSE

Battling over the Future of Social Security

Following our success in helping pass the Medicare Modernization Act, with its all-important prescription drug benefit, the Democrats, who had long been AARP allies, were furious that we had worked with Republicans on the Medicare legislation. They continued to criticize the new law—and slam AARP—around the country.

After our work with President George W. Bush and his White House staff on Medicare, our relationship with the administration was cordial but not exactly chummy. During the Medicare debate, we had talked with the White House and the Social Security Administration about holding a series of events the following year (2004) on the status of Social Security. We wanted a national dialogue on how the program could be strengthened as the huge baby boom generation aged.

Barry Jackson, who reported to Karl Rove, President Bush's chief political advisor, told us they wanted another nongovernment sponsor, the National Association of Manufacturers, in addition to AARP. They were suspicious of us on Social Security, and we were suspicious of them. Jim Lockhart, deputy commissioner at Social Security and a strong White House ally, was our primary contact there. Eventually, these community events were scrapped. This was virtually the only discussion between us and the White House about Social Security during that period. It was essentially dormant as a policy or political issue during 2003 and 2004.

The presidential election of 2004 was hard fought between President Bush and Senator John Kerry. While we knew the Republicans, including the president, had long been skeptical of Social Security as part of "big government," it did not surface as a major campaign issue. The president did say—as one among many topics in his campaign speeches—that he continued to favor private accounts as part of the program. But it seemed to be nowhere near the top of his list of goals for a second term.

At a June 2004 meeting of the Leadership Council of Aging Organizations, an umbrella group of nonprofits that I, as CEO of AARP, was taking our turn to chair, a Kerry policy staffer said that Senator Kerry, as president, would "fix" Social Security without cutting benefits or raising taxes. When one of our group asked how he would do that, the Kerry staffer said they would grow the economy. During the campaign, Kerry said that Social Security was fine as it was. He offered no plan except to say that "the best thing to do to protect Social Security is to put America back to work in jobs that pay more." He did criticize Bush for his idea of carving out private accounts.

At our big annual member event in October 2004—in the heat of the presidential campaign—First Lady Laura Bush came to speak on behalf of the president. She was gracious and friendly and gave a good speech about her husband and where he wanted to take the country. John Kerry, who did attend, stayed secluded back stage—I guess a snub for our Medicare work—until his time came to speak. He chided AARP management for supporting the Medicare legislation, and he promised to protect Social Security.

Skirting the issue was typical of the general approach most politicians took to Social Security. Long called the "third rail" of American politics, the program was sacrosanct—and explosive. It is the public pension for older Americans, and for many, the only income they have in old age. It provides a base of income for retirement years, financial protection for disabled workers and their dependents, and income for the families of workers who died. So seniors, politicians, and everyone else well understood what was at stake: don't mess with Social Security.

Created under Franklin D. Roosevelt during the Great Depression, the program has grown into one of the most important government protections in American history. Everyone (or almost everyone) contributes via payroll taxes, and everyone who contributes is guaranteed participation in the benefits, not as a charity but as a right. It is an earned benefit—not welfare.

While preserving and strengthening Social Security for future generations was and continues to be a core AARP goal, it did not appear to be on the political horizon in the near future. Instead, we were focused on getting the new Medicare improvements running smoothly and looking ahead to what we anticipated would be a major debate over health care reform in 2005 and beyond.

So we were caught flat-footed when, just two days after Bush won the November 2004 election over Kerry, he announced his intention to radically transform Social Security. He said in a press conference that he had earned a lot of political capital, and he was going to spend a good portion of it to give workers the opportunity to invest some of their Social Security taxes in personal private investment accounts. The president said, "We must lead on Social Security because the system is not going to be whole for our children and grandchildren."

We were surprised—and alarmed—by his announcement. The White House was under no obligation to signal their intentions and plans to AARP, but since we were the nation's largest organization dealing with aging issues and had worked with them on Medicare, it might have been a good idea to let us know.

But beyond that, the idea of private accounts carved out of Social Security taxes seemed to us and many others to be simply a bad idea. It did not meet the goal of a guaranteed benefit that would be there and be fair for all generations. And it would divert resources from the program and worsen the challenge of long-term solvency.

Bush's announcement was a surprise not only because it was so sudden after his reelection but also because he made it a centerpiece of his new four-year term. Looking back, we saw that he had mentioned private accounts in Social Security in his inaugural address in 2001, and later that year he formed a Commission to Strengthen Social Security, which included consideration of private accounts as part of its work. At the time he said, "Personal savings accounts will transform Social Security from a government IOU into personal property and real assets; property that workers will own in their own names and that they can pass along to their children."

The commission's interim report in 2001 called Social Security a "broken system," an inaccurate charge that compelled us to respond. I issued a public statement saying that "the President's Social Security Commission continues to work toward a predetermined outcome—a dramatic overhaul—that would lead to cuts in guaranteed benefits and shift financial risk to individuals."

The commission's final report came out at the end of 2001 and contained several options for personal accounts. It didn't receive much media or public attention. One reason was the continued focus on the September 2001 attacks on the World Trade Center and the Pentagon. In addition, the stock market was sliding downward, wiping out investors' wealth and probably cooling enthusiasm among Republicans for private accounts carved out of Social Security. Republican congresswoman (now senator) Shelley Moore Capito (R-WV), in a tight race for reelection in 2004, said she was "opposed to putting Social Security funds in the stock market and investing it willy-nilly, like Russian roulette." And the National Republican Congressional Committee said that "Republicans are opposed to privatization and are opposed to any proposal that would cut benefits, raise taxes, or raise the retirement age."

But the president and his advisors kept the idea alive. When he dramatically resurrected it after his reelection, he painted a picture of a modern Social Security for the 21st century that would give millions of young workers the chance to control and invest their own retirement money. We saw that as a reasonable, even attractive idea, but only if the private investments were *in addition* to Social Security, not carved out of payroll taxes. We saw the foundation of a secure retirement as resting on four pillars: a solvent Social Security system; individual retirement savings and employer pensions; the ability to work and to continue to earn; and adequate and affordable health care and long-term care coverage.

The Bush plan failed our test of a guaranteed basic income floor for all Americans. We saw it as a major step away from solvency—defined in policy terms as the ability of the Social Security trust funds at any point in time to pay the full scheduled benefits in the law on a timely basis. The program had already reached a point where annual benefits being paid out were greater than the annual revenues from payroll taxes, and the gap was projected to widen in coming decades. Solvency was the long-term problem that needed to be addressed, and the Bush plan didn't measure up.

I quietly asked long-time Republican congressman Ralph Regula (R-OH), a member of the House Appropriations Committee, what he thought of the Bush plan for private accounts coming out

of Social Security. He said he was against it because it would create winners and losers, and "the losers will be coming back to us
[Congress] to be made whole."

But now the President had won a tough election and kicked off
his second term by announcing to the nation that he was determined to transform a bedrock program for all Americans. There
would be no turning back for the White House. Here was a president who *would* mess with Social Security. We had to respond, and
we did, full bore, with every resource we had.

The battle over the future of Social Security wore on for eight
frenetic months. In the end, the White House was stymied. Like
Ralph Regula, some Republicans quietly stayed out of the argument. Democrats strongly opposed the Bush plan and adamantly
rejected private accounts. But they also avoided facing up to the
Social Security solvency problem. The Democrats saw Social Security, like Medicare, as *their* program and didn't want a Republican president in the kitchen. As for AARP, we carried the fight
around the country with lobbying, advertising, and other media;
a barrage of volunteers and grassroots activity; and hard work with
like-minded partners.

When it was over, the partial privatizing of Social Security was
off the table as a viable issue. The administration, its allies in the
business community, and Republicans in general put the blame for
the defeat on AARP. This was the other side of the partisan coin
from the Medicare debate, when we had worked with Republicans
and the Democrats blamed us for passage of the Medicare prescription drug bill.

Were we changing sides just to even things out? Absolutely not.
I called our position the pragmatic center. Our responsibility was
to assess the issues through the lens of our principles and policies
and to stake out positions that we believed served our members
and the country.

Forming a Plan of Attack

We moved past our surprise at the president's post-election press conference to a determination that we would take a leading role in opposition. We had already scheduled a meeting of our state directors and headquarters team for just a few days later. It gave us the opportunity to announce our plan to vigorously oppose the White House initiative on private accounts. Since we had recently worked with the administration on Medicare, some of our state directors wondered whether we would now seek a compromise on private accounts. I said, "No, we're going to stick to our policy and our principles, and the only way to do this is to get out front, work hard, be smart in our opposition, and commit the resources it will take to win."

Just a few days later, David Certner, our director of federal affairs, laid out a clear case for our position. He wrote: "We have to move on two fronts: substantive and political. On the political front, we have to convince Congressional Republicans that it is not in their best interest to take on private accounts. . . . It is a fight they cannot win. . . . They will face strong public and AARP opposition. On substance . . . our best arguments include: the fact that the diversion of funds weakens Social Security financially and will lead to cuts in guaranteed benefits, the overwhelming transition costs, and the added risk that does not belong in the Social Security benefit."

Certner and our policy advocacy team recommended that in the short term we had to keep Congress from moving forward on any proposals for private carve-out accounts because they risked a public backlash in the midterm elections. In the longer term we would continue to pursue the responsible course of recommending ways to create solvency for the program and take this issue to the public for discussion and understanding.

We translated that strategy memo into a call-to-action statement from Marie Smith, our president, and me to our full membership in the *AARP Bulletin*. Now our position was clear, public, and unequivocal—no private accounts carved out of the Social Security program.

At our board meeting the following week, we outlined our plan of attack. I made clear what it would take in the way of resources. We had begun a new phase of public opinion research, and I explained that, while we clearly had great credibility on the issue, the idea of private accounts seemed to have strong appeal for younger workers, many of whom doubted that Social Security would be there for them when they eventually retired. We would have to convince all age groups and cut through the Social Security policy weeds with clear, compelling messages. The board was solidly in favor of our counterattack, and now everything was in place to act.

Our survey research and focus group responses were sobering, although unsurprising, based on what we already knew. If you weren't well versed in the facts, the president's pitch seemed simple and persuasive: "It's your money; you can do better with it than the government, which is taking Social Security down a path toward bankruptcy." Private accounts sounded attractive, especially to younger audiences, who trusted themselves more than they trusted the government. This attitude was based partly on the perception that the money for future benefits had already been spent (the trust fund had been "stolen"). Many younger workers thought they would have control and choice in how they invested their Social Security money in anticipation of retirement.

The research suggested that talking about the transition costs of private accounts was probably not an attractive strategy. These costs were enormous—they would impose the double expense of paying current benefits while borrowing to fund the private accounts. But younger people seemed to think that the transition costs suggested short-term pain for long-term gain (the private accounts).

The approach that seemed most promising was to convince people of two things: First, privatization would mean cuts to guaranteed benefits and greater federal debt. Second, it wouldn't be that difficult to stabilize Social Security for everyone without drastic measures like private accounts. We concluded that the public was much more interested in reforms that returned Social Security to fiscal health than in wholesale changes to a system that they largely favored and that had been working for many decades.

We found that people's views differed by audience segment:

- Age was a key variable, and political affiliation also made a difference. Young Democrats were attracted to private accounts until they were linked to the Bush administration. Young Republicans were probably out of reach of our arguments. Those 30 to 39 years old seemed most favorably inclined toward private accounts, while younger Americans (20 to 29) were more disposed toward Social Security per se and least likely to favor a Bush administration proposal. Among older audiences, most Republicans and virtually all Democrats rejected the idea.
- African Americans were solid supporters of Social Security and least likely to favor private accounts.
- Hispanics were more interested in private accounts than the public as a whole, perhaps because this segment skewed younger. But Hispanics tended to reconsider their support when they saw that privatization could result in benefit cuts and increased debt.
- Women overall were most favorably disposed toward Social Security and least in favor of private accounts. While conservative women supported the administration, moderates were likely to oppose the Bush plan.

Now we set out to craft persuasive speeches, articles, interviews, testimony, mailings, and advertising based on our research findings and woven into an effective, anti–private accounts campaign against the power and reach of the administration and its allies. In all, we spent some $33 million on the effort, not including the staff we assigned full time to the campaign. It was a substantial investment in time and money and a total revamping of our agenda for the year. But it was worth it.

The White House was floating the idea that the large cost of transitioning to private accounts was manageable. They argued that an added trillion dollars or so to the national debt was tolerable; Social Security was already carrying a huge debt, so adding more would not roil the stock markets, and the outcome would be worth the cost.

On the last working day of 2004, I called Karl Rove at the White House to try to end the year on a positive note. Our conversation was barely civil. He expressed surprise that we had not been aware that the big Social Security push would come right after the election and said they were going to win on this issue. Rove claimed that John Kerry had tried to use Social Security as a scare tactic during the campaign, and now AARP was taking Kerry's position. I said we would like to work with them on solvency but would not accept private accounts. The best he and I could manage at the end of the call was a "happy holidays" and a pledge to talk again.

We began the new year with a major ad buy starting January 4, 2005, the day Congress came back into session. Our plan was to start fast and aggressively and to stake out the policy and political terrain first. Kevin Donnellan called it our shock-and-awe campaign. We appointed a single coordinator for the whole Social Security defense effort, Hop Backus, who set up an opposition research group (the "blue team") to monitor the other side's activities and messages and offer counter-strategies and arguments. They were an effective resource and dove so deeply into the opposition perspective that they began to think like them. Everybody at AARP was on board with this initiative.

Our master guideline for this campaign was called the "2005 Social Security Operational Plan." This comprehensive plan covered all our resources, strategies, and tactics and was based on three goals: in the short term, defeat any proposal to create private accounts in Social Security; in the intermediate term, position AARP as the leading voice in the debate for achieving Social Security solvency; and in the long term, enable Americans to rely on a Social Security system that is solvent and maintains a guaranteed benefit and income protection. The integration of our internal communications was probably the best it had ever been. We were solid and organized.

In the Senate we would need 40 votes to sustain a filibuster to block legislation, if it came to that. Senate minority leader Harry Reid (D-NV), who was still smarting from our Medicare campaign with the Republicans, wanted to know if we would hold firm on this issue. Of course we would, I told him. Most (but not all) Republican senators stood with the White House on private accounts, but we took pains to keep lines of communication open with all of them.

On the House side, it was more complicated. We prepared a list of members in competitive districts and ranked them in three tiers based on our assessment of whether they were likely to support our position against private accounts. Our lobbyists, plus two former congressmen (one Republican and one Democrat), met with the staff of each selected member and often the members themselves. The idea wasn't just to persuade but also to offer information, research, and assistance. These discussions with Senate and House members and their staffs continued throughout the debate. We were determined to keep members informed and impressed with our resolve, our resources, and our staying power.

No organization, AARP included, can tackle a problem and an opposition this formidable alone. We reached out to organizations that were compatible with us in fighting against the idea of carving private accounts out of Social Security. We formed a coalition that included the National Council of Churches, state Public Interest Research Groups, the Consortium for Citizens with Disabilities, and others. Some of these groups needed resources to tackle the issue, and we provided grants and other help. One of our more creative choices as an ally was Rock the Vote, a youth-focused group that helped us establish credibility among young workers, students, and families.

Mobilizing the Grassroots

With everything in place, we set out to raise a groundswell of awareness in the first three months of the new year and to generate an avalanche of public opposition that policy makers couldn't avoid. We sent more than 2 million alerts to our members, asking them to contact their members of Congress, including their offices in their home districts. We could have generated many more congressional contacts, but we held back. As Kevin Donnellan said, "We had the ability to shut down the switchboard with a huge volume of calls. We didn't want to go quite that far, but we did want to drive our message home."

What did the media think of all this? They naturally thrived on the combat between the Republicans and the Democrats and between us and the White House and anyone else favoring private accounts. Since we had just sided with the administration on Medicare, our opposition to their Social Security plan was immediate news. Getting media coverage for our story was hardly a problem.

The January 15, 2005, issue of *National Journal,* a publication followed carefully by Washington's political community, featured a cover photo of a confident George Bush donning a Stetson hat. In the upper corner of the cover was the notation "AARP on the Offensive." This was our first media initiative, and we laid down the gauntlet. The opening paragraph of the interview with John Rother, David Certner, and me stated, "As President Bush set out this month to tell Americans why they should embrace his approach to overhauling Social Security, he ran into a large, immovable object: the 35 million-plus-member AARP. The nation's largest advocacy group for the elderly strongly opposes Bush's central idea— allowing individuals to divert some of their payroll taxes into private accounts—and has kicked off an opposition campaign."

In the *National Journal* interview we emphasized our key points: private accounts are not the answer to the Social Security shortfall, neither Congress nor the public sees private accounts as a priority, and there are much better ways to make Social Security whole. We offered three incremental steps to solvency: increase wages subject to the Social Security payroll tax from $90,000 to $120,000 (this would solve about 43 percent of the problem); allow the government to invest a portion of the trust fund assets in total market index funds like other countries (15 percent of the shortfall), and put all newly hired state and local workers into the Social Security system (9 percent). We also offered an olive branch to the administration: let's work together to make sure the program is strong and ready for future generations. I knew this would be read all over town.

The media coverage was getting our message across. Shortly after the *National Journal* piece, the *Chicago Tribune* ran a story headlined "AARP: Don't Mess with Social Security." It began with a quote from a Pittsburgh retiree named Jack Heim, who said he looked forward to giving a message to his two senators, Rick Santorum and Arlen Specter: "Don't destroy the greatest program in the world." The story went on to say that we had launched a "multimillion-dollar campaign to defeat Bush's plan using newspaper ads, phone banks, pollsters, and an army of activists" and quoted Senator John McCain: "It's going to be very difficult to get Social Security [reform] without them."

As for "reform," the reporter indirectly quoted me as saying that we were eager to address the program's long-term financial challenges—just not the way Bush envisioned. And my direct quote followed: "We are dead set against carving private accounts out of Social Security money; we are speaking out now, while the agenda is being set." The article outlined the reasons for our opposition and our ideas for reaching Social Security solvency. Arizona Republican senator Jon Kyl was quoted as saying that he had already met with members of the local AARP at home and described himself as "intrigued" by private accounts. Asked by the reporter if the AARP members were equally intrigued, Kyl "smiled and said, 'Not so much.'" The story also carried our olive branch—a truce proposal—to the administration: we were eager to work on a bipartisan solution, as long as it did not tamper with the traditional approach to supporting beneficiaries.

The *New York Times* and media across the country carried our story. And our ads, speeches, and extensive local member meetings were also having an effect.

One of our print ads was headlined, "Winners and losers are stock market terms. Do you really want them to become retirement terms?" Another showed a retirement-age couple with one of them saying, "If we feel like gambling, we'll play the slots." The concluding message to each of the ads was: "Let's not turn Social Security into Social Insecurity. While the program needs to be strengthened, private accounts that take money out of Social Security are not the answer and will hurt all generations. Call your legislators and urge them to oppose private accounts that put Social Security at risk."

One TV spot, created by our advertising agency GSD&M, was based on the well-tested concept that AARP was a voice for our members and the country: "If one person could do it alone, the world wouldn't need AARP." It featured a woman calling a President Bush look-alike to ask him to make Social Security solvent.

He replied that he'd get right to work on that. Another was a man with a tin cup, collecting money for Social Security, with the same tagline. But of course, one person could not do it alone.

This was a powerful message, and it was accurate. We *were* a voice and advocate for our members and the country. A good example came my way from New Jersey. We had been working there on reducing property taxes to help older people remain in their homes. Doug Johnson, a New Jersey staffer, sent me a note from a woman who wrote, "I just wanted to thank you personally and AARP for your help and your advocacy. You saved my home for me, and I will never forget it." That kind of message will make you get up and go to work every morning.

For good measure and a little fun, we even had a truck circling the streets around the Capitol with a billboard sign that read, "Oppose private accounts that take money out of Social Security." We used it as a prop at a January press conference where AARP president Marie Smith and I talked about our big push against the president's plan but again offered to work with the administration. I stated that Social Security had a long-term problem, and it was important to address it. I said, "That's why we're pleased that the president has put Social Security reform high on his agenda. Our goal, like his, is long-term solvency and fiscal soundness." And again, we stated examples of how to fix the shortfall without drastic measures.

The White House reaction was predictable; they were plenty angry over there. We joked among ourselves that we wouldn't be invited to any more White House holiday parties. But we had hints that not all Republicans were going along with private accounts. In a meeting Senate majority leader Bill Frist (R-TN) asked us to back off on our campaign until the president offered a much more detailed blueprint for Social Security. We admired Senator Frist for his evenhandedness and the work we had done together on prescription drugs and Medicare (see chapter 4). But I respectfully said that we had to speak out forcefully now because the White House was presenting the problem in a distorted way, saying that the only choice was between private accounts and the collapse of Social Security. Senator Frist admitted that there was widespread skepticism in the Senate regarding the Bush plan.

Chris Hansen, our chief lobbyist, was a key liaison to the White House. He got an earful with every contact. Chris joked that when he was chief of government relations at Boeing, his main job had been to explain Boeing's position to Democrats; now he was trying to explain AARP's position to Republicans, and he was getting yelled at every day.

The White House rolled out its artillery. The president made a number of speeches promoting his plan, and Vice President Dick Cheney did as well. Budget director Josh Bolton (now head of the Business Roundtable) spoke to the US Chamber of Commerce, a strong supporter of private accounts. Ken Mehlman, who had been campaign director for Bush's successful reelection and was now chairman of the Republican National Committee, announced that the GOP election apparatus—their voter database, surrogates, volunteers, and hundreds of thousands of precinct captains—would now be focused on Social Security.

Other formidable groups supporting the White House Social Security offensive included the Business Roundtable (made up of major company CEOs), the National Association of Manufacturers, and an alliance called the Coalition for the Modernization and Protection of America's Social Security (COMPASS). The White House was bringing others into the fight, with the potential to spend tens of millions of dollars. Peter Wehner, the president's director of strategic initiatives, circulated an e-mail saying, "If we succeed in reforming Social Security, it will rank as one of the most significant conservative governing achievements ever. . . . For the first time in six decades, the Social Security battle is one we can win." He went on to call for not only instituting private accounts but also adjusting benefits in the program. This was shaping up to be a huge battle, and we knew it. But our opposition didn't get off to the fast start that we had.

Our research was sound, and our message was good. We were not just opposed to something; we had solutions to offer. And we had an effective team of spokespersons. Our president, Marie Smith, and other board members, our state directors, our advocacy team, and our senior management all spoke out effectively. I debated Congressman Paul Ryan (R-WI)—an up-and-coming power in the House and later Speaker and vice presidential running mate with Mitt Romney—on a Bloomberg radio program. He had a vision for smaller government and private enterprise regarding Social Security, but I think I held my own. We had a vision too.

All this made Social Security a front-page story, and we saw nervousness among some Republican members of Congress, especially in the House, where they all had to stand for reelection the following year. Not many were publicly campaigning for private accounts. Democrats were busy speaking out against the Bush plan.

In the Senate, it was a different story. Senator Lindsey Graham (R-SC), seeking a bipartisan solution, enlisted Senators Chuck Grassley (R-IA) and Judd Gregg (R-NH) on his side of the aisle and Senators Max Baucus (D-MT) and Ben Nelson (D-NE)—and sometimes Blanche Lincoln (D-AK) and Joe Lieberman (D-CT)—on the Democratic side.

The House and Senate Republicans issued their own playbook, as we had, with research-tested messages. Among their arguments: Social Security must be fixed *now*; it's your money and your choice; the cost of fixing it today is far less than fixing it tomorrow; with a nest egg you can reach your retirement goals, have peace of mind in retirement, and leave a legacy. Also: AARP is a liberal organization, it's using scare tactics, it's just protecting the status quo, and it doesn't represent you (if you're under 50).

In his February State of the Union address, President Bush spoke favorably about the important institution of Social Security and how it was symbolic of trust between generations. He asked the nation to join together to save the program. And he offered a variety of options. His plan would phase private accounts gradually into the system starting in 2009. The money would be invested in mutual funds. As workers grew older, the fund would shift more of its resources into bonds, which are generally less risky than stocks. This was one of the options proposed by the Commission he had convened back in 2001.

The day after his State of the Union address, President Bush began a cross-country campaign to try to get Democrats in red states to support his plan. His first target was Democratic senator Kent Conrad of North Dakota, whom I admired as a pragmatist. Conrad was working with Senator Judd Gregg, a New Hampshire Republican on the Finance Committee, to apply reasonable adjustments to Social Security. As both said, "It's just math." It was math, but it was also politics. (Years later I talked with Senator Gregg, who said we could fix Social Security "in 10 minutes.") Conrad told the president he remained opposed to private accounts because they would trigger a massive increase in the deficit.

In whichever red state Bush visited, we ran newspaper ads thanking the incumbent Democrat for holding fast against private accounts. Senate Democrats threatened to filibuster to block any legislation. We lobbied to get Democrats to sign a letter calling for a plan that "minimizes the need for additional federal borrowing"; 43 out of 44 Democratic senators signed the letter, which presented a filibuster-proof and veto-proof wall against private accounts. Our lobbying and policy team did a lot of work keeping senators informed, running thank-you ads back home, providing policy research and options, and working hard in the states.

I called our strategy "talk and fight," because we were forceful in public in every way, but behind the scenes we were talking to members of both parties about how to move beyond the dispute to a solvency agreement. Both Republicans and Democrats were telling us that our campaign was working and that private accounts were not going to fly. A number of Republicans were angry about our advertising and other aggressive tactics, but they got the message. In turn, we made it clear that we were not going to attack any member of Congress.

One House leader who didn't agree that we were beating back private accounts was Tom DeLay (R-TX). We had worked together, albeit grudgingly, on Medicare (see chapter 4), and now David Certner and I went to see him about Social Security. He greeted us with a bit of warmth, and we chatted about the success we had had together on Medicare. Then I brought up Social Security and explained our position. DeLay said, "If that's where you are, then we'll fight." I said OK, and the meeting was over. He denounced us in the House as "hypocritical and irresponsible." Nothing new there from "The Hammer."

Another Republican who wasn't giving up was the president himself. He set off on a trip to visit 60 cities in 60 days to promote private accounts. We resolved to be in each city, waiting for him. We held sessions either the day before or the day after the president was in town. As a result, we were part of each story about the Bush visit. A good example was the president's whistle-stop in Raleigh, NC, where we commanded public attention even before *Air Force One* landed. The headline in the *Raleigh News and Observer* was "Opponents Gear Up to Take On President." The story went on to say, "AARP, the influential senior citizens' lobby, joined with other groups . . . to denounce the idea of allowing younger workers to invest part of their Social Security taxes in private savings accounts. The group's North Carolina spokesman said such a plan could jeopardize [the program] by undermining its finances, putting savings at risk, reducing benefits and tearing holes in the safety net for the elderly."

The *Washington Post* reported on the president's stop in Iowa: "In the punch-for-punch debate over Social Security, AARP is working hard to keep the White House on the ropes. When President Bush arrives in Iowa today to talk up his private-accounts proposal, the senior citizens group plans to counter him with two news conferences, the release of a national poll, full-page newspaper ads and commercials on radio and television."

But it wasn't just the media. Our volunteers were out, they were knowledgeable, and they were animated. The White House had promised that those 55 and older would not be involved in private accounts and that their benefits would remain untouched. That backfired, because, as our research showed, older people didn't just want a Social Security check; they wanted the program to be there for their children and grandchildren.

Our AARP president, Marie Smith, was a powerful speaker and leader for us on this issue, just as she had been with Medicare. Marie's career had been in the Social Security Administration, and she knew what she was talking about. On one of her campaign trips, Marie went to a conservative district in Connecticut, represented by Republican congressman Chris Shays. She was ready for heavy pushback on our position. Instead, Marie got a warm response and heard plenty of criticism about a representative from the Social Security Administration who had tried to convince the crowd of the virtues of private accounts. Marie came back to say that this debate was breaking in our favor.

Our research supported her point of view. An early February tracking poll showed that AARP had a 76 percent level of trust on how to reform Social Security. The president was at 43 percent. Later that month I took that information with me to a White House lunch with Karl Rove and Al Hubbard, chief economic advisor. Rove was decidedly unhappy. He called our campaign unfair and misleading. There was no give on his part to move beyond private accounts to focus on solvency. Instead the two worked to convince me that their plan was reasonable and sound.

I went back to the White House a few weeks later with Chris Hansen and two of our Social Security experts, Evelyn Morton and Laurel Beedon. Hubbard had Chuck Blahous, their Social Security guy, and Keith Hennessey. The discussion got wonky, but it was no less contentious than the earlier lunch. We wanted to discuss solvency options; they were firm on private accounts, and they repeated the same rant about our unfair media and grassroots campaign.

Now the national dispute got even hotter, and some of it focused on us. The lobbying group COMPASS launched a campaign that they claimed would spend $20 million and recruit 100,000 volunteers on behalf of private accounts. USA Next, an obscure group we barely knew, posted an online picture of a US soldier with a big red X on him and another of two men kissing. The caption was "The REAL AARP agenda." We didn't bother to respond. Another group ran a TV spot comparing Social Security to the Titanic— about to go under.

Bush surrogates fanned out across the country to sell private accounts. Our coalition ramped up activities, and by the time of the congressional spring recess, we felt things were going our way. Yes, the president had his bully pulpit, but the private sector proponents of private accounts—the Chamber of Commerce, the Business Roundtable, the National Association of Manufacturers, and others—never did expend the money or effort we had expected (we had estimated that our opposition would marshall its forces and commit as much as $650 million to the fight). Why? It wasn't clear. Wall Street would have benefited from workers investing their Social Security money. The Chamber, under CEO Tom Donohue, was nearly always a reliable partner of Republican administrations. What about all the big corporations under the

Business Roundtable banner? We speculated that there were several reasons. One was that we got out in front fast and early and established strong arguments for our position before our opposition did. And with our substantial volunteer force, we had a formidable grassroots presence across the country that couldn't be matched. Chris Hansen, our veteran lobbyist and a political warrior, added another theory: "In the end, most companies never contributed because . . . corporate lobbyists are shrewd. They weren't about to sink money into a lost cause. . . . They were not about to spend a lot of money on something that was not well thought out and was going nowhere. . . . The business campaign never really got started."

Another reason might have been that big companies saw the same problems with the Bush plan that Congressman Regula suggested: there would be winners and losers. If Social Security went south, companies would have had more responsibility for pensions for their employees and retirees. Wall Street firms might have liked private account investments in the stock market, but other companies had other interests. Whatever the reasons for the tepid support from Corporate America for private accounts, we decided not to let up, and in fact to double down on our effort.

We ran an ad campaign targeted at workers aged 30 to 49, which research showed were favorable to private accounts. We wanted to burn in the idea that transitioning to private accounts would create huge amounts of public debt that would damage the American economy and hurt workers and their families.

Then we unleashed our advertising bombshell. GSD&M, our ad agency, presented a concept that we quickly tested and produced. It was a TV spot with a woman standing in her kitchen while a plumber tells her there's only one way to fix her clogged sink: "We're going to have to tear down the entire house." "What?!" she says, just before the ad cuts to scenes of a bulldozer roaring through her living room, a crane ripping the roof off, and the whole house crashing down. A voice-over says, "If you had a problem with the kitchen sink, you wouldn't tear down the entire house. So why dismantle Social Security when it can be fixed with just a few moderate changes? Reform is necessary, but diverting money into private accounts is just too drastic. It could add up to $2 trillion more in debt and lead to huge benefit cuts."

We ran that spot heavily, to great effect. The opposition cried foul. Al Hubbard told me and others that it was a distortion. He said we should have shown a house full of termites, rotting away like Social Security. We ran the spot some more.

The president implied that he would consider a raise in the wage base on which Social Security taxes are calculated. Senate majority leader Bill Frist and House Speaker Denny Hastert said that would be considered a tax increase and was therefore unacceptable. I talked to Speaker Hastert, who said confidentially, "The president got us into this soup, but he has longer legs than we do."

A new survey in March showed that public support for private accounts was continuing to decline and that AARP had a higher trust level than the president and congressional leaders. This wasn't our poll; it was conducted by the Pew Research Center for the People and the Press.

With congressional Republicans reluctant to move legislation and Democrats strongly opposed, the idea of private accounts carved out of Social Security was stalled. Among the Republicans who did not support the idea was Olympia Snowe (R-ME), who considered private accounts a bad idea for Republicans and for the country. She told David Certner and me, "No matter how much Chuck Grassley [Senator Charles Grassley, chairman of the Senate Finance Committee] yells, I'm not backing down."

In late April the administration changed the centerpiece of its strategy from private accounts to Social Security solvency. This was where we had wanted to focus the debate in the first place.

We said we were committed to working in a bipartisan fashion to help ensure that Social Security would remain strong for all Americans and offered basic principles for moving forward: a risk-free retirement benefit for all who contribute, disability and survivor benefits, full participation for everyone, adequate benefits for low-wage retirees, benefits based on one's contributions into the program, and annual adjustments that kept up with the standard of living.

President Bush said he wanted to make the program "permanently solvent" and added, "I propose that future generations receive benefits equal to or greater than today's seniors get. I believe a reformed system should protect those who depend on Social Security the most. So, I propose . . . a system . . . where benefits for low-income workers will grow faster than benefits for people who are better off."

But the administration called for progressive price indexing tied to increases in consumer prices rather than wages (Congress had set the existing formula in 1977). Low earners would be kept on the existing formula, but for everyone else, his plan would substantially reduce the relative value of the Social Security benefit.

Some estimated that this proposal would cut benefits drastically over the coming years. We said it had the potential to cause most people to view Social Security as more akin to a welfare program, and we weren't alone. Even Trent Lott, the conservative Republican senator from Mississippi, made the same point. Things were going nowhere.

The White House encouraged members of Congress to offer new proposals. Three Republican senators—Lindsey Graham and Jim DeMint, both of South Carolina, and Rick Santorum of Pennsylvania—came up with a complex plan for private accounts. We and others pointed out that it would not address solvency and would increase the deficit. Chris Hansen and I recalled with some amusement that earlier in the year when we had visited Senator

DeMint's office to talk about Social Security, he had called us "communists." Chris and I were probably two of the most committed capitalists in all of AARP.

In the House, Jim McCrery (R-LA) and several others came up with an even more complicated concept, which he admitted would essentially double-count the surplus funds going into the program over the coming years. I had high regard for Congressman McCrery but had to tell him we couldn't support his plan.

I talked to Senator Mitch McConnell (R-KY), who said, "Now is the time to work on solvency. Go tell your Democrat friends that it's possible." I said I would, and I did. (McConnell liked to call me a Democrat.) But the Democrats showed little interest in reforming Social Security during a Bush presidency. Bipartisanship was not alive and well.

The Beginning of the End

In August the TV program *60 Minutes* did a feature on AARP. It began, "Earlier this month, Social Security turned 70. Some Americans, including President Bush, think the retirement program is ripe for overhaul. But after a six-month-long campaign, Mr. Bush has made little headway in convincing Americans that a radical change of Social Security is a good idea. As CBS news correspondent Dan Rather reports, the group most responsible for opposing the president's Social Security reform plan is the AARP." The program referred to the earlier Medicare legislation and said "the bill passed Congress only after Novelli threw AARP's support behind it at the last minute. . . . Instead of cheers, the move brought . . . a torrent of criticism from Democrats and members . . . but AARP is now waging a much bigger political battle, with much higher stakes: It is fighting Mr. Bush's plan to overhaul Social Security."

Rather went on to discuss our reasons for opposing the Bush plan, and the *60 Minutes* piece concluded that "AARP seems to be winning the battle for public and political opinion. Polls show only one-quarter of Americans approve the President's handling of the issue. And leading Republican senators are, so far, unwilling to embrace privatization." The program ended with me saying that our strength "comes from our members. It's because they vote. It's because they're politically active."

There was no official epitaph or sounding of taps, but private accounts carved out of Social Security had passed away. The president declared that he wasn't giving up, but the White House went on to other issues, including energy and trade legislation. We shelved the rest of our ad campaign and ended our grassroots activity. Our teammates at Rock the Vote had the last word, with an e-mail to a million young people, urging them to "get the facts and don't get played." It ended with, "Social Security—it will be here for you."

We celebrated a job well done. But there were costs—the resources and time committed to the fight, which we didn't begrudge, but also the animosity that came from a bruising battle with an incumbent president and many in his party. Just as we had angered the Democrats in the Medicare win for prescription drug coverage, now our stock among many Republicans was at an all-time low. As Harry Truman said about politics, "If you want a friend, get a dog."

The biggest cost, however, was that although we had won a major battle, we had not won the war for Social Security solvency. And the greying of America continues.

In 2010 President Obama appointed a National Commission on Fiscal Responsibility and Reform, chaired by former Clinton White House chief of staff Erskine Bowles and former senator Alan Simpson (R-WY). It was a time of concern about America's growing debt (the total indebtedness of the nation) and deficit (the annual shortfall).

Shortly after, the Bipartisan Policy Center (BPC) assembled a commission chaired by former senator Pete Domenici (R-NM) and Alice Rivlin, who had been President Clinton's Office of Management and Budget director and the first head of the Congressional Budget Office. I had left AARP by then and was invited to join the Dominici-Rivlin commission with a bipartisan group of former mayors, governors, labor leaders, and cabinet secretaries—an impressive and truly diverse group.

Both commissions recognized the unsustainable fiscal situation in which the nation found itself, and both asserted that Social Security was one of the key issues to be addressed. Our group said there were two huge challenges: accelerating growth and job creation, and reducing future deficits to stabilize the debt so that it is no longer growing faster than the economy.

In testifying before the Joint Select Committee on Deficit Reduction, Pete Domenici and Alice Rivlin called for cooperation across party lines and a "grand bargain" that would encourage growth and stabilize the country's fiscal situation. They were clear and strong in saying that this was a historic opportunity, and if the country were not put on the right track, the consequences both to the economy and to public confidence could be dire.

Our commission made a number of public appearances, and I participated in presenting our proposals for Social Security solvency. The program was continuing to experience shortfalls, and we aimed at strengthening Social Security so it "can pay benefits in a fair and equitable way for the next 75 years and beyond."

The Bowles-Simpson Commission's proposals on Social Security were weighted more heavily toward Social Security benefit reductions than ours. According to the Center on Budget and Policy Priorities, "the Dominici-Rivlin plan is much better balanced." It turned out to be a moot point. Neither commission's recommendations led to meaningful policy change, and the country continued on its path of huge debt and deficits.

And where is Social Security today? Nothing much has changed. We still need the adjustments necessary to achieve solvency so that upcoming retirees and the generations that follow will be secure in their old age. In March 2019 Joan Ruff, the chair of AARP's board and an attorney and employee benefits expert, testified before the House Social Security Subcommittee of the Ways and Means Committee. She said the retirement security of millions of American will *increasingly* depend on Social Security because of diminishing pensions, inadequate retirement savings, and longer life expectancies.

Among middle-income households aged 55–64 with a defined-contribution plan or individual retirement account, Ruff said, the median savings for retirement is only $100,000—nowhere near what is needed. And half of American workers are in jobs with no retirement plan at all. She pointed out that even those workers lucky enough to have access to a workplace retirement plan are likelier than ever to find that Social Security is the only lifetime, inflation-protected, guaranteed source of retirement income that most Americans will have—and it is an *earned* benefit.

She said the same thing politicians have been hearing for many years: the Social Security program has enough funding to pay full benefits until 2034, but if something isn't done, benefits could be substantially reduced through the remainder of the century. She proposed a national discussion on the issue, the same thing we wanted to do with the Bush White House over a decade before.

Our world of toxic partisanship and political warfare has us stymied; we're not getting things done for ourselves or for future generations. We need to get mad, and we need to get organized. It's up to all of us to demand change. And in the meantime, be sure to save for retirement.

In the political world, today's opponents can become tomorrow's partners. The Business Roundtable, which had supported the Bush plan for private accounts, became AARP allies just a couple of years later. Nancy LeaMond and I worked to make peace and enlist them in support of health care reform. John Castellani, their CEO and a smart Washington strategist (who later went on to become president of PhRMA, the association of US drug companies that had been our primary foe in the fight over prescription drug coverage in Medicare), said, "Yes, we'll go into a coalition with you. You kicked our butts on Social Security; now let's work together to get something done on health care." We formed Divided We Fail (DWF), with the two of us plus the Service Employees International Union (SEIU), with Andy Stern as its leader, and the National Federation of Independent Business (NFIB) headed by Todd Stottlemyer. We could hardly agree on what day of the week it was, but we were together on the dire need to reform health care, and we were a formidable lobbying team. It showed how divergent interest groups—strange bedfellows—can get something done.

The eventual legislation, the Affordable Care Act, which came to be known as Obamacare, was a partisan victory for Democrats, and there were plenty of casualties along the way. Divided We Fail was a strong advocacy effort that extended into the Obama presidency, and Barack Obama talked about DWF in town hall meetings as he made health care reform a key part of his agenda.

Moving On

As AARP's 50th anniversary approached, I was in my prime as CEO and thinking about what was next for me. I believe in renewal: doing good work and moving on. In 2008 we celebrated AARP's "Big 50," as we liked to say in our magazine about those hitting their 50th birthdays. The *Washington Post* did a feature that said,

> AARP's 40 million members, many of them more than capable of finding a voting booth on Election Day, make it the country's single largest organization—that is, if you don't count a little outfit called the Roman Catholic Church. . . . Five years ago it helped President Bush persuade Congress to add prescription drug benefits to

Medicare. Two years later, AARP flexed again, leading opposition to Bush's plan for private Social Security accounts. . . . "It's the largest, most effective lobbying group in D.C. and probably the world," said James Thurber, an American University government professor who studies lobbying. "It can stimulate people out there very quickly and get them to push back on issues. Just the threat of AARP going against you gets people to change their minds."

The article referred to me as "avuncular" (I looked it up) and said,

At the age of 49, Novelli left Porter Novelli . . . to devote himself full time to social issues. His first stop was CARE, which combats global poverty, then the Campaign for Tobacco-Free Kids. He joined AARP in 2000, becoming chief executive the following year. His mission was to lasso the millions of baby boomers becoming old enough to join up. . . . [AARP] now has a $1.3 billion budget and 2,400 employees. It generates more than $1 billion in revenue, a stream produced by $12.50-a-year membership fees, grants and investments, royalties from endorsing everything from health insurance to motorcycle insurance, and by selling advertising space in its publications ($483,000 for a full-page ad in the magazine). Novelli . . . poured money into its lobbying operation, expanded the number of state offices and led AARP into the 2003 fight over Medicare reform. AARP's alliance with Bush prompted rebukes from a traditional ally, the Democratic Party, which painted Novelli as a Republican shill. Some 60,000 AARPers canceled their memberships, and senior citizens showed up outside headquarters to protest. Novelli, a registered independent, maintained a pragmatist's steady hand, telling reporters that the Bush plan was not perfect, but "you're not going to get perfect legislation in this day and age." Two years later, AARP countered the president's push to offer private Social Security accounts [and] Bush's plan was headed for oblivion. The two episodes, Novelli said, are evidence that AARP is "down the middle."

I "retired" from AARP the next year—2009—to head for Georgetown. The *National Journal* wrote, "Some who have worked with the hard-driving executive say that the job has taken a toll because of the difficulty of implementing his ambitious plans for overhauling the organization." But that wasn't my reason for moving on. Hard work was never my problem. It was just time to renew. When I gave my goodbye speech, I said I thought we had done pretty well. I reminded our employees of who we are—leaders— and so we need to stand tall and up front. And I told them I was confident they would continue to serve our members and all generations to make this country and the world a better place.

I left AARP with tremendous pride in what we had accomplished. We played a key role in passing the Medicare Modernization Act, making prescription drugs available to millions of Americans for the first time, and then we helped implement the changes it achieved. We fought successfully against using Social Security payroll money to fund private accounts outside Social Security. This move would have introduced real risk into our bedrock safety-net system and would have been enormously expensive to implement.

And we won a lot of key victories at the state level. The one I'm most fond of was working with Jeannine English, then president of AARP California (later AARP's national volunteer president), and Governor Arnold Schwarzenegger to win Proposition 11. It took state legislative redistricting out of the hands of legislators and put it into a citizen commission. Today redistricting remains as big a problem for good government as ever. The Supreme Court has ruled that racial gerrymandering is illegal, but it can't seem to do the same with partisan gerrymandering. But we made a difference in California.

Along the way we doubled AARP's revenues, added 5 million members, and internationalized the organization. Ethel was right: it's a great privilege to serve, not to be served. And it doesn't hurt to be able to visit a member of Congress about a key issue and point out that up to a quarter of the voters in her district are AARP members. AARP is listed among America's greatest brands, but it isn't like most others. I call it a "warrior brand," because the organization is in so many policy battles.

Today AARP's CEO is Jo Ann Jenkins. She and I had worked together on the board of AARP Services, Inc. Jo Ann and her team are still fighting the good fight—advancing health care reform, bringing down the cost of prescription drugs, protecting Social Security, and empowering people to choose how they live as they age. Sometimes the more things change, the more they stay the same.

CHAPTER SIX

THE OPPORTUNITIES AND CHALLENGES OF OUR RAPIDLY AGING SOCIETY

I left AARP for the campus at Georgetown University, but I didn't leave behind my commitment to working on aging issues. The aging of America (and the world) presents both opportunities and challenges, and now—being in a business school—I am promoting companies, products, and services that can not only be profitable, but also create social value for older Americans and their families and, in fact, all of society. And I am focused on helping to reform advanced illness and end-of-life care in this country.

The Aging of Society

I once gave a talk to a group of AARP members in Kentucky. A woman raised her hand and asked if I knew that women outlived men. Yes, I did, I said. She responded, "Well, what are you gonna do about it?" There was a lot we were *trying* to do, including focusing on men's health and wellness (as well as women's). And of course, she was right; women do outlive men. The extreme example of this is among centenarians: for every 100 women in this age cohort, there are only 20.7 men.

We're all no doubt aware that the world's population is aging, and the United States is no exception. Globally, there are nearly a billion people over the age of 60 alive today—about 13 percent of the total population—and that number is more than twice as many as in 1980. It is estimated that by 2050, that number will double again, to nearly 2.1 billion, exceeding 20 percent of the world's population. We're in the midst of the biggest population shift in history.

According to the US Census Bureau, the number of Americans 65 and older is expanding rapidly (some 10,000 Americans turn 65 every day) and will accelerate in the next 20 years, fueled by the baby-boom generation (those born between 1946 and 1964). By 2035 people 65 and older will outnumber those younger than 18. The average US life expectancy is 84, but the rise in longevity may be slowing or even reversing among some segments of our population, possibly owing to obesity and the illnesses associated with it (such as diabetes) and to addiction, including the opioid epidemic.

This greying of society has huge implications—both positive and negative. Older Americans represent not just a demographic wave, but a consumer, workforce, and social phenomenon as well. What do people want as they age? It's not very different from what younger people want. AARP research indicates five things: health and health care, financial security, to contribute and be productive, to connect with their communities, and the opportunity for recreation—to have some fun.

That last one, recreation, may not seem as important as the others, but it is. Play is part of physical and mental health, family life, and staying fit and sharp. I recall when my parents were retired and living part of the year in Florida. My dad had just shot an 88 on the local golf course and was griping about it. First, he had lost a few bucks betting on the round, and second, he just missed shooting his age—he was 87 at the time. He had started playing golf when he was a kid, caddying during the Depression, and he had worked hard his whole life. Recreation was important.

In general, today's older people are in better health than previous generations. Part of this is due to improved health care and nutrition. And part of it is environmental, like basic sanitation and changes in the kind of work we do. Fewer Americans perform the backbreaking labor that inspired the line in the old song, "You worked so hard you died standing up." I come from a family of steelworkers in the Pittsburgh area, and when that generation retired, they were truly *tired*. I remember my Uncle Andy coming home from work one day, setting his lunch pail down on the porch, and saying, "That's it. I'm retired." And he was.

Paul Irving, chairman of the Milken Institute Center for the Future of Aging, has written about the opportunities of an aging society: how communities can prepare for older, increasingly diverse populations; the business of aging, in which companies and investors need to think and act differently about older workers and older consumers; and healthy aging—promoting wellness and productivity.

On the economics of aging, Paul quotes Bank of America Merrill Lynch projections that the global spending power of those 60 and older was slated to reach $15 trillion annually by 2020, while the McKinsey Global Institute concludes that the 60-and-over population, one of our few engines of economic expansion, is on track to generate half of all urban consumption growth in this country between 2015 and 2030. The over-60 population holds the majority of wealth worldwide and 70 percent of disposable income in the United States. But that's not the same as being wealthy. The average net worth for someone aged 65-70 is about $193,000, of which approximately $130,000 is in the form of home equity. For low-income elders, the picture is a lot worse. Still, it's no wonder that the financial services industry has always had a focus on older people as they plan for and enter retirement.

But the opportunities of an aging society go well beyond financial services. Companies in all industries can improve their own bottom lines while improving people's quality of life and the American economy as well, by creating products and services that address the desires and challenges of aging. In other words, doing well by doing good.

Among these many opportunities, there are at least three major areas to consider: accommodating an older workforce in our greying society; enabling older people to live as independently and as well as they can, with as much control over their lives as possible; and the needs of family caregivers.

The Older Workforce

I don't often think of myself as an older worker, but I am. I never gave a thought to "retiring" when I was 65. Now I always put "retiring" and "retirement" in quotes because they often don't have the old meaning anymore and are being constantly redefined. Satchel Paige, the ageless pitcher from the old Negro leagues and the major leagues, once asked, "How old would you be if you didn't know how old you are?" A very good question.

"Retirement" is full of possibilities, but it isn't easy. Everybody seems to go about it differently. A common piece of advice for those transitioning from work to not work is "Don't agree to anything for at least six months while you figure things out." And then there are those who say they "flunked retirement" and changed directions, including going back to work. One of the saddest "retirement" stories I've heard comes from Japan. I was in Tokyo, being interviewed by a Japanese reporter who asked what I knew about divorce among older Americans. AARP had just done a story on it, and so I had some information. I told him that divorce among older Americans was growing—in the past 25 years divorce among those 50 and older had doubled. It was often initiated by the wife, and many husbands never saw it coming.

The Japanese interpreter broke in to say that Japan was about to revise its pension laws to give wives more legal rights to their husbands' pensions. As a result, they expected to see a spike in divorces among older Japanese couples. She explained that Japanese salarymen tend to work six days a week, go out drinking at night, and play golf on Sunday. When they retire, they are lost. Their wives don't know what to do with them and can't get them out of the house. The women refer to them as "wet fallen leaves"—they can't sweep them out of the way. What a fate—working hard for a lifetime only to become a wet fallen leaf.

The simple fact is, there is no set pattern for aging. It's a continuum, and we all enter life stages in different ways and at different times. Many people work longer because they have to. They can't afford to stop working even if they want to. And then there are people like me, who are fortunate to be in good health; who have opportunities for engaging, productive work; and who keep on keeping on (Satchel Paige again: "Don't look back; something may be gaining on you.").

Older workers have been part of the employment scene for years, but many companies are still catching up to this trend. One reason to develop sound policies and practices for hiring and retaining older workers is the need for skilled workers in today's world. Another is the quality of older workers themselves. They tend to be loyal, experienced (of course), good at problem solving, and reliable, and they often have an institutional memory that can contribute to a positive corporate culture. They can also serve as mentors to younger workers. And since older consumers are a big market for many organizations, it can help to have older employees who can relate to the consumers they serve. There are useful frameworks and guiding principles for companies to apply in building and nurturing an older workforce. The Global Coalition on Aging has a set, as does the Milken Institute Center for the Future of Aging.

Melissa Gong Mitchell is head of the Global Coalition on Aging, a research and advocacy organization that advises businesses on how to take advantage of the opportunities that stem from an aging population. She believes that "older people are the future of the workplace." She sees employers gaining competitive advantages from nurturing an older workforce, although older workers do have some different needs to be addressed.

One of those needs is training. There is evidence that older workers don't learn new tasks and technical skills the same way younger workers do, so attention to methods of training and learning are important. Another dimension is flexibility. This issue is getting attention beyond just older workers as companies learn that employees of all ages benefit from flexibility in work hours and venues, as long as the work gets done. Catering specifically to older workers, Home Depot and CVS Health have "snowbird" programs, which enable workers to move south for the winter months, if they wish, and still have employment with the companies.

There are also cultural differences among workers of different ages. Peter Cappelli, a Wharton School professor, and I wrote a book called *Managing the Older Worker: How to Prepare for the New Organizational Order* (Peter did most of the work!). We discussed the challenges of creating a productive environment between younger and older employees. For example, imagine that you are a 70-year-old woman sitting across the desk from your 32-year-old supervisor, who just happens to remind you of your daughter. You may well be saying to yourself, How can I report to this kid? At the same time, the supervisor is wondering, Is she trainable? Will she be able to measure up? The two of you have a difficult time figuring this out and relating to each other. But 20 or 25 years ago, men on the job were asking themselves and each other, Can I report to a woman? Today that question has been answered. Women are running companies, universities, military operations, major non-profits, ministries, and every other kind of organization. We'll figure out the challenge of age differences in the workforce as well.

It's tempting to paint a rosy picture about older workers, and much of it is accurate. Laura Carstensen at the Stanford Center on Longevity finds that older workers tend to be healthy, experienced, and satisfied with their work. They are usually motivated, have a good work ethic, and care more about making a contribution and less about advancing up the career ladder.

Still, there is a persistent innate bias against older workers in the United States. AARP has studied this, and Jo Ann Jenkins, AARP's CEO, often speaks out on the subject. She says, "Today it is socially unacceptable to ignore, ridicule, or stereotype someone based on their gender, race, or sexual orientation. So why is it still acceptable to do this to people based on their age?" There are estimated to be more entrepreneurs in this country over the age of 50 than under. This is probably due to several factors, including the experience they have gained, some money they may have set aside to invest in a new enterprise, and an interest in creating a legacy. But there is another reason as well—the prejudice against older workers that drives people out of the workforce and makes it difficult to get back in.

This issue is not easy to deal with. Some years ago I was on the board of overseers of the School of Arts and Sciences at Penn. At one of our meetings the dean announced that the school was unable to bring in as many new faculty members as he wanted because some of the old faculty wouldn't retire. I took issue with that. I asked him why they didn't have performance standards by which to measure faculty that would enable the school to retain high-performing older professors and separate out those who weren't getting it done. I made the comparison with firefighters. Regardless of age, you need to be able to perform to stay on the job. The dean and other school administrators smiled at my naivete and went on. I learned over time, including at Georgetown, that evaluating tenured faculty based on performance is far harder than it seems. That's true of other professions as well.

As Jo Ann Jenkins and others have pointed out, the five-generation workforce is an emerging reality. Companies and other organizations that embrace this, prepare for it, and adapt to it will have a competitive advantage over those that don't.

Enabling People to Live Independently

Research shows what we probably always knew—that successful aging is enhanced by regular exercise and staying engaged and connected. My motto has always been, If you have a moving part, move it, and always take the stairs. Unfortunately, the Pew Research Center reports that those 60 and older now spend more than half their daily leisure time—4 hours and 16 minutes—in front of screens, mostly watching TV or videos. This is a rise of almost half an hour per day over the past decade, while screen time among younger people has stayed the same.

Charlotte Yeh, chief medical officer at AARP Services, Inc. (the taxpaying subsidiary of AARP the parent), studies successful aging and often focuses on the social determinants of aging, including loneliness, social isolation (the opposite of being engaged), hearing loss, and lack of a sense of purpose. Charlotte found, for example, that hearing loss is associated with an increased risk of dementia, falls, and depression. It has been linked to poorer job performance and lower salaries. It is also a serious condition that can lead to isolation and loneliness. Charlotte notes that technology can help seniors adapt, but because of the stigma of hearing loss, the average older adult waits 7–10 years to get a hearing device, and only 20–30 percent of all adults who could benefit from a hearing device ever get one. Charlotte also shows that a sense of purpose in life really matters and is associated with a wide range of better health outcomes, including reduced risk of mortality, stroke, type 2 diabetes, heart attacks, and Alzheimer's disease. And people with a sense of purpose also tend to have lower health care costs. She also reports that optimism and a positive view of aging have a substantial impact on our health, adding 7.5 years to life.

Technology has a huge role to play in helping people to live independently and as well as possible as they age. A good example of a company doing well by doing good in the aging market is Philips, the global tech company. They issued a statement that serves them and all their stakeholders well: "We firmly believe that the challenges around the health and well-being of our planet offer substantial business opportunities, creating value for our company as well as society at large."

Several years ago, Philips wanted to get out in front in the areas of health and health care. So they assembled a group of outsiders, including me, from several related fields to advise them on creating a framework to address two ambitious goals: productive, healthy, secure citizens, and prosperous, equitable societies across all generations. The company wanted to use the thinking that came out of our group to develop new products and services, but that was almost a by-product. They called it the Philips Center for Health and Well-Being Active Aging Think Tank.

We focused on two key factors for healthy aging: staying independent and being engaged. We looked at the evidence showing that aging populations affect nearly every aspect of society, including health care, the work force, retirement security, government debt and deficits, housing and community living, consumer behavior, volunteering, recreation, and lifelong learning. As we began to zero in on where Philips could make a difference, the company asked me to involve our Georgetown Business for Impact center in research and planning so the company could expand its market for assistive technology and help older people live as independently as possible. We found that the vast majority of older people want to live in their own homes as they age—no big surprise there—but most homes just aren't designed well to accommodate older residents. There are opportunities here for housing redesign.

Diane Ty, who led this work, conducted an interesting study on adult caregivers and those receiving care (often a parent). She found that older people often want to be active online but that their adult caregiver children may not have the time or inclination to help them. It isn't that elders avoid being engaged with today's online connectivity, as we may think; it's that they need help and sometimes can't get it.

Our work with Philips evolved into our AgingWell Hub at Georgetown. With Philips as our founding partner, we created a partnership among companies, nonprofits, and government, including The Hartford, MedStar Health, AARP, Merck, and the Alzheimer's Association. The first Hub product was a caregiver journey map that documented the specific steps and process of a middle-aged, married woman with children caring for an elderly parent with Alzheimer's. This wasn't anecdotal; it was evidence based, and it applied design thinking to better understand the experience of a family caregiver. The journey map has been useful to companies, patient groups, and others to indicate opportunities for providing caregivers with support and solutions. The map leveraged expertise from many players and is now a resource for OpenIDEO's global innovation challenge on caregiving sponsored by UnitedHealthcare and AARP, MedStar Health's use of information and support to family caregivers, and the National Alliance for Caregiving in their advocacy with policymakers. In addition, the US Department of Veterans Affairs adapted the map into a military caregiver journey. Our AgingWell Hub also worked with Transamerica on a cost calculator that enables families to calculate the financial cost of caring for a member with Alzheimer's at each step along the way.

Many other companies are moving into what we might call the business of aging with creative ideas. Robert Wray, a retired US Navy rear admiral and founder of the home tech company Blue-Star SeniorTech says, "There's no shortage of technology development and creation, and there's no shortage of seniors in need. The problem is connecting the innovation with the seniors who need it." He identifies products in three categories: safety (such as fall detection and other sensors that automatically call for help); health (such as monitoring devices that measure heart rate, glucose levels, and other factors and alert health professionals as needed); and connecting (primarily information technology for communicating with family). Some research, however, suggests that not all seniors may be pleased with their adult children closely monitoring their activities. They may feel that their independence is being compromised, and families will have to deal with that.

I recently met with a for-profit start-up company, Edenbridge Health, led by geriatrician Stephen Gordon, that is seeking capital to create community living places for the frail elderly. They want to create "purpose-driven senior centers" that will minimize hospital care and create "true partnerships with families and caregivers." They and other newcomers may find venture capitalists increasingly interested in the elder care market as it expands.

Another example of a start-up moving into "the business of aging" is Home Care Genie. This is an aging-in-place insurance product for older adults and seniors (ages 50 to 75), paired with a coaching service that helps members navigate and access a range of social and support services that can enhance their ability to stay in their homes.

Joe Coughlin, founder and director of the Massachusetts Institute of Technology AgeLab, created the multidisciplinary research program to understand the behavior of the 50-plus population, the role of technology and design in their lives, and the role innovation can play in improving their quality of life. He and his team at the AgeLab work with many start-up companies, entrepreneurs, and well-established companies on the leading edge of the business of aging. But he recognizes that most businesses still don't know how to take advantage of the opportunities offered by this fast-growing market. In his book *The Longevity Economy: Unlocking the World's Fastest-Growing, Most Misunderstood Market*, Joe writes that many businesses are hampered by ageist attitudes and misperceptions about who older people are and what they want and need. Successfully addressing this market, he says, "starts with businesses recognizing older consumers, listening closely to their demands, and building them better tools with which to interact with the world around them. It starts with bold leaders willing to erect a new narrative of possibility in old age."

The Challenge of Advanced Illness and End-of-Life Care

Back when the Robert Wood Johnson Foundation was investing in the start of our Campaign for Tobacco-Free Kids, it was also funding a new initiative called Last Acts to expand palliative care in the United States. They asked me to look at the program, and I became fascinated with the challenges involved in this huge social issue. It seemed like an opportunity to make a positive difference at a critical juncture in the aging process. Years later, as I was leaving AARP, a reporter asked me what was next for me. Among other things, I told him I planned to work on advanced illness and end-of-life care. "You mean death?" he asked? Well, yeah.

We've probably all seen the T-shirt: "Life's a Bitch. Then You Die." It may be amusing, but it isn't really true. Most people enjoy life, and we usually don't want to think about the end.

There's a wistful story among gerontologists about how everyone should live in good health to a ripe old age, well into our 90s, and then have it end with a quick bullet—fired by a jealous lover. Romantic, yes? But we all know that isn't the way most people in America head off into the great beyond. Dying in our society is often painful, isolating, and costly to families and the nation. Here are excerpts from three stories that vividly spell this out:

First, from my colleague Tom Koutsoumpas (more on Tom later):

> Another trip to the emergency room in the middle of a frigid night was not what Mom wanted, nor was it what my sister . . . and I wanted for her. Our mother was a proud woman who had lived independently for years with multiple chronic conditions. However, she was 85 years old, frail, and on this night, she had the symptoms of a mild stroke, so what else could we do? This was a recurring cycle over many years. Late at night, simple answers to simple questions did not come quickly, but were discovered only after putting Mom through tiresome rounds of ER protocol—CT and MRI scans and countless forms to fill out. Communication among the numerous specialists treating mom was seriously lacking.

And here is a story by Michael Wolff in *New York* magazine:

> The costs for my mother, who is 86 and who, for the past 18 months, has not been able to walk, talk, or to address her most minimal needs and who . . . is absent short term memory, come in at about $17,000 a month. And while her [long-term care] insurance hardly covers all of that, I'm certainly grateful she had the foresight to carry such a policy. . . . [But it] helps finance some of the greatest misery and suffering human beings have yet devised. . . . Everybody would manage his or her parent's decline differently. We all mess it up. We agreed with a cardiologist to perform surgery on my mother when she was 84. It did not occur to us to say: "You want to do major heart surgery on an 84-year-old woman showing progressive signs of dementia? . . . Are you nuts?" The operation . . . repaired my mother's heart. "She can live for years," according to the surgeon (who we were never to see again). . . . But before, where we were gently sinking, now we were in free fall. She was reduced to a terrified creature—losing language skills by the minute. "She certainly seems agitated," the

psychiatrist sent to administer anti-psychotic drugs told me, "and so do you." Six weeks and something like $250,000 in hospital bills later (paid by Medicare—or that is, by you) she was returned, a shadow being, to . . . her assisted living apartment.

Finally, an e-mail to me from a college classmate about the final year of her partner's life; she titled it "Coordinated Health Care: Who's in Charge?":

Here is a list of specialists he had to go to see regularly: head and neck surgeons (four in the same practice), medical oncologist, radiation oncologist, cardiologist, urologist, dermatologist, gastroenterologist, internist, two integrated medicine MDs, dentist, speech and swallowing therapist, and lymphoma therapist . . . and visits with a pulmonary surgeon, plastic surgeon, oral surgeon, ophthalmologist and palliative care specialist. We thought the integrated care MDs or the internal medicine MD would be more involved in the coordination, but even they were focused on their individual contributions. . . . There were massive numbers of prescription drugs, ordered at two different pharmacies, many . . . in liquid form, crushable or powdered, some requiring pre-certification from the insurance company, taking days and even weeks to complete. I now look at the entirety of his medical history as a series of hurricanes that hit him, which he survived because his immune system . . . like levees, held. Finally, the storm was too strong, the aging process weakened him, and the levees broke.

You've heard and perhaps lived through similar stories. So have I, including my father's extremely traumatic experience of two weeks in an intensive care unit after he had suffered a stroke, despite his request to my brother, Jerry, and me about not wanting aggressive end-of-life treatment.

Advanced illness usually—but certainly not always—occurs among the frail elderly, when one or more chronic conditions, such as cancer or heart or vascular disease, progress to the point where general health and functioning decline, response to curative treatment is reduced, and care needs increase. Trips to the emergency room and hospitalizations frequently occur, prognosis and treatment plans become uncertain, patient goals and preferences may change, and often there is stress and a feeling of crisis among patients and their families.

What is it that people actually want when they are seriously ill and know they may be approaching the end? Research shows that they want to be at home, with family and friends; to have their pain and other symptoms managed; to have their spiritual wishes honored; and probably above all, to avoid impoverishing their families because of their illness.

And when asked the difficult question "Where do you want to die?" the large majority of Americans answer, "At home." Instead, many people die in hospitals, often victims of overmedication, infection, and unwanted treatment. Doctors know all this, which may explain why 72 percent of them die at home, according to an article by Ravi Parikh and Andrew MacPherson.

So, despite what seriously ill people want, that isn't what they usually receive. They are often given aggressive treatment, even when it may be inconsistent with patient and family wishes and understanding. Often that treatment occurs when there is little chance of prolonging a quality life and when it may even have the opposite effect. And this punishing experience can burden families and the nation with huge costs. The National Academy of Medicine reports that some 5 percent of patients account for nearly half of total spending on health care. Over half of these individuals are 65 and older, and many are frail elderly with multiple chronic diseases and near the end of life.

Physicians are dedicated, caring people. No doctor sets out to provide "assault-and-battery care," as some advanced illness treatment has been described. A powerful statement on this came from Atul Gawande in his 2014 book, *Being Mortal*. I interviewed Atul about his book, and he lamented that physicians find it so difficult to discuss "the larger truth" (about serious illness) and communicate honestly with patients and families. They are trained to cure, and so they have real difficulties in facing patient problems they cannot "solve" and in deciding when to "fix things" and when not to. His conclusion: "Modern medicine has not served aging and seriously ill Americans very well."

The Michael Wolff story demonstrates that reality. Technology, the great blessing of our age in so many ways, has the perverse potential to keep people "alive" no matter what they want or what state they're in. The surgery described in that story also is an example of a national trend: it has been estimated that those 65 and older undergo probably over half of all surgical procedures. And it isn't a surprise that older surgical patients experience worse results than younger ones.

Atul is not alone in his observation. Many other physicians also recognize the problem. Angelo Volandes, in his 2015 book, *The Conversation*, says, "The health care system is teeming with brilliant scientists, but there is a dearth of effective communicators and advocates." As a result, he concludes, much like Gawande, that the "discrepancy between the type of medical care people want at the end of life and the type . . . they actually receive . . . is largely due to the failure of doctors to have discussions with patients about . . . life's final chapter."

Today's clinical teams tend to be just that—teams. Nurses play an important and expanded role, and chaplains, social workers, and others also contribute, with physicians usually functioning as team leaders. But the problems persist. Not even chaplains find their training adequate. As Joan Paddock Maxwell wrote in *Soul Support: Memoir of a Hospital Chaplain*, "There's no recognized school for hospital chaplains—but many hoops to jump through. . . . You'll know you're really a chaplain when someone calls 'chaplain' in a hospital corridor and you turn around. . . . I visited all the patients receiving palliative care in the hospital. . . . The stakes were so high, and spiritual matters are often of prime importance in the foxholes of the dying."

Of course, this isn't just a clinicians' problem. Patients and families have a difficult time with serious illness—preparing for it and facing up to it. At AARP we had research showing that adult children were loath to broach the issue with aging parents, while the parents themselves were more likely to want to discuss it. I think the reluctance to discuss serious illness is changing; it is becoming a more open topic.

A few years ago, Norm Glickman, the chairman of my college reunion, called to ask me to speak at the event. "Talk about whatever you want," he said, "whatever is current and on your mind." I said, "OK, I'll talk about dying better in America." Norm snorted over the phone. "That's jolly," he said. "We'll get maybe three people to come to that, with their martinis." But more than a hundred people packed the room at Irvine Auditorium at Penn, and we had to bring in extra chairs. People, certainly including those my age, aren't afraid to talk about it.

But the challenge is still *how* to address the issue. US senator Johnny Isakson (R-GA), who retired from the Senate due to his own illness, is a strong advocate of advanced illness legislative action. He talked about his own family: "I was the son of a mother and father who suffered from two . . . terrible diseases . . . cancer and Alzheimer's. Having not discussed the what if's when my mom was of sound mind and body, we were guessing in trying to figure out the right thing to do." Senator Isakson is not alone in trying to guess his way through these problems.

I attended a seminar at a hospital in Pennsylvania where various real-life scenarios were discussed. One example: a comatose woman was admitted to the emergency room, the man with her was not her husband (and therefore not a decision-maker), and her next of kin were in Greece and didn't speak English. What to do? The doctors and nurses tried to stabilize the patient and referred the problem to their ethics committee. (The woman died before the committee could take up the question.)

Amy Berman knows how to talk about it—from a deeply personal perspective. Amy is a nurse and a senior executive at the John A. Hartford Foundation. And she is a breast cancer patient at a serious stage in her illness. She speaks at meetings and conferences all across the country and tells a powerful story. When she was diagnosed, Amy sought several medical opinions. She was advised to undergo extensive and aggressive treatment, including a mastectomy, chemotherapy, and radiation. She asked if that would cure her or arrest the disease. When the physician answered that it was unlikely, Amy opted for palliative care—medicine to manage her pain and slow the spread of the cancer while she continued her career and an active life. A decade later, Amy is still working hard, experiencing what she calls a "really great life." She is hoping for a "Niagara Falls experience," by which she means a continued active life until the very last days, followed by a precipitous decline—Niagara Falls. Amy is a role model for many in the field, and her story represents not just courage, but one rational way to deal with advanced illness.

Like Amy, Lucy Kalanithi discusses advanced illness from a deeply personal perspective. Her husband, the late physician Paul Kalinithi, wrote about his own end-of-life experience, succumbing to lung cancer. Lucy finished her husband's well-known book, *When Breath Becomes Air*, and today is a compassionate speaker about advanced illness and family relationships. She also serves as a board member of our Coalition to Transform Advanced Care.

BJ Miller, a palliative care physician—and also a member of our Coalition board—and his coauthor, Shoshana Berger, address the complexity of these problems in their recent book, *A Beginner's Guide to the End: Practical Advice for Living Life and Facing Death*.

This is a layman's guidebook for dealing with serious illness. It covers virtually the whole journey, from beginning the paperwork to the very end. Experts often say that loss of control over one's life is particularly difficult, and BJ and Shoshana try to bring control back into the picture. But, as they point out, not everyone wants *total* control. The book covers the contingency that someone might not want to know about a prognosis: "You can say, 'No thanks, I opt out.'" No matter what we prefer, as Atul Gwande says in his book, "We all want to be the authors of our lives."

Now, with the coronavirus pandemic, things are even more difficult. Physicians and nurses have to talk to grieving families about critical care patients via video instead of in person. Personal protective equipment has been in short supply. Everyone involved is under intense pressure to make critical life-and-death decisions. Policy discussions at national, state, and local levels are taking place about the number of cases and fatalities. The whole world is dealing with these issues.

Under normal (nonpandemic) circumstances, choosing which patients will be saved and which may not is a foreign concept in the United States. Back in 2009, when Congress was debating health care reform, opponents used the scare tactic of warning about "death panels." But it was false. I spoke to a physician who was treating (if that's the right word) an elderly woman on a ventilator. Every week he called the woman's daughter to tell her it was highly unlikely that her mother would get better. And each time the daughter said, "Doctor, please understand, we are a family that believes in miracles." In this case, the mother continued to receive the treatment her family wanted for her. So, absent a pandemic, discussions about advanced illness is not about "pulling the plug on grandma."

Consider a young mother with advanced cancer. She may want every possible form of treatment she can get—experimental drugs, surgery, radiation, chemotherapy—and she may "fight hard" to the very end. She must be given every chance to do so, with the care she needs and wants.

Research suggests, however, that when people with advanced illness and their families get and understand the information they need, they often choose less aggressive treatment and more comfort-based care and support. This approach often moves the focus of care out of the hospital and into homes and communities.

Palliative care, sometimes called comfort care, can be administered at any time during an illness, not just during serious illness or at the end of life. It is sometimes confused with hospice care, which centers on medical care to help someone with a terminal illness live as well as possible for as long as possible, increasing quality of life.

Advanced illness and end of life lie before all of us, and the challenges are clear. We have a rapidly aging population, a health system ill equipped to provide care for advanced illness, and patients and families uninformed and conflicted by difficult decisions. The result: greater risk of more hospitalizations and potentially unwanted, aggressive treatment; conflicting medical advice; and a much higher cost of care to families and to the nation. The way we die in our society is a medicalized and painful process that too often occurs in a hospital room or hospital intensive care unit.

This is a difficult problem to solve, but not an impossible one. We need to put patients and families at the center of treatment, following their choices as well as sound clinical advice—a shared decision-making. The bottom line: we can die better in America.

Starting the Coalition to Transform Advanced Care (C-TAC)

When I began to think through how to tackle this large and growing social issue, I started where most big challenges begin, with the need for resources. I went to Pete Peterson. He had been secretary of commerce under President Nixon and had gone to Wall Street to make his fortune. The son of Greek immigrants and a strong believer in America and our economic health, he was particularly concerned about the nation's enormous debt. I thought I could connect this concern to advanced illness.

The first time I sat down with Pete, he was mad at me. Or more accurately, he was angry at AARP, and I was a handy target. It was late 2003, and he and I were on a discussion panel at the Council on Foreign Relations in New York. Pete's anger stemmed from what he perceived as AARP's lack of cooperation over the proposed balanced budget amendment to the US Constitution several years earlier (before my tenure). He and I debated and discussed fairness in spending across generations and the importance of fiscal responsibility. At the end of the discussion, Pete surprised me by leaning into the microphone, looking my way, and saying, "This is a reasonable man." We became friendly, and I served on his foundation's advisory committee.

Pete and David Walker, former US comptroller general, produced a documentary, *I.O.U.S.A.,* about the threat of runaway deficits and national debt. They premiered it in Omaha and invited several people, including me, to participate in a panel discussion after the film was shown. But first Pete held a press conference with David, himself, and Warren Buffett, an old friend of Pete's who had appeared in the film. I think Pete was mightily surprised when Buffett, in his press conference remarks, largely expressed indifference about the threat of the US going over a fiscal cliff. "We'll work our way out of it," Buffett claimed. Pete didn't believe that for a minute. That was back in 2006, and it's still the argument among many. Will the economy respond to the big tax cut of 2017 with increased revenues, and will we grow our way out of fiscal disaster? Pete never bought that kind of reasoning, and neither do I. And now, with the economic shock of the coronavirus, we have an even bigger mountain to climb.

My pitch to Pete about advanced illness and end-of-life care was that we can't solve our national debt problem until we get health care spending under control, and we can't do that without controlling spending near the end of life. Pete saw the logic in that and gave me a start-up grant to get things off the ground. Since then, he and his son Michael, now president of the Peter G. Peterson Foundation, have provided additional grants to form and expand our Coalition to Transform Advanced Care (C-TAC) and build a national alliance. Pete was our catalyst. He believed in us and in the importance of our mission.

An additional delight in knowing Pete was finding that his wife was Joan Ganz Cooney, one of the founders of *Sesame Street* who had influenced me to apply marketing to ideas, issues, and causes (see the Introduction). A few years ago, I went to New York because Pete was ailing, and I wanted to thank him, possibly for the last time, for his faith in our work. Michael was there, and we had a nice chat. Pete passed away not long after, and I was grateful to have had the opportunity to say thanks—for being a real American patriot who was dedicated to raising public and policymaker awareness about America's long-term fiscal challenges, and for believing in C-TAC.

Not long after Pete provided the initial seed grant, I met Tom Koutsoumpas, a health care policy expert whose personal story of coping with advanced illness (told earlier in this chapter) animated his work in this area. Tom, who had helped develop the Medicare hospice benefit and been a senior executive at UnitedHealthcare, is now the CEO of Capital Caring Health, one of the largest non-profit hospice and palliative care organizations in the United States, operating in Virginia, Maryland, and Washington, DC. Tom and I became instant friends and teammates, and we co-founded C-TAC with this big goal: *all Americans with advanced illness will receive comprehensive, high-quality, person-centered care that is consistent with their goals and values and honors their dignity.* In other words, we wanted to close that big gap between what patients and their families want when serious illness occurs and what they receive now in the American health care system.

When Tom and I cofounded the Coalition to Transform Advanced Care, we soon assembled a great team, which is always the key to progress and success. David Longnecker, who had been chief medical officer for the University of Pennsylvania Health System and a senior executive at the Association of American Medical Colleges, joined us as a volunteer executive (Tom and I call David and other committed volunteers—including ourselves—"dollar-a-year men," after the executives who volunteered in World War II).

Marian Grant, a remarkable palliative care nurse and professor who earlier in life had been a marketing executive on Procter & Gamble's CoverGirl cosmetics business, is our outreach and clinical expert. Marian is a true change agent. She says, "Maybe it was an early midlife crisis, or maybe it was the fear that bringing the world a better lipstick wasn't going to get me through the pearly gates, but . . . after a lot of soul-searching, I took a big pay cut and left the corporate world to become a nurse, and I've never looked back." Cheryl Matheis, an attorney and an effective and accomplished senior executive at AARP, came aboard with deep experience in health and health care. Brad Stuart, a superb writer and passionate advocate for patients with serious illness, is our chief medical officer. And a young guy with a master's degree in philosophy, Jon Broyles, came in at a bottom rung, worked hard, learned the trade, and today is our leader as executive director and informal chief storyteller. We have other talented teammates as well. As always, mission attracts talent, and a talented, dedicated team moves mountains.

Why the acronym C-TAC? It sounds like an airport, or maybe a medical procedure. When we started the Campaign for Tobacco-Free Kids, we purposely put children front and center, believing that the tobacco industry would have second thoughts about attacking an organization dedicated to protecting kids. And we used the word "campaign" to signify action and movement. With the Coalition to Transform Advanced Care, we didn't want to get too obvious. The "death panel" fearmongers were out and about, and we thought discretion might be the better part of valor. Later we tried to change from "Coalition" to "Campaign" (again, to connote action), but our board was wary. They thought it might suggest a short-term effort, like a political campaign. So here we are: C-TAC. We're used to it now, and so is the community in which we operate.

As we got going, we were aware that, as in so many fields of public interest and social impact, there's already lots going on, with many players occupying different niches. For example, the Center to Advance Palliative Care (CAPC), led by a nationally known physician, Diane Meier, has been making progress for years in promoting palliative care in hospital settings and at the community level. Ellen Goodman, the former syndicated columnist with the *Boston Globe*, founded the Conversation Project to encourage families to discuss advance directives and to have other conversations, including with physicians, to avoid the guesswork that Senator Johnny Isakson and so many others have had to puzzle out. There are many others across the spectrum.

The National Academy of Medicine formed a committee on which I served and issued a report in 2015—*Dying in America: Improving Quality and Honoring Individual Preferences Near the End of Life*. Our report covered the progress being made and said, "A substantial body of evidence shows that broad improvements to end-of-life care are within reach. . . . Improving the quality and availability of medical and social services for patients and their families could not only enhance quality of life through the end of life, but may also contribute to a more sustainable care system."

We presented six major recommendations: improved delivery of comprehensive care, improved clinician-patient communication and advance care planning, increased professional education, reform of policies and payment systems, public education and engagement, and better measurement of performance and results. Today we see progress in each of these areas, but much more work remains to be done.

That same year, Tom Koutsoumpas and I—with Boe Workman, the editor of this book—produced a C-TAC volume called *A Roadmap for Success: Transforming Advanced Illness Care in America*. We summarized nearly the whole field, covering the need to put patients and families first, the role of spirituality, strategies for employers and their employees who are caregivers, needed policy reform, and care delivery models. We ended with a call to action—we *can* achieve the goal of "enabling all Americans, especially the sickest and most vulnerable, to receive comprehensive, high-quality, person- and family-centered care that is consistent with their goals and values and honors their dignity." We added, "The mortality rate in America is still 100 percent. None of us are going to come out of this alive anyhow, so we might as well get this done."

Our basic C-TAC approach is not to reinvent wheels but to support what is already working. We positioned our organization to be a strong, national voice and a catalyst—a big tent—to promote the growing movement that can benefit from shared goals and information and, as the National Academy of Medicine report called for, common measurement of performance and results.

Like much of America's health care system, advanced illness care is fragmented, creating burdens for patients and families. While palliative care can contribute to higher quality of, and perhaps longer, life, timely referral to palliative care needs to be accelerated. And as Atul Gawande and others have said, clinicians need to help patients choose the care they want, which often is focused on reducing pain and suffering. Frequent clinician-patient conversations about values, goals, and preferences are needed to avoid unwanted treatment.

Based on all this and what was happening in the field, we initiated four C-TAC strategies:

- Support *public engagement* to assist patients and their families with advance directives and other early decisions and to help them understand their options and make more informed decisions about treatment for serious illness.
- Educate *health professionals (clinicians)* to become better at communicating effectively with patients and families and engaging them in appropriate treatment decisions.
- Build on and promote *clinical and community models* that work. These best-practice models already exist, and we can promote this high-quality, coordinated care across all settings, especially in the home and community.
- Drive policy change through effective *advocacy*—legislative and regulatory. This is the one strategy where C-TAC needs to take the lead, working with our coalition partners, because there aren't enough others engaged.

Building the Coalition

As has been evident throughout this book, coalitions are hard to build, to maintain, to make cohesive, and to use as funding sources. C-TAC is no different. Coalition members are often just names on a page, but we were determined that this would be different. We followed the maxim of being nonpartisan but political—a necessity to create policy change. It took time to create a broad, national coalition in advanced illness and end-of-life care.

Two of our first and most important coalition members were the American Hospital Association and the American Heart Association. I had worked together with Rich Umbdenstock, then CEO of the hospital association, on health issues when I was at AARP. He brought his association into C-TAC early and with enthusiasm. Tom and I asked him if reducing aggressive advanced illness care would have a negative economic effect on American hospitals. Rich said it was certainly possible but that the writing was on the wall and that hospitals needed to make health care more affordable and sustainable. When Rich stepped down as CEO, he joined our C-TAC board, and his successor, Rick Pollack, has been a strong C-TAC supporter.

I asked Nancy Brown, the CEO of the American Heart Association, to bring her organization into C-TAC. She didn't hesitate. While there has been tremendous progress in reducing death and illness from heart disease and stroke, Nancy said, the later stages of the continuum—advanced illness—needed much more attention. She not only brought the heart association on board but also, like Rich, has been a highly valued board member.

Today C-TAC is a broad alliance of some 140 stakeholders, including patient and consumer groups (e.g., AARP, American Heart Association, National Alliance for Caregiving); health systems (e.g., Gundersen Health System, Kaiser Permanente, MedStar Health); professional associations (e.g., American Society of Clinical Oncology, Association of American Medical Colleges, American Academy of Home Care Medicine); faith-based organizations (Christian, Jewish, and Muslim); health insurance companies (e.g., Cigna, Aetna, Highmark); and hospice and palliative care groups (e.g., National Partnership for Hospice Innovation, Minnesota Network of Hospice and Palliative Care).

In most of the work I've done in social change, I have found that faith-based organizations often play critical roles—either for or against your objectives. When evangelical Christians decided that smoking was a serious hazard for children, they got involved in tobacco control. And when Islamic leaders told women in Egypt that contraception was not to be practiced, it had a negative effect on our Family of the Future reproductive health program when I was at Porter Novelli. (Effat Ramadan, the executive director of Family of the Future, successfully recruited other imams who preached that contraception was in women's and families' best interest.)

In advanced illness and end-of-life care, faith-based groups have been vitally important. Rabbi Richard Address and the Reverend Tyrone Pitts, a Baptist minister, were early leaders. They come from different religious traditions but are great teammates who can really inspire a crowd. The Reverend Gus Reyes in Texas is also a key partner. Our Interfaith and Diversity Workgroup reaches into communities with information on how religious organizations can support family caregivers and provide training for faith leaders, who in turn engage local "navigators" and parishioners.

Community-level support is critical. Diane Meier, the head of the Center to Advance Palliative Care, stresses the need to combine clinical and community services to keep people out of hospitals and other institutions. Meals on Wheels (MOW) is an excellent example of an effective community service. Ellie Hollander, our chief people officer when I was at AARP, now heads Meals on Wheels America. She and her strategy officer, Lucy Theilheimer (also an AARP alumna), have shown that MOW reduces social isolation, improves health and quality of life, and enables elders recently discharged from the hospital to live independently at home.

As the movement has grown, state and community coalitions have formed across the country. Our role is to support these groups and to share information among them, as well as to encourage new ones to spring up. One of the most successful state coalitions is the Massachusetts Coalition for Serious Illness Care, led by Andrew Dreyfus, CEO of Blue Cross Blue Shield of Massachusetts, with more than 100 state-based organizations. California's coalition has been successful in getting state legislation enacted. And the Oregon Coalition for Living Well with Serious Illness began with

Massachusetts as a useful model. Alliances are underway in Arizona, Michigan, New Jersey, and North Carolina. To advance state action, we produced a case study of the Massachusetts program for use by others. And we've done roundtables across the country to listen and learn.

Some two decades ago, Gundersen Health System began Respecting Choices, an initiative in LaCrosse, Wisconsin, designed to improve advanced illness planning among health professionals, individuals, and families. Bud Hammes, who started the initiative, believed that communication was the key to effective care that honored patients' wishes and values. After its local success, Respecting Choices grew into a national and international program that is evidence based and well documented. A few years ago, Gundersen, a member of C-TAC, asked us to manage Respecting Choices and help scale it up. Today the program, now led by Stephanie Anderson, is a powerful model of advance care planning and community involvement in more than 130 health systems and medical centers, with more than 10,000 trained facilitators worldwide.

National Policy Advocacy

We are determined not to duplicate initiatives being undertaken by others, but it became clear that there was a substantial shortfall in national policy advocacy. One of our first steps was to develop a policy agenda based on the National Academy of Medicine report *Dying in America* and other priorities identified by our members and discussions with Congress and the administration. These include reform of the delivery system (including payment), better access to advance directives for patients and families, resources for family caregivers, and expansion of the advanced illness care workforce.

Our advocacy on Capitol Hill is truly bipartisan, based on the very human reality that everyone—senators, representatives, their staffs, and everyone else—has a personal story about advanced illness. Talk to a United States senator about any aspect of this issue, and she is apt to say, "First let me tell you about my mother." Personal experiences bind us together. We advocate as a coalition team with many of our members. Comprehensive legislative reform is unlikely, if not impossible, in today's political climate. But incremental change is possible, and it's happening.

The Chronic Care Act of 2017 expanded the use of telehealth and broadened the definition of supplemental benefits that Medicare Advantage plans can offer to include home-based palliative care, nutrition, and transportation support for those with chronic illness. The Bipartisan Budget Act of 2018 included provisions to study long-term care planning, extend a model program on care at home, and make Medicare benefits more flexible. Also in 2018, a new law mandated a national strategy to support family caregivers and improve caregiver coordination across government programs. Another important piece of legislation would improve training of health care workers, expand research, and educate health consumers and professionals in palliative care. It passed the House, and now we are working to pass it in the Senate. Keeping congressional members and staff informed and engaged is a key part of any successful advocacy program, so we conduct Hill briefings and participate in congressional hearings.

Progress is also taking place on the regulatory front. The Center for Medicare and Medicaid Innovation is launching a primary care model, including a track that would pay for interdisciplinary care at home for those with serious illness. This model is based on one created by C-TAC, along with one developed by the American Academy of Hospice and Palliative Medicine. Our comments on various proposed rules have succeeded in adding advance care planning into various Medicare programs and excluding those receiving palliative care from some opioid restrictions.

Measuring Progress

Every program, every alliance needs metrics to assess performance and results. It's important to keep score. In the National Academy of Medicine report *Dying in America*, we called for improved measurement and accountability. So, in the growing movement to improve advanced illness and end-of-life care in America, how are we doing? Are we making progress? If so, how much? In all honesty, we don't know.

Some national and state government statistics and organizational measures are being collected, but there is no comprehensive effort to measure progress and make midcourse corrections. As with policy advocacy, this is an area where we decided C-TAC had to lead. We began our Advanced Care Transformation Index (ACT Index) several years ago to evaluate efforts in states and nationally to improve the quality of life for those with advanced illness and their families. The idea is not just to measure progress, as important as that is, but also to identify opportunities and encourage improved care, to increase patient and family satisfaction, to lower costs, and to support caregivers.

Our first steps were to appoint an expert task force and to collect dozens of possible metrics from existing databases at federal and state levels. Ideally, we want to use current sources so we don't have to set up a data collection structure. We chose 37 measures that we combined into a single composite measure, or index. The component measures include percentage of deaths at home (most people want to die at home rather than in a hospital or other institution), hospital and hospice days per decedent in last two years of life, total Medicare spending in the last two years of life, person-centered and family care (as judged by patients and families), and percentage of adults who went without care in the past year owing to cost of care.

We calculated a composite score for each state, and it wasn't surprising to see wide variations. Maine, New Hampshire, and North Dakota performed the best, while North Carolina, West Virginia, and Kentucky were at the other end of the scale.

We have been refining the index and taking it to various states to gauge their interest in improving their efforts in advanced illness and end-of-life care. The Arizona Hospital and Healthcare Association and Arizona End of Life Care Partnership are pilot partners. We have an ACT Index "calculator" to enable states to compare their performance with any other state on any set of years for any performance metric they choose. They can see how their overall index score would change based on the areas they want to improve.

The "Business" of Caregiving

There are tough jobs in this world, and then there are the really tough jobs. Being a family caregiver is one of those. The demands on people (mostly women) taking care of older family members and other loved ones are intense and growing even more difficult. As our older population increases, more people will have greater needs and require care. The United Hospital Fund and AARP did a study showing that demands on caregivers are growing and becoming more complex. Tasks like caring for wounds, managing multiple medications, and giving injections, which were once the province of medical professionals, now fall to family members. Caregivers, as well as those they care for, are more and more on their own.

This is a huge "industry," if you want to call it that. The National Alliance for Caregiving estimates that more than 40 million Americans provide care for a chronically ill, disabled, or aged family member or friend in any given year. Many of these caregivers are also working at full-time or part-time jobs. Estimates are that about $450 billion worth of free caregiving is delivered annually by and to American families. Health and long-term care, insurance, housing, and other industries are built around it. And public policies are designed, or should be, to foster better care.

In my work with and for older Americans, I've seen a lot of research on caregivers: how it affects their health, their employment, and their wallets. But I've never seen the truly vivid intensity of caregiving until C-TAC and the Cigna Foundation collaborated on a digital ethnography containing some 7,000 conversations from websites where caregivers talked about the reality of their lives. You can study statistics and summaries and surveys, but you have to read the actual words of real people in distress to appreciate the challenges of caregiving. The C-TAC/Cigna ethnography gathered caregivers' comments on many aspects of their lives:

- state of mind (mental fatigue, loneliness, anger, helplessness, anxiety, grief);
- crimped social lives (resentment toward their families, difficulties having other relationships, inability to leave their patients, feeling neglected);
- health status (stress, emotional and physical decline, insomnia);
- finances (higher medical bills, compromised careers, part-time jobs to pay bills); and
- support (lack of help from their families, the need to go online to talk to other caregivers).

The most common words used among these caregivers were "help," "sad," "exhausted," and "stress." Reading their comments knocks you off your chair. Here are just a few:

- "At first I cried because of the thought of losing him."
- "It does get hard. . . . I cry a lot in the shower . . . but God is going to take care of it all."
- "I've never experienced such pain."

- "I feel like I'm going crazy."
- "I feel as though I'm at my breaking point in caring for her."
- "I'm exhausted beyond belief."
- "I'm tired, scared, and want her home emotionally, but want a life for myself, too."
- "I tried to get him to go back to the hospital so I could get some respite [but] he absolutely refuses. Now I am exhausted and feel guilty."
- "My mum's conditions are hemorrhaging stroke, heart deceases [sic] and now she is [sic] osteoporosis, I'm so scared, confused."
- I'm mad, I do everything at the house at 4 o'clock in the morning to bedtime plus still work."

There are many, many more, but you get the picture. You may be (or have been) one of these caregivers, and you certainly know some of them. Former First Lady Rosalynn Carter once said, "There are only four kinds of people in the world: those who have been caregivers, those who are currently caregivers, those who will be caregivers, and those who will need caregivers." That sums it up pretty well. Today the Rosalynn Carter Institute for Caregiving is working on research, policies, and partnerships to support caregivers' health and resilience.

Now what can we do to make this better? C-TAC has several members, including the National Alliance for Caregiving, directly focused on these issues. They and other organizations offer tips, hotlines, online sites, including chat rooms, and other support. There is a good deal of policy advocacy to improve family caregivers' situations in their communities, jobs, and homes. We and others are working to advance all this. But caregiving is still, and will remain, one of the toughest jobs in the world.

Alexandra (Alex) Drane is committed to doing something about it. A self-described "serial entrepreneur" and a member of our

C-TAC board, Alex has started and grown several companies, including Eliza Corporation, that apply health care technology to "help people live happier, healthier, and more productive lives." She jokes that her business philosophy is "Don't go under!" Alex concluded that "health is life, and when life goes wrong, health goes wrong." Life going wrong includes "work, financial, relationship, and *caregiving* stress, which are killing us."

Alex's sister-in-law died young, and Alex herself survived a brain tumor that required nine-and-a-half hours of surgery. She learned a lesson from that ordeal: "If you might be dead tomorrow, you don't worry about the BS. Make the most of every minute." And now, with a family and a busy career, she did something I would never have thought of. Alex became a cashier at Walmart. Talk about understanding customer needs and doing real research—this is it. As she serves customers on her nine-hour shifts, she talks to them and to her coworkers, and she learns. "Is Mentos your favorite candy?" Alex asked the woman who was buying 10 rolls of Mentos. The woman said they were for her mother who suffered from Alzheimer's and for the nurses helping take care of her. "Always get extra for the nurses."

Alex learned a lot from her checkout vantage point, which she shared in a panel discussion at our C-TAC national summit with two other women who also were Walmart cashiers. Then, partnering with Walmart and MassOptions, she started an organization—Archangels—to honor and support caregivers. She still does her cashier job on occasion, and she and other cashiers wear lapel pins asking if a customer is a caregiver. Here's the message: "Archangels: We think caregivers are our country's unsung heroes. Thank you for all you do—and we want to help support you. For free help with things like home care, transportation, financial assistance, and food—go to massoptions.org or call toll free 1-844-422-6277." Alex's own motto is "Caregivers are everywhere. Love on them, and give them a lift."

The American Cancer Society is also active in caregiver support, with a hotline that fields some 1.2 million calls a year for patient and caregiver assistance. AARP also makes caregiver research, advocacy, and direct support a high priority.

Lee Woodruff, who was once a Porter Novelli account executive, went through caregiving purgatory when her husband, Bob, a national ABC News anchor, suffered a roadside-bomb injury in Iraq. Lee wrote a best-selling book about it, and she and Bob founded the Bob Woodruff Foundation to assist wounded service veterans and their families. But with all that's going on, there's a tremendous amount of work to do, and there are many opportunities to make a difference in caregivers' enormously difficult lives.

A controversial issue in this area is medical aid in dying, when a physician provides a competent, terminally ill patient—at the patient's request—with a prescription for a lethal dose of medicine that the patient intends to use to end his or her own life. Today some 22 percent of Americans live in a jurisdiction where medical aid in dying is authorized, either through statute or court decision. This includes nine states—California, Colorado, Hawaii, Maine, Montana, New Jersey, Oregon, Vermont, and Washington—plus the District of Columbia. Public polls indicate strong approval of this policy; in a May 2018 Gallup survey, 72 percent of registered voters supported medical aid in dying. Kim Callinan, CEO of Compassion & Choices, the primary organization advocating for this option, calls it "dignity and choice at life's end." At C-TAC we have stayed neutral on the subject because we believe the controversy surrounding aid in dying can overshadow the larger issues we are pursuing.

The Power of Story

Storytelling is a hot commodity today, from TED talks to fireside chats to corporate sales meetings to NPR's Story Corps. Everyone loves stories; they can inspire, anger, motivate, and sell. Alex

Drane likes to talk about the power of statistics and stories in combination. But I find that many of these stories lack a strategy. They may be hugely entertaining, but from a social change or a commercial standpoint, there often isn't a sufficient purpose behind the tale.

Robyn Castellani is a storyteller; her company, Castle & Spark, is entirely devoted to strategic narratives. She works with clients to build narratives around "the need, the adversary, and the core promise—the emotional appeal that will get people to engage." Robyn draws on a Yale study that followed adults for 20 years and found that people who had a positive view of aging in midlife lived an average of 7.6 years longer than those who had a negative view. She says that hundreds of studies prove the "life-changing magic of a productive story." I am a strong proponent of bringing strategies to life through effective storytelling, and that's what we try to do at C-TAC as well as in the other issues, movements, and campaigns I'm involved in. Robyn is a big help. As I tell my students, partners, and colleagues and try to do myself: tell your story, sell your story, live your story.

Jon Broyles, the executive director of C-TAC, is a storyteller who has been able to combine statistics (that is, evidence) with strategy in our stories. A key objective is to help patients and their caregivers and surrogates understand their options in dealing with serious illness and engage with clinicians in shared treatment decision-making. To make this possible, the clinicians themselves (often physicians, who usually are the decision-makers) must be willing to listen and relate to patients and families, and then to involve them in decisions about care—to help people be the authors of their lives, as Atul Gawande put it. Clinicians aren't well trained for this. And seriously ill people and their stressed-out families are seldom in a coping mode.

Every year we have a C-TAC National Summit on Advanced Illness Care that brings together health care leaders from around the country—from hospitals and health systems, insurance companies, employers, faith groups, and consumer advocates—to share best practices, assess the state of play, and advance the movement. Jon uses stories at the summit to spark and inspire our participants. Here are two examples:

DRIVING MISS NORMA

An elderly woman in upstate Michigan, Norma Bauerschmidt, known to her family as Miss Norma, was feeling poorly and went to the doctor. The diagnosis was uterine cancer, and the physician told her the treatment was a combination of surgery, radiation, and chemotherapy. Miss Norma stood up (all five feet of her) and said, "I'm ninety years old. I'm hitting the road." And she did, with her son, Tim; his wife, Ramie (they call themselves "professional nomads"); and the family poodle, Ringo, in their motor home. They went wherever Miss Norma wished: the Grand Canyon, Cape Canaveral, Bar Harbor, Yellowstone, Albuquerque, Presque Isle, New Orleans, Mexico's Baja California Peninsula, and Cheyenne, among many other destinations. Miss Norma went up in a hot air balloon (with Ringo), rode a horse, and made an "educational" visit to a cannabis dispensary.

Tim, Ramie, and Ringo stood on stage at our National Summit and told Miss Norma's story. She met new people, tried new foods, tasted life, and left this world with humor, love, and family.

Tim and Ramie told about later reading Miss Norma's diary and how she focused on life. They wrote a book, *Driving Miss Norma: One Family's Journey Saying "Yes" to Living*. In the book they said:

> The most remarkable thing we discovered about Mom's diary was not what was in it but what was missing. She did not write a single word about cancer . . . [or] about seeing herself on television or being recognized on the street. She did not write about the fear of dying or illness at all. Instead, she talked about life, living, and the little things that brought her happiness: a sturdy wheelchair and someone to push her; the sight of

mama and baby goats; cookies and peppermint patties; getting a good hair perm; the gift of a Santa hat and a new bar of soap; and food to enjoy along with family, friends, and her trusty sidekick, Ringo.

Jon enlisted Tim Bauerschmidt and Ramie Liddle as C-TAC's first Caregiver Fellows. They speak and blog about their experience as caregivers and about our work as a voice for the movement.

THE BLUE CHAIR

At a later Summit, Jon invited Shirley Roberson, a dignified, quiet woman with breast cancer, to tell her story. She was unhappy with her doctor because she didn't think he was listening to her and was not including her in the deeply personal process of her advanced illness. She made a big, difficult decision—to change doctors. When the new physician came into the room to meet with her, he carried a chart (it turned out to be the wrong one) and began to tell her about the course of her treatment. Shirley endured this for a few minutes and then snapped. She saw a chair across the room and blurted out, "What I want to say to you is stop talking and go sit in that blue chair. While sitting in the blue chair you must not talk. You must listen. I get to talk. Do you understand what I'm asking you to do?"

The young doctor looked at Ms. Roberson and then meekly sat down—in the blue chair. She started talking; she told him about herself, her family, her concerns about her illness and the course of her treatment, and her hopes for recovery. After a while a relationship formed, and she and the doctor proceeded to discuss a course of action. Now he was dealing with a woman, a human being, not just a patient. Our Summit audience was spellbound—physicians, patient advocates, all of us. For the rest of the Summit we had blue chairs on stage, and they became the symbol of understanding and dialogue. Today in the C-TAC office we refer to the Blue Chair when we mean to say, "Listen to a new point of view. Just listen." This is part of what Robyn Castellani calls strategic empathy.

"Driving Miss Norma" and "The Blue Chair" have different messages but similar conclusions. Miss Norma received a diagnosis, understood the prognosis, and elected to forgo treatment. Shirley Roberson very much wanted treatment, but she also wanted to understand it and be part of it, and she wanted the physician to understand her. Again, they both wanted to be the authors of their lives. How do we make that the key to reforming advanced illness and end-of-life care in America? How do we use public engagement and clinician support and training to create shared and informed treatment decision-making? We're working on it.

At our most recent Summit, we unveiled our moon shot, a huge step up to galvanize and accelerate the movement and serve as a rallying point—by calling for improving the lives of 6 million Americans in stages of advanced illness and end of life. Jon said that 6 million has to start with one, and he asked each board member on stage to identify the first person we would help. I named my college roommate and lifelong friend George Edelstein, who went from being a successful lawyer at the Justice Department to a long, lonely period of serious depression. His former wife and Fran and I became his support system. I said I wanted my first of those 6 million to be George. Six months after our Summit, George died from Covid-19. He remains my image of the person I want to help.

Even though we need better metrics—our Advanced Care Transformation (ACT) Index and other measures—it's clear that a lot of progress is being made toward the goal of having all Americans with advanced illness receive high-quality care that meets their goals and values. The movement is growing at national, state, and community levels.

The baby boomers, a feisty generation, are aging and are already making a difference; they're unlikely to passively accept the treatment their parents endured. As Beth McGroarty, head of research for the Global Wellness Summit said about boomers, "They are basically saying, 'I refuse to have a terrible death.'"

The National Academy of Medicine report *Dying in America* has informed the professional community and policy makers. The death panel scaremongers have receded into the background. There is much more, and much better, media attention to these issues. Recent regulations to have Medicare compensate clinicians for advance planning discussions with patients, demonstrations of alternative payment models, and other steps are promising.

And policy makers are well aware that we can't afford the huge costs to taxpayers, to government, to the health system, and especially to families and individuals. The number-one concern for people with serious illness is the fear of incurring a financial burden for themselves and their families.

A big reason why change is afoot is the personal stories, from Senator Isakson and other lawmakers to Amy Berman to Miss Norma and Shirley Roberson. Another moving story is that of former First Lady Barbara Bush, who passed away in 2019 with the announcement that she would not continue to seek treatment for an illness that had repeatedly hospitalized her. Instead, she opted for palliative care and spent the rest of her days with her family. This was her choice, as the author of her life.

As for C-TAC, we're energized and on the move. Stay tuned, and get involved (www.thectac.org). You may already be a caregiver or part of this issue in some other important way. There's lots to do and a role for just about everyone. For companies, nonprofits, and many others, this is a big opportunity to do well by doing good.

CHAPTER SEVEN

BLENDING PROFIT AND PURPOSE

*Building an Academic Center for Today's
and Tomorrow's Leaders*

Business school students believe in capitalism and in business—that's obvious. But often having been out in the real world before coming back for their MBA degrees, they realize that the marketplace is a grey area where both good things and bad things happen. In class, I draw a long line across the white board—a continuum of social responsibility—with the most responsible companies at the far left and the most irresponsible at the far right (that would be the tobacco companies in my view, and in the view of most students). Then I ask, Where does ExxonMobil belong on this continuum? Goldman Sachs? Walmart? Toyota? McDonald's? This sparks plenty of debate, and students conclude that companies can be responsible and (often at the same time) misbehave. As consumers, investors, regulators, and prospective and current employees, we can and must influence their performance.

I often hear from graduates years later in the scrum of business life who tell me about what they are doing to make a difference. To them, life is about making a decent living and about making things better. A good example is Jenny Heflin, who left her mark here at Georgetown and then went to Accenture, where she led some of the company's key corporate citizenship partnerships over the next six years. She quotes a phrase common among Accenture leaders that comes from Marian Wright Edelman: "Service is the rent you pay for being." Jenny's role was primarily to facilitate grants to nonprofits and lead pro bono consulting assignments, monitor progress, and help them grow. Now she's a senior manager in the firm's public service leadership team, where most of her clients are state and local governments and universities. Jenny says that companies have to get into the communities in which they operate. Her advice to current students is to "get hands-on experience at Georgetown, and then when you go out, practice corporate citizenship."

I had always wanted to have an academic chapter in my career, where I could reach students, work with them, and prepare them to do well by doing good. Near the end of my tenure at AARP, a reporter asked me "What's next for you?" I said I wanted to join a top-level university with a good gym, have the opportunity to teach and build something, and audit some anthropology courses on the side. Georgetown turned out to be that place. And although I haven't had the time to audit courses, all the rest of it has come to pass, even beyond what I had imagined.

The university is on a hilltop in the Georgetown section of Washington, DC, with a total enrollment of some 19,000 students at the main campus and downtown, where the law school and the school of continuing studies are located. It was founded by Jesuits in 1789, the year the US Constitution was ratified, and the joke is that our bureaucracy operates at 1789 speed. That's not far from the truth, but I think it's probably typical of most academic institutions. They aren't private sector companies on the move, that's for sure.

I'm a Hoya, and a proud one. I've come to have enormously high regard for Georgetown University. But it took me awhile to really discover what it was all about. We started Porter Novelli in George-town, just a few blocks from the university. Some of our staff used to play basketball at lunchtime in the Georgetown gym, and—aside from delivering several guest lectures over the years—that was the extent of my connection to the school.

When I came here I had a passing knowledge of Jesuits and their history, but I had little understanding of Jesuit values. It turns out that the commitment to "Women and men for others" is real and permeates the university. Although most of the students are not Catholic, that credo is everywhere. In an age of ethical ambiguity, it's a powerful idea. This is the only university I've ever seen with a cemetery in the middle of the campus—the resting place of many of the Jesuits who built this place. That and the general management of universities reminds me of the quote usually attributed to Erskine Bowles (who had headed the University of North Carolina) about how being president of a university is like being president of a graveyard: "You can talk all you want, but nobody is listening."

When I was exiting AARP, the dean of Georgetown's Mc-Donough School of Business was George Daly. We met through Alan Andreasen, a Georgetown professor and one of our social marketing academic gurus from my Porter Novelli days. George and I hit it off, and he invited me to join the faculty.

I've had some great views of the world in my various incarnations. From my Porter Novelli office on Broadway in New York, I could see the bustle and action of Manhattan. I had an inspiring view of the US Capitol from my AARP office. But my favorite view of all time, I think, is from my Georgetown office window. It is like a stadium skybox, overlooking the football and lacrosse field. I see the men's and women's teams practicing out there almost every morning. In my days at Penn, our football team often practiced at 7:00 a.m., which we thought was ungodly. These Georgetown jocks are out there even earlier.

Athletics begets leadership, I am convinced. A great example of this is Karin Corbett, the women's lacrosse coach at Penn. Ask her what she does, and Karin will tell you she's a teacher. She works on building leaders with high standards, personal responsibility, and accountability. Karin says that college students can become self-absorbed, and although they want to give back, they need to understand how. She has a community service program in which her players mentor inner-city Philadelphia kids on campus and in the community. Karin has her players write assessments of their own performance, as well the team's. She tracks their progress later in their careers, and they tell her they are well prepared for the real world. Karin says this is what's important, and the lacrosse wins will come. And they do; she's won 11 Ivy League championships and 229 victories. Jesse Cantrill, my lacrosse buddy and fellow midfielder, and I always look forward to alumni lacrosse day on Franklin Field, where we watch the women's and men's teams go at it and see old friends.

Distinguished Professor of the Practice

I have a fancy title at Georgetown—Distinguished Professor of the Practice—that I don't pay much attention to. (I try to get Fran to call me Distinguished Professor, but she won't do it.) Truth be told, I'm not really an academic. I never finished the PhD I pursued at New York University when I was at Unilever and Wells Rich Greene. (I'm also one merit badge short of my Eagle Scout award.) A professor of the practice is supposed to have real-world, professional experience that students value. I have that, and the MBA students relate to it. They have been in the workforce for several years between their undergraduate and MBA programs, and they are realists to the core. No fluff, no puff for them.

The students are my favorite part of Georgetown. It's a highly competitive institution, and the students in the business school and across the university are real achievers. I go home happy every night because I see tomorrow's leaders in action.

Years ago, when I coached the youth soccer team of my sons, Peter and Alex, sometimes for fun I'd tell the kids to line up by IQ. They would mill around for a bit and then all jostle to get into the front of the line. There's a bit of that in academe—lots of very bright people quite willing to display their knowledge. I've always been aware that I am seldom, or even ever, the smartest person in the room. Knowing that is actually an advantage.

It took me a while to realize that professors of the practice are not always highly regarded by some of the true academic professors, who work extremely hard for years to get tenure. They do extensive research and compete to be published in highly selective, peer-reviewed journals. They teach while also laboring on faculty committees to make the university and the business school function. They consult when they can, to supplement their incomes and to gather data for still more papers. Being a professor on the tenure track can be a demanding job.

I've spent my entire marketing and management career applying research and data, but I'm not a researcher myself. There are serious questions about who reads all the academic research papers that are published. Some studies suggest that many papers have very small audiences. As the American academic model comes under more scrutiny, the cost to universities (and therefore to the parents and students) of this method of scorekeeping is coming into question. Still, I appreciate some of this work. My colleague down the hall, David Walker, a long-tenured professor of economics, is always working on academic papers, and he passes some of them on to me. I especially liked several analyses he did on predicting political elections on the basis of economic indicators. That's useful information.

Several of my business school colleagues here, including Tom Cooke, an expert in business law and federal income taxation, and

Charlie Skuba, a marketing professor and head of a major portion of our executive education program, are strong professionals who, like me, are not on the tenure track. I doubt that it even occurs to them. It certainly doesn't bother me, and it does have its advantages.

Years ago, in my Porter Novelli life, I was invited to guest lecture in a social marketing course at Columbia University in New York. I walked across the campus and asked a student for the location of the building. She asked who the professor was, and when I told her, she said, "He's famous." When I inquired what he was famous for, she said, "For being a great teacher." I've never forgotten that. What praise—a great teacher. When I taught social marketing and health communication at the University of Maryland, I thought I was pretty good. Now, teaching in the MBA program at Georgetown, I do well, but I don't think I can call myself a great teacher. It's something I aspire to become.

I created two MBA courses at Georgetown: Corporate Social Responsibility, and Leadership and Management of Nonprofit Organizations. Both are woven throughout this book. The course on corporate social responsibility provides "an overview and examination of the rationale, role, and practices of corporations in creating core business objectives, strategies, and competencies to *do well* (improve financial and other business performances and build wealth for shareholders) and at the same time to *do good* (improve society and create social value for multiple stakeholders)." Students really dig into this. They have plenty of criticisms of corporate performance, as they should. Not all companies are in front of the curve; for many, it's hard to find the sweet spot where financial and social value converge.

Students who take the nonprofit course often come from that sector, and many are in business school because they want to make nonprofit organizations better or change the direction of their career. Although the course aims to develop students' capacity to thrive, lead, and succeed in the nonprofit community, there are also students from corporate backgrounds who want to know what nonprofits are all about. I welcome them because when they return to business or government or another field, their understanding of nonprofits will help them engage in partnerships, nonprofit board service, and volunteering, as well as in their potential roles as donors. In this course, as in the corporate social responsibility course, there are plenty of skeptics and critics; many believe that nonprofits are inefficient and often ineffective. Some of them base this attitude on their personal experience, and I'm sure there is ample justification. My own experience (with AARP, the Campaign for Tobacco-Free Kids, American Cancer Society, American Heart Association, and Kaboom!) is that most nonprofits have the opportunity and ability to be great organizations. Our students can help make it happen. Now Tom Nelson, who was chief operating officer at AARP with me, teaches this course. He is also the president and CEO of Share Our Strength / No Kid Hungry, which is a major force in combating child hunger in the United States. Tom loves his job, and he loves teaching.

My current teaching assignments are two required MBA courses: Ethical Leadership for Business and Society, and Managing the Enterprise. Every business school in America, maybe every school of any kind, proclaims that it creates leaders. I've had the opportunity to work with effective leaders, from senators and cabinet secretaries to business and nonprofit executives. And I've given a great deal of thought to critiquing my own leadership abilities, which I think of as a work in progress. There's a vast literature—academic and popular—on leadership. I've combined the readings with my own experience and come to a conclusion that might be considered obvious—leadership really, really matters.

Leaders set the direction, but not alone. They aren't prophets who return from fasting alone in the wilderness with a vision. Visions usually come from collaboration and teamwork. But leaders have to own the vision, set the direction, and take us there. It's not about yelling "Charge up that hill!" It's much more about "Come with me." Ethel Percy Andrus, the founder of AARP, was a leader. Steve Schroeder was a leader. History tells us about other leaders who, like Ethel, got mad about the way things were, organized their forces and resources, and created lasting change. Leaders *do* things. They *act*, often with courage and in the face of risk.

There's a story about Walt Disney and his brother when they conceived the idea of Disneyland. His brother said that they first needed to build the hotels. But Walt said, "No, first we build the castle." The lesson is that building a hotel is management, but building a castle is leadership. And of course, we need both.

In my course on ethical leadership, I tell the students—who are about to reenter the workforce and are looking for some spark and inspiration—that I can't really teach them leadership. That is, nobody is going to walk out of the classroom transformed into a great leader. What I can do is give them the direction and tools to practice leadership over a career and to become strong leaders over time. We examine what defines leadership, what leaders owe business and society, what motivates people to act ethically or not, what inclines us to follow some people but not others, what it takes to motivate teams and entire organizations, and how to become a more effective leader. Some people are natural leaders, but I'm convinced that leadership is not innate; we can learn and develop our leadership skills. And you don't have to be in the top spot to lead. Former secretary of state Colin Powell, whom I admire, taught me that, and I've seen it work. Powell said, "Have you ever noticed that people will personally commit to certain individuals who, on paper or on the organization chart, possess little authority, but instead have pizzazz, drive, expertise, and genuine caring for teammates?"

I recently heard from Alex Triplett, a US Army officer who took my leadership course. He's returned to active duty and is determined to be an even better leader than he is now. Leadership transcends disciplines and sectors, including military and civilian life.

One model I like for thinking about and teaching leadership is a business case study called "Invictus: Introducing Leadership Competencies, Character, and Commitment" from the Ivey Business School at Western University in Canada. A faculty group there conducted interviews across the world with business, government, and other executives. They wanted to assess the role that leadership played in the global financial and economic crisis of 2008–2009. They asked: Would better leadership have made a difference? Their conclusion: yes.

The authors (Gerard Seijts, Jeffrey Gandz, and Mary Crossan) base leadership on three dimensions: commitment, competence, and character. The "leaders" who were involved in fomenting the crisis had commitment, to be sure. They were competent in their trades and crafts. Where they fell short was in elements of character (such as integrity, accountability, humanity, and especially judgment). The overall lesson for leadership development is that competencies determine what you *can* do, commitment determines what you *want* to do, and character determines what you *will* do.

One of the toughest tasks of leadership is to transform an organization's culture in order to achieve big goals. We've probably all heard Peter Drucker's comment that culture eats strategy for breakfast every day. Culture can be simply defined as "the way we do things around here," and one definition of leadership is the ability to change culture.

With the help of others, I essentially built the cultures of the start-ups Porter Novelli and the Campaign for Tobacco-Free Kids. I was completely influenced by—and submerged in—the cultures of Unilever, Wells Rich Greene, the Peace Corps, and CREEP (the parent of our November Group), although I do think I was able to provide some leadership from the middle of the ranks. It was AARP where I set out to change the culture of a large organization. I wanted us to be more strategic, more nimble, better users of our resources, and much more aggressive about social impact and policy advocacy. My approach was to blend the top people already on board with outstanding newcomers, set bold goals, create a tone of leadership from the top, encourage leadership in the ranks, and carry out "management by walking around" by working with just about every state office and headquarters unit in the organization. Did it work? While it's hard to quantify culture change, we achieved a great deal and made a difference inside and outside the organization.

I ask my MBA students to write a diary describing their experience as a leader and how they intend to build on this over time. They are asked to include the advice they would have given themselves when they were younger. I tell them that in three years they should go back to read and update it. I hear from former students who do just that. These diaries are heartfelt and powerful stories of what they have already accomplished and what they intend to do. They often include ethical conflicts they have faced. Students' goals vary a great deal: run a family business, rise in the ranks of the military, lead a company or a nonprofit, contribute to solving a major social problem like human trafficking, or just leave the world a better place. But they are clear-eyed and analytical about how to get there. Although grading is my least favorite part of teaching, I always look forward to reading these diaries.

I like to be provocative with students and to make an important point about ethical behavior. Read the *Wall Street Journal* any day of the week, and there are stories of corporate (and government and nonprofit) misbehavior. I use excerpts from a book called *Get Rich Cheating: The Crooked Path to Easy Street*, a satire by Jeff Kreisler. Here's the gist of the book: Why not cheat? Everyone's doing it. You can too, and you can do it better than everyone else.

Cheating isn't wrong or bad, and it won't send you to hell. That's just talk from a weak culture that doesn't want you to succeed. Why cheat? Simple: money, money, money.

The students reject this philosophy of dishonesty so completely that it's hard to get a decent discussion going. They've all seen cheating in their careers, and they are repelled by it. I don't think they're faking honesty; I believe they embrace it. I'm encouraged. Recently, during the coronavirus pandemic shutdown, I've been teaching via online video. I asked a Chinese student about her point of view on *Get Rich Cheating*. She got up from her chair and returned with her infant in her lap. She said simply, "This is why I don't cheat."

Students today are often misjudged. We hear that young people are lazy, more interested in the life side of the work-life balance, willing to change jobs at the drop of a hat. Based on the students I teach and work with, I don't find that portrayal accurate. To be sure, my older generation has a different view. Throughout my career, I've been guided by this philosophy: you can't always out-think your competition, and you can't always outspend them, but you can almost always outwork them. Young people today look askance at this approach. I have two daughters-in-law from Spain, one from Madrid and the other from Barcelona. One said to me, "I don't live to work like you do; I work to live." The other considered my work philosophy and said, "What happened to your Italian genes? Italians aren't supposed to think that way." And they didn't even know about my FILO approach (first in, last out of the office).

I've observed, however, that students do work hard. They care. I hear them in the classroom, in the halls, and in the gym talking about their study habits, the papers and exams they have due, the part-time (or even full-time) jobs they have, and the hours they put in. They just do it differently. Their idea seems to be: I'll work when and where I want, and I will get the work done. As has been said, work is a thing, not a place. Plus, they have far more opportunities today. I overheard two business school undergraduates in the locker room at our gym. One asked if the other got the summer internship he was chasing. The answer was yes; the company had offered him three locations: London, Hong Kong, or New York. He went on to say that his girlfriend chose New York. Wow. In my day at that age, I was bussing tables in Ocean City. Times change.

Creating Georgetown Business for Impact

When Dean George Daly invited me to join the McDonough School of Business faculty, he said, "Bill, besides teaching, I know you want to create something here. What do you have in mind?" I said I wanted to build a center for social change. "This is a business school," said George. "Can't you call it something else?" I said, "How about a center for social enterprise?" George loved that idea. We shook hands, and I went to work.

With George's encouragement I set out to create the Global Social Enterprise Initiative (GSEI). Several MBA students worked with me on the competitive analysis, the overall concept and structure, and cost and revenue projections (no money was forthcoming from the business school or university for our program), and helped me present it to the faculty for approval.

Our premise was that leading and managing a corporation requires an understanding of how to build social and environmental strategies into the core business and that this approach can improve financial performance as well as create greater good for other stakeholders and society as a whole.

Citing substantial student demand for this, we said our vision was to create new generations of leaders who make responsible management decisions that create economic *and* social value across the globe. We pointed out to the faculty executive committee that civil society (nonprofits, universities, faith-based organizations, and associations) and government also had important roles to play. Our big goal was to be the best academic institution in the country for teaching and practicing the triple bottom line: people, planet, profit. The faculty voted to approve, and we were ready to go. Later, we changed the name from the Global Social Enterprise Initiative to Georgetown Business for Impact.

One of our founding students was Rahul Pasarnikar, who had come to Georgetown specifically to study business and social impact. Rahul later went to McKinsey for several years as a consultant and now is the director of business development for CRED (Create Real Economic Destiny), which is led by former US secretary of education Arne Duncan and works to reduce gun violence in Chicago. It is part of the Emerson Collective, a social change organization focused on education, immigration reform, the environment, media and journalism, and health. Founded by Laurene Powell Jobs, the Emerson Collective uses philanthropy, impact investing, advocacy, and community engagement as tools to spur change in the United States and abroad. Rahul is a good example of blending business and social good.

It took a while for us to get Business for Impact up and running (1789 speed?), but eventually we were underway. We knew that we were behind other universities from the outset. Harvard, Wharton (at Penn), Duke, Stanford, and other schools had been in this space for a long time. We saw our primary competitive advantage as being in Washington, where the policy action is (or should be), where numerous multinational institutions (such as the World Bank) reside, and where just about every major corporation in the country has an office or membership in a trade association. Inside the university we promoted our initiative (doing well *by* doing good) as in keeping with Georgetown's Jesuit values and our business school's commitment to being in service to business *and* society.

We've had several deans of the business school since George Daly. David Thomas, who followed George, also had a strong affinity for our work. Today David is the president of Morehouse College. Our current dean, Paul Almeida, is a real champion for our cause. He is an entrepreneur himself, having built the school's executive education program. Paul specializes in strategy and international business. And his theme couldn't be more Jesuit or more in keeping with our purpose: to be the best *in* the world and the best *for* the world.

Like Porter Novelli and the Campaign for Tobacco-Free Kids and other new ventures I've been involved with, Business for Impact was a true start-up operation. Being inside a university has some advantages in terms of existing infrastructure, but basically start-ups are pretty much the same regardless of the sector—for profit, nonprofit, or education.

Bank of America

Ladan Manteghi came on board as our executive director. She had been with me at AARP, where she directed our international work and served as a problem solver. She has many skills, including kickboxing, but I don't think she's had to use that in her business dealings—yet. Ladan is a persuasive person, and she and others helped us get our first big break: a substantial grant from Bank of America. This good fortune reminded me of starting the Campaign for Tobacco-Free Kids. A strong financial backer at the beginning makes a huge difference. The word EMILY ("early money is like yeast") comes to mind.

It took a while to hit our strategic stride with Bank of America. In an early conversation I asked one of their executives what areas of interest they had. He said, "We're a bank; we do well when the economy is strong, so let's work on economic issues that are relevant to us and you." Kerry Sullivan, president of the bank's Charitable Foundation, reinforced that message and called our partnership a great opportunity to work together on job creation and economic development, which she called "critical issues facing our communities." We're doing that and more. In addition, the bank has a penchant for what we came to call "rock star events"—we did one with Bono, another with Warren Buffett, and a third with Ken Burns.

Bono gave an impressive, inspiring speech on global economic and human development. And it was fascinating to see the blocks-long line of students waiting to get into the event with Warren Buffett in 2013, when Buffett was 83 years old and going strong as the Oracle of Omaha and CEO of Berkshire Hathaway. Bank of America CEO Brian Moynihan asked Buffett about where the country was headed. Though forever optimistic, Buffett said that "inequality is getting wider," and he stressed that we needed to figure out how to "share the bounty." He also gave our students some investing tips: he said you didn't have to be that smart to succeed as an investor ("If you've got an IQ of 160, sell 30 points; you don't need them."), and he advised buying what you know—like Coca-Cola—which he drank throughout his talk with Brian.

Before each rock star event, we held a roundtable discussion with Brian and our students. They asked excellent questions, and Brian obviously enjoyed the give and take. On the issue of companies' investing in communities at home, he told the students that if you want your business to succeed, treat your communities well and they will treat you well in return. He stressed that investments in communities are vital to corporate success. This advice contrasted with lots of classroom discussion about moving jobs overseas for cheaper labor.

These roundtable discussions reinforced the value of having businesspeople connect with students. The sparks don't always fly, but they often do. Students value real-world perspective and practical experience, and business leaders relish talking to students. They think they have experience and wisdom to share, and most of the time, it's true.

Today our partnership with Bank of America is going strong, and we are working together on an analysis of social enterprise and workforce development throughout the United States.

Nestlé

Nestlé came to us with a possible strategy to address the growing obesity rate. Obesity and overweight together affect two-thirds of American adults and about 30 percent of the global population. Child obesity rates in the United States are now at 18.5 percent, equivalent to 13.7 million children. Nestlé executives said they want to support consumers in making healthy, balanced food choices that enhance quality of life and contribute to a healthier future. The proposed strategy, supported by a study from the McKinsey Global Institute, was "portion guidance." McKinsey analyzed some 70 possibilities and concluded that no single intervention is likely to have much impact but that combating the problem on a large, multi-front scale could have big effects in terms of improving population health, reducing health care costs, and increasing productivity. My quick, simplistic summation of this strategy was "don't eat the whole pizza."

Nestlé invited us to build a multisector leadership program—a coalition—and they would provide upfront resources to help launch it. Diane Ty took the lead for our team. It took us over a year, and now we have an alliance of manufacturers, nonprofits (including public health and watchdog groups), institutional feeding organizations, restaurants, academics, and government working together. Diane concluded that reducing portions wasn't enough. So we broadened the concept to portion *balance*, which includes volume, proportionality, and quality.

With our Portion Balance Coalition members involved, we set three goals: to build consumer demand for portion-balanced foods and beverages, to work on the supply side (restaurants, institutional food-service companies, take-home purchases from stores), and to share best practices among our participants and the public. As out-of-home eating becomes a larger share of household total food spending, especially among millennials, it's important to make consumers aware of the calorie consumption that goes along with it. Getting restaurants to change their menus is a tall order, but they will respond to consumer demand. With many local restaurants and regional and national chains traditionally competing on volume and serving large portions, consumer interest in healthier diets and sustainability provide an opportunity to change the value proposition to something other than volume.

We've completed initial consumer research and identified a key target segment: fence-sitters. They know what they need to do to be healthy, and they want to engage in the right behaviors. Still, this will be a challenge in terms of individual behavior change. It reminds me of a discussion I had in my Porter Novelli days with a senior officer of the US Navy who wanted to develop a wellness program for noncommissioned officers. He said that many of them were skilled technicians who tried to reenlist but had gained so much weight they were over their body mass index limits. I asked him what they were doing about this, and he said, "We make 'em taller. You'd be surprised how many guys come in at 5'9" or so and are now listed—on paper—at 6'2"."

We are now using our research to develop a consumer campaign for our many coalition members to use. Not all our partners are comfortable with each other, but it's another example of needing everyone at the table to make a difference.

VF Corporation

VF Corporation is one of the world's largest apparel, footwear, and accessories companies. It manages supply chains, including manufacturing, for its many brands, including Timberland, The North Face, Vans, and others. This relationship began when I was invited to serve on VF's Responsible Sourcing Advisory Council. I took two MBA student leaders, Becky Arnold and Jackie Bakalarski, with me on a council trip to VF's contract factories in the Dominican Republic and Nicaragua. They interviewed factory workers and presented their findings to our advisory council and VF management. When they returned, Becky and Jackie blogged about their experience and moderated listening sessions (large focus groups) with students from Georgetown and other Washington-area universities. Later I took additional trips to see factories in Cambodia and Vietnam.

These listening sessions, corroborated by quantitative studies, showed that millennials purchase apparel and footwear primarily on the basis of fashion, fit, and price. No surprise there. But before many of these younger consumers (and tomorrow's leaders) will even consider buying a brand or an item, they want to know that the company behind them is acting responsibly in how it treats the workers who make those products.

VF deals primarily with contract factories in Africa, Asia, and Latin America. The company regards these contract employees—mostly women—as their own. To deliver on this commitment, VF's Worker and Community Development program surveys the workers, assesses their health and social needs (such as clean water, after-school programs for their children, eyeglasses, protection from sexual harassment on the job) and then addresses those needs with on-the-ground initiatives delivered through CARE, UNICEF, and others. Jazz Smith-Khaira, the global senior manager for work and community development at VF, says, "If you speak with any worker from Bangladesh to the Dominican Republic, the reason they're working is to provide a better future for their families."

The competition among apparel companies is fierce at the retail level, but some worker programs in low-income countries can be more efficient when conducted *in cooperation with* competitors, including Levi's, Target, and Williams-Sonoma. And VF's work extends beyond workers and families to include protecting the environment. Our Georgetown students are now engaged with VF to plan a case competition for a number of universities. The challenge will be to come up with strategic, creative ways to tell the VF story. I also plan to take more students to visit factories with our VF advisory council.

Chevron

Chevron has been working for many years with the Nigerian government in oil extraction in the Niger Delta region of Nigeria. Early on, the company established the Niger Delta Partnership Initiative (NDPI) with local NGOs, international aid agencies, other companies, and the Nigerian government to support communities there in job creation and economic development, public safety, and other initiatives. We have been involved with NDPI and its local, Nigerian-led partner for several years.

Now, after a decade of work, Chevron wants to assess progress. Our Business for Impact team is researching and writing a case study of its activities, focusing on what has and has not been successful and what might improve performance. The study is designed to provide insights and recommendations that can be shared with other companies, NGOs, and governments working in public-private partnerships. To discuss these findings and conclusions, we will hold a conference at Georgetown of global development leaders, incorporate their ideas into the case study, and publish it. Chevron's goal is not just to improve conditions where they are doing business but to share their experience and advance private sector involvement in international development.

AB InBev

AB InBev is the world's largest beer company, with global distribution and sales. It formed its own foundation to promote responsible drinking, starting in nine pilot cities and then moving beyond that. We are part of this effort, starting with a pilot program to reduce underage drinking in a low-income community within Johannesburg, South Africa. Gael O'Sullivan, our program director, is an experienced hand at social marketing and international development. She also oversees our Chevron work.

While a baseline study was underway of youth and adults, Gael organized qualitative research among youth in the community. The results, while not surprising, were grim. Kids lack money for the most basic needs like food, school fees, and clean clothes. Many live without fathers or other male figures in crowded homes and with domestic violence. The researchers coined the term "kidulthood" to represent the heavy responsibilities kids face at very young ages. And alcohol use is ubiquitous. Youth live among drunk people at home, in the streets, and in the many informal taverns ("shebeens").

The response to these problems is going to have to go far beyond responsible drinking messages. These kids need improved community safety and support, safe spaces and facilities, enforcement of alcohol sales laws, school and sports programs, and other structural changes. The AB InBev Foundation and our Business for Impact are now in discussions with community leaders to see what we can do together. What we learn and do here may be useful elsewhere, including in so-called developed societies like our own.

Jobs for People with Disabilities

It's just plain hard for people with disabilities to find jobs in America. Only about 35 percent of adults with disabilities are employed, compared with nearly 80 percent of all work-eligible adults. In partnership with the US Department of Labor and the Viscardi Center, a leader in disability issues, our research showed that many corporate human resource officers seldom even think of disability as a diversity category. Fortunately, many companies do have programs to hire, train, and retain people with disabilities. We want to help close the disability gap. John Kemp, the head of Viscardi, a lawyer and himself disabled (and a Hoya), is a national leader on this issue. We're working together to support effective employment programs and to encourage more companies to take action. Among other things, we hold disability inclusion events to bring together companies that are making progress with other companies that are just getting started. Walgreens, Bank of America, Starbucks, Marriott, PwC, and others have impressive programs. So do Santander Bank, Omnicom and Porter Novelli, Northrop Gruman, Accenture, and Signal Group. Recently we connected with former US senator Tom Harkin of Iowa, whom I had worked with in tobacco control when he was in the Senate. Tom is a long-time advocate for people with disabilities, and we plan to work together.

This problem is not intractable, but it is stubborn and resistant to change. We need to create pipelines for qualified job candidates, communicate the positive experiences of people with disabilities at different career stages and in different sectors, and encourage disability inclusion as part of corporate values. One of our Business for Impact teammates, Lauren Gilbert, is our inspiration for all this. She has researched these issues, is a representative to Georgetown's Working Group on Disability, and knows firsthand the challenges and opportunities of having a disability.

Rural Opportunity Initiative

Matt McKenna is a triple-strength leader: business, nonprofit, and government. He created and directs our Rural Opportunity Initiative (ROI) to promote financially and socially sustainable rural development in partnership with federal and state governments, land-grant universities, and the private sector. The main thrust is to drive private investment to create rural prosperity. Matt sees a misalignment—scarce and expensive capital that often doesn't meet the needs of rural business owners, workers, and communities.

The challenge is to unite investors with businesses that can deliver both financial and social returns in rural America. Matt, working with colleague Ladan Manteghi, is looking to capital market and financial tools that bring the scale of urban investment opportunities to rural America. Georgetown is not a land-grant or rural state university, but we are in the nation's policy capital. And Matt has recruited Iowa State, Mississippi State, Purdue, and the US Department of Agriculture as partners in ROI. Several banks and other investors have joined in. As Matt says, "We're making good progress working with private investment to drive rural prosperity." Our students are especially interested in ROI because it combines public-private partnerships, business, and social impact in a unique way.

New Strategies

Our Business for Impact initiatives go well beyond the traditional education and research activities of a university—they are rooted in *action*. We want to demonstrate that social impact is achievable, especially when working across sectors: private, public, and civil society.

Some of our other partnerships involve aging independently and with well-being (see chapter 6 about our AgingWell Hub); designing new models of benefits, training, and certification for the 21st-century workforce; and promoting the value and importance of science and scientific research to the American public.

Our largest program is New Strategies, which I mentioned in the Introduction of this book as a winning example of cross-sector partnerships. There is a tried and true saying among nonprofit organizations: "no money, no mission." I know this firsthand; I've lived it. The most important social missions in the world won't go anywhere without the resources to pursue and achieve them. Our response to this is New Strategies. It began as the brainchild of Curt Weeden, a former Johnson & Johnson executive who probably knows more about nonprofit operations, including fundraising, than anyone else in the country. Curt grew his program to a reasonable size but wanted to expand it beyond that, and he wanted to make sure it had a permanent home. It does with us.

New Strategies is an intensive four-day workshop focused on just one topic: helping nonprofit CEOs and other senior-level executives (such as chief development officers) build revenues to pursue their missions. Today some 250 nonprofit executives a year come to Georgetown for these workshops, which are followed by webinars, online newsletters, and consulting assistance. To date, nearly 1,000 nonprofit execs from every conceivable sector—social, education, health care, arts and culture, humanitarian assistance, and environment—have participated. Topics include corporate funding, cause marketing, data analytics, social media campaigns, and impact investing. One of the strongest elements of New Strategies is how these experienced nonprofit leaders share information and strategies among themselves during and after the workshops.

What does it cost them to attend? Nothing. Corporations pick up the entire tab. Some 26 companies and their foundations, including American Express, Target, Nike, Thrivent, JP Morgan Chase, Aetna, Merck, General Mills, Procter & Gamble, Bristol Myers Squibb, and Coca-Cola fund the program. They send their nonprofit partners because they want them to do well, and they want to strengthen the entire nonprofit sector. Bernard Boudreaux, previously a key leader in Target Corporation's social responsibility efforts, leads our work. He, Chico Rosemond (our program director), and Curt are planning to expand in order to increase their effect on the nonprofit sector. The sponsoring companies want to know what's working, and so do we. Our annual surveys show that our nonprofit "graduates" are putting New

Strategies ideas into place and building their revenue base. These are truly successful partnerships in action.

Building Social Movements

Several years ago, Leslie Crutchfield joined our team as a research fellow to write a book on social movements. She had already co-written the best-selling nonprofit leadership book *Forces for Good: The Six Practices of High-Impact Nonprofits*. Leslie had been a senior advisor at FSG, the social impact consulting firm begun by Harvard's Michael Porter and Mark Kramer, who wrote the seminal article in the *Harvard Business Review* on shared value (see Introduction). Leslie's latest book, *How Change Happens: Why Some Social Movements Succeed While Others Don't*, came out in 2018 and is popular and well regarded among company and nonprofit executives tackling social impact. It's an important book at an important time—when social movements are springing up in response to everything from criminal justice to a rapidly warming planet. Leslie studied drunk driving, tobacco use, gay marriage, guns, and other issues of the first decades of the century. No, she didn't find a magic bullet, no perfect recipe, no "movement in a box" that we can apply to social impact. But she does show how the messy world of social change works—and doesn't work. One of her chapters is devoted to the role of corporations in making a positive difference for themselves and for society. She finds they are much more involved today in speaking out on public issues in ways that involve their employees and appeal to their customers.

The underlying theme in Leslie's book is optimism. Most big, important social and environmental problems seem daunting and almost beyond solution, but she shows us otherwise. Strong leadership (she calls it being "leaderful"), good strategies, perseverance, and effective grassroots involvement can move mountains. We've used Leslie's findings to accelerate large-scale movements in combating the opioid epidemic and advancing science education and support. Leslie took over from Ladan Manteghi as executive director of our Business for Impact center and also teaches our corporate social responsibility course.

Educating Business Impact Leaders of Tomorrow

Our mission hasn't changed—help solve today's most pressing problems by delivering world-class education, impactful student experience, and direct action in partnership with companies, non-profits, and government. But as our program has grown and matured, we've gained more and more momentum. A big part of that has been our emergence as a magnet for students.

Our business school, and in fact Georgetown in general, has traditionally been a top source of employees in Wall Street finance and investment banking. But equally important at Georgetown is the Jesuit value of "women and men in service to others." We believe that students can have both. We want every student who walks out the door to understand that there is not just one bottom line but three: people, planet, profit. Students see that companies are moving in this direction, and companies realize that students and young graduates are as well. I like the cartoon of a company's interviewer saying to a young prospect: "We're looking for someone with an MBA, five years of sales and marketing experience, and a low carbon footprint."

So the need is for competence *and* commitment. A good example is the pharmaceutical executive who told our students about distributing anti-malarial drugs in Africa. A student said to him afterward, "I want to come work for you and save the world!" The speaker said, "Saving the world is good, but I need people who understand supply chains."

Our student participation began with Rahul Pasarnikar and a handful of others. Today we have well over 170 students involved, with about 30 of them serving as student leaders—engaged as researchers, writers, analysts, organizers, speakers, interns, and ambassadors for the program. I call it "student power," and it's our biggest asset. Most are from our business school, but others—both graduates and undergraduates—are in Georgetown's schools of foreign service, public policy, nursing and health studies, law, and medicine. As we grew, we were able to provide opportunities for students to attend conferences and other events across the country, gain internships in areas of interest, enter pitch contests, and receive funding and support for projects they want to develop. Several partner companies, including Bank of America and the international law firm Reed Smith, are investing in this. Students want to network with executives, learn about new ventures, secure internships and volunteer opportunities , and, of course, get jobs. Joe Weinstein and Christine Kidwell, who coordinate our student program, have organized it into tiers based on student availability and commitment. They hold orientation sessions, require and vet applications, and offer paid and volunteer engagements on virtually every partnership and program we have.

With student interest so high, we've taken another step: launching a certificate program at the MBA level. It is among the first US classroom certificate programs to focus on sustainable business and the triple bottom line as core strategies for corporate success. This new certificate is attractive to students who want to take tailored courses, hone their skills, and demonstrate competence as they enter the job market. And like our program itself, the certificate fits our promise of educating global leaders to make a positive impact.

Periodically we survey our participating graduate students— whose backgrounds seem representative of our business students as a whole—to gauge their attitudes and opinions. On average, they have worked for four to eight years before entering graduate school, with many coming from finance, consulting, government or public policy, education, and nonprofits. After graduation, they often intend to restart their careers in consulting and finance or investing, with fewer aiming for the nonprofit world. Their long-term career goals include becoming executives in large corporations, starting new businesses (including social development enterprises), impact investing, and politics. They also see volunteering, consumer purchasing, and other personal, everyday actions as ways to make a social difference.

But regardless of where they intend to work, they understand that all business sectors can contribute to positive social and environmental change. Why? They cite business innovation, capital and other resources, job creation, overall size and revenues, and a general belief that business can be more efficient than other sectors. This capacity for creating both financial and social impact, in students' minds, requires corporate *responsibility*—to apply the right values, to create cultures that respect society, to be accountable, and to encourage other companies to be responsible. Our students also recognize the role of government, including the importance of correcting for market failures.

Kenneth Turner, one of our graduates, is now at Johnson & Johnson, leading innovative finance projects that improve access to health care for vulnerable populations. He had previously been with the US Agency for International Development and the World Economic Forum. Kenneth's career goal is to continue leading impactful global programs that leverage innovation and technology. He got a good grounding in his MBA studies by consulting for a social venture in educational technology—building its youth health and wellness curriculum—and doing a social entrepreneurship research project. Kenneth says, "The private sector, public sector, and civil society organizations all play a critical role in advancing social and environmental impact."

Chris Musser puzzled over where to take a job after graduation. He wanted to make money, and make a difference. He interviewed with several top consulting firms and also considered a nonprofit path. He said a lightbulb went on when he read an article in my class about Milton Friedman's assertion that the only role of business is to make a profit. Chris's realization—his "powerful moment" as he recalls it—was that Friedman's position is "not the case." In another course I invited Jim Clifton, chairman of Gallup, to speak on leadership. Chris sat in, although he wasn't in the class. He was considering a job offer in Gallup's consulting operation, and Jim knew it. Chris listened to his potential CEO and took the Gallup job. Now, he says, he is in a culture of entrepreneurship and is thinking about how to quantify the value of purpose.

Katie Glaser, one of our undergraduate student leaders, majors in accounting and had been offered an accounting job when she graduates. Instead, Katie began to explore other directions. She says she has had "the chance to get hands-on experience in social impact and met professionals from a variety of backgrounds . . . with nonprofits and corporations and gained insights into the types of career paths out there." She wants "to join a company that has its own mission-based ESG framework and is creatively involved in being environmentally and socially mindful." She found her spot; Katie accepted an offer to join EY in its financial services advisory practice in strategic and management consulting for financial services companies. This is going to be a good start for Katie. We tell our students that they can pursue any position within a corporation and contribute to the organization's doing well by doing good. Katie is going to do a great job at EY and have a successful career with a purpose.

Shelbi Smolak came from retail banking and wants to "pivot from my career in banking to a mission-driven role." She's working on our AgingWell Hub and thinking about her future. I asked her if she thought it was possible to stay in banking and still achieve a mission-driven purpose, and her response was "yes but . . ." Shelbi says in her banking work she had been too caught up in personnel matters and operations as the regulatory environment continued to change and evolve. She thinks she could stay in banking and find purpose, especially as "the fintech and non-bank bank space expands." Shelbi is keeping her options open and exploring what an impact-driven firm might look like. She will find her path.

When Daniela Fernandez came to Business for Impact as a freshman, she declared at her first meeting that she wanted to save the oceans. Could we help her do that? She had learned about the problem on a trip to the United Nations and asked herself, Why am I the only young person here? She started the Sustainable Ocean Alliance (SOA), and her first step was to organize a conference. Over time, Daniela seeded chapters at other universities and kept growing her annual conferences. By the time she graduated, SOA was really taking off. She had won the Peter Benchley Ocean Award and was named one of *Glamour* magazine's top 10 college women of the year. We provided a stipend to enable her to devote herself full time to her nonprofit startup, and Daniela took her operation to San Francisco. She is a natural at organizing and a persuasive leader. Today Daniela has substantial funding and is investing in companies working in ocean cleanup technology. I reconnected with her at an event in San Francisco, where she spoke to our alumni about her cause. One example she gave of her investment strategy is with a company creating drinking straws out of seaweed. We were catalysts, but Daniela is cause and effect.

Based on my experience working with students in Georgetown Business for Impact and teaching my classes, I have confidence that today's up-and-coming generation will strive and achieve. Social responsibility ranks high on their list when they're choosing where to work and where to stay employed. We have a world full of problems, but the future, if these young leaders have anything to do with it, is bright. And, as we see in the next chapter, they have ample opportunity to make a difference.

CHAPTER EIGHT

YOUR PURPOSE

*People and Organizations
Making a Difference*

Problems worthy of attack prove their worth by attacking back.

This is a battle cry for me. It is modified from an aphorism attributed to Danish mathematician Piet Hein. It spells out what we're up against: big, tough social, economic, and environmental problems that won't go away by themselves. They don't respond to sitting on our hands and hoping for the best. Muddling through is not a good strategy.

Today, this is where we are with global warming. This is where we are with the opioid epidemic; rising health care costs (including the "financial toxicity" of treating cancer as science advances); obesity and overweight (now affecting many countries); gun safety (especially in the United States, where gun violence is proliferating); south-to-north migration into Europe, the United States, and other regions; and socioeconomic and racial inequality. There are many more. The coronavirus pandemic may be just one of other pandemics to follow. These problems have global consequences, and they also come directly to the streets and neighborhoods and towns in which we live.

Why should we care? And even if we do, can we really make a positive, sustainable difference? Should we be the ones to attack these challenges? For most of the people in this book, for me, and I think for you, the answer is a strong "yes." Many of us feel a moral obligation to do something. Whether or not you share that view, there is also the practical matter of our families' and communities' futures being at stake. We need to fix these problems.

Many people want to leave things a little better than they found them. At AARP, our research showed the power of legacy—individuals want to be remembered as having been here and done something. We don't want to have just "visited this world," as the poet Mary Oliver expressed it. Others have found it helps to ask, What did you do with the dash? It refers to the dash that will be on each of our tombstones: "Here lies Abraham Lincoln, 1809–1865." In other words, what did we do with the time between being born and going off into the great unknown?

We can all make a difference; we can all leave things better than we found them. Sometimes those differences might affect just a few people. I recall sitting in a grade school classroom in Philadelphia, knees up, in a chair sized for a little kid. I was there to watch a retired sanitation worker and AARP volunteer teach reading to a group of children, which he did with great enthusiasm. He said, "There's nothing better than showing first, second, and third graders how to read." The principal loved this volunteer's work.

In fall 2019 Fran and I went to the annual Kidsave gala. We go every year, and we strongly support the organization, first because of its powerful mission, and second because it was cofounded and led by Terry Baugh and Randi Thompson, two Porter Novelli alumnae. They were successful businesswomen who each adopted children (Terry from Russia, Randi in the United States) and then pivoted to helping kids grow up in families and connected to caring adults. They put their business skills to work "with governments and communities worldwide to see that no orphan or foster child is forgotten, and every child grows up in a family with love and hope for a successful future." Terry and Randi developed their Family Visit Model, enabling older kids from foster care and orphanages to spend weekends and school breaks with families who agree to host them in their homes and introduce them to other families. This model results in lots of love, with frequent adoptions and mentoring. Through these family visits in the United States and abroad, Kidsave and its partners have placed thousands of kids from Colombia, Kazakhstan, Russia, Sierra Leone, and the United States with adoptive families. Because Terry was "retiring," the gala was bittersweet.

She and Randi are practical, no-nonsense business types. Terry had a consulting practice where both women worked when they decided to start Kidsave. Randi plunged into their first summer program for overseas orphans. With Randi working from her bedroom office, Kidsave provided 177 kids with summer vacations with families, and nearly all of them were then adopted as a result. Terry kept her day job, working both on her consulting practice and on Kidsave; the idea was to use her consulting work to fund their nonprofit enterprise. But she soon discovered that this dual existence wasn't getting it done, so she and Randi went into Kidsave full time. They had some rough patches, but today Kidsave is a going concern, to the benefit of children around the world.

There are many examples of successful businesspeople like Terry and Randi, who cross the bridge into the nonprofit sector, or who travel the opposite way, from nonprofit work to the corporate sector. I've gone back and forth in both directions and even detoured to a third destination (government). Not everyone makes these transitions work, but many succeed. Equally important are those who stay right where they are—in companies big and small, in nonprofits, and in government—and make change happen from there. The big opportunity today is for companies to do well by doing good. There are critics and criticisms galore (more on this later). But managing for global good is trending in the right direction. That's not altruism; it's an important pathway to business success.

The Changing Landscape of Corporate Social Responsibility (CSR)

About 10 years ago McKinsey analysts looked at the landscape and projected what they thought the future would bring. They issued a report called *Whither CSR? Shaping the Future: Solving Social Problems through Business Strategy: Pathways to Sustainable Value Creation in 2020.* A number of their predictions are coming to pass. They anticipated that multinational companies would increasingly reach potential customers in low-income countries (the base of the pyramid) by working with government, multilateral, and nonprofit partners. This is clearly happening. The United Nations has formed the Connecting Business Initiative. The UN Development Programme (UNDP) increasingly "supports the private sector and foundations to become transformative partners in development through research, advocacy for inclusive business, facilitation of public-private dialogue and multi-stakeholder partnerships." UNDP also says the private sector plays an essential role in humanitarian preparedness, response, and recovery efforts. And with climate change bringing increasing environmental emergencies, this kind of partnership will become more important.

The US Agency for International Development (USAID) created its Private Sector Engagement Policy to "work hand-in-hand with the private sector to design and deliver our development and humanitarian programs in all sectors." The agency calls it a "more sustainable . . . shift in [the] journey to self-reliance."

Many consumer-goods companies see the base of the pyramid as an opportunity to expand their businesses, create goodwill, and earn a "license to operate" as worthy corporate citizens. Half of Unilever's sales today are reported to be from developing countries. Merck for Mothers, sponsored by the global pharmaceutical company Merck (known as MSD outside Canada and the United States), focuses on reducing maternal mortality across the world. Merck for Mothers partners with the World Health Organization, USAID, and many others. Julie Gerberding, whom I worked with when she headed the Centers for Disease Control and Prevention and who is now an executive at Merck, said that one of the initiative's collaborations supports pregnant women in refugee camps on several Greek islands where, as she puts it, many of the pregnancies are "forced."

One of my alma maters, CARE, reports that "the private sector has a critical role to play in reducing poverty—in job creation, technological innovation, the provision of goods and services and overall economic development and growth." This is very different from my days working at CARE, when we collaborated with USAID and others. Back then, the private sector was thought of mostly as a funder or marginal partner. Governments and NGOs were seen as the key players in development work.

Of course, the role of business in international development is not always positive. Deforestation and the use of child labor on hundreds of thousands of cocoa farms in West Africa are difficult, persistent problems. Mars, Hershey, Nestlé, and Ferraro are among the companies that depend on certification by NGOs that child labor is not being employed. Many consumers are willing to pay more for chocolate products from certified cocoa, but the certification process is difficult to perform and very spotty. Desperately poor farmers try to avoid or fake it, and the companies continue to wrestle with the problem. In an October 2019 *Washington Post* article, the Ferraro Group (a confectionary company) said it is using its own monitoring and control systems in addition to NGO certification efforts, and Mars pledged to continue to work with farming communities to assure that "100 percent of our cocoa is responsibly sourced and traceable by 2025." It won't be easy, to say the least.

In McKinsey's look into the future, it also predicted that companies will be increasingly held accountable for social issues along their entire supply chains. This is certainly the case today. There was a time when a company might say it didn't track (and was therefore not accountable for) conditions where their products were sourced. Today regulators, watchdog groups, and consumers reject that argument; companies are responsible for their entire supply chains and are establishing industrywide labor and environmental standards. VF Corporation shows how companies can take responsibility for apparel and footwear sourcing, including when the people making those products are contract employees (see chapter 7).

Tom Glaser, who left VF (where he was president, supply chain) to join Tapestry, Inc. as chief operations officer, calls this shift a journey for the whole industry. While responsible sourcing was evolving over the years, Tom says the 2013 collapse of the Rana Plaza garment factory in Bangladesh, where more than 1,300 workers died and another 2,500 were injured, "was the really big change for me. We all needed to do more. Checking boxes on compliance and standards was just not enough." Tom asks, "What's it like to sit on the factory floor as a worker? Are these employees safe, protected, and respected?" He thinks of value creation as helping factory workers while also making his employees proud to work for a company that cares. Tom compares the business environment his 21-year-old daughter, a business major (see Katie Glaser in chapter 7), is entering with what he saw when he was 21. Back then corporate philosophy consisted of the Milton Friedman mantra that the business of business is business (that is, profit). Now, Tom says, "the aperture of stockholder value has broadened. And consumers are concerned with the environment and with people's well-being." Tom takes a broad view: "We can help other countries build their social capital, and this gives us a license to operate. This is how to be financially successful."

In its predictions, McKinsey also wondered where public opinion would come down on these changes. Would people argue that sustainable value creation is really corporate greed dressed up to look like something else? Or would businesses meet public expectations and be more trusted as corporate citizens? The jury is still out on these questions, and debate continues, but more and more corporations are taking advantage of the positives that Babson College (see Introduction) and others have identified.

Walmart has come in for its share of criticism over the years. When I headed AARP, I met with Lee Scott, then the company's CEO. One of his executives had visited me earlier to inquire about working together. Scott asked why we didn't seem to want to enter into partnerships with Walmart. I answered that they were often cited for questionable practices, such as paying such low wages that many of their employees were on Medicaid. I thought he would argue with me, but instead he said, "You know, it took me several years to realize we had a problem, and a few more years to figure out what to do about it. But now we're making progress."

One of Walmart's positive steps was to address criticism about the huge amount of solid waste it generated through discarded packaging, which often ended up in landfills throughout the country. In response, Walmart worked with its 66,000 vendors, the Environmental Defense Fund, and other groups to cut packaging weight and volume. It created a packaging scorecard and declared a goal of becoming packaging-neutral by 2025 (that is, recovering as much material as was used in the packaging that flows through its stores). The technological challenges were considerable, and consumers had to get used to changes, including smaller and lighter packages. The result so far has been a substantial cost savings for the company and its suppliers, as well as environmental gains for society. Over a decade, Walmart has reported diverting 82 percent of materials from US landfills and an average of 71 percent in international markets. This is a good example of Babson College's finding that a focus on financial and social value can increase sales, reduce costs, or both. Today Walmart, like many big corporations, has its detractors as well as its proponents. But through its foundation and its everyday business practices, Walmart is contributing in ways that seek to benefit society.

Socially responsible actions can also help mitigate corporate risk. Barie Carmichael was Dow Corning's chief communications officer during the silicone breast implant controversy. She and coauthor Brian Moriarty wrote about this in a June 2018 article for the Conference Board. They pointed out the growing and "unprecedented potential for near-instant business disruption" and reputational risk in today's social media age. Corporate management and boards are increasingly aware of this risk and are taking action, often through closer oversight and stewardship of company resources. Coca-Cola, like other big food and beverage companies, is a major user of water throughout the world. Consequently, Coke is focused on improving its own water use and contributing to clean-water policies and practices. Nestlé is also concerned with clean water, and like Coca-Cola, sells bottled water. Both companies are working to protect water supplies and water quality. General Mills mitigates risk and contributes to the environment by pursuing a target of reducing absolute greenhouse gas emissions by 28 percent across its value chain—from farm to fork to landfill, as they put it—over 10 years.

Goldman Sachs has had a troubled reputation among the public, legislators, regulators, and many thought leaders. The company was roundly criticized in the wake of the financial crisis in 2007–2008, when it was alleged that Goldman misled investors and profited from the implosion of the mortgage market. Congress held a special Goldman Sachs hearing (before the Senate Permanent Subcommittee on Investigations) as well as hearings for all the investment banks. The Justice Department and the Securities and Exchange Commission (SEC) investigated, and Goldman reached a settlement for $550 million. The company denied any wrongdoing and said it would conduct a "comprehensive examination of our business standards and practices" as well as pursuing more disclosure and better relationships with clients.

In the midst of this furor, Goldman Sachs announced a $100 million program with a five-year goal of helping 10,000 women become more skilled and more successful business entrepreneurs. Drawing on its in-house business skills, Goldman set up courses at partner universities. By 2011 the company said that the program 10,000 Women was on track to meet its goals and that 70 percent of participants had increased their business revenues. In 2011, to help even more women, Goldman entered a partnership with the US State Department. At that point the program had already reached women in more than 20 developing countries. Since then, Goldman has also partnered with a unit of the World Bank, set up programs in some 56 countries, and invested well over $1 billion to assist more than 50,000 women. This is a story Goldman is proud to tell. By itself, 10,000 Women isn't going to offset the criticisms, but it does represent a positive and responsible step forward.

An even greater Goldman contribution to the triple bottom line is its sustainable finance program. By the end of 2018, the company had gone beyond $80 billion toward its goal of financing or investing $150 billion in clean energy by 2025. Then, in mid-2019, it restructured to set up a sustainable finance group to place a greater focus on impact investing and financing sustainable commercial projects. The focus is on working across corporate functions to mitigate climate change and foster "more inclusive economic growth." Kevin Smith, a vice president who had already been engaged in environmental, social, and governance (ESG) programs, joined the new sustainable finance group. He called it "a big growth opportunity for Goldman clients and to put capital to work for social and environmental good." Kevin is well aware of the criticisms big financial companies face. His response is "We deal with it, and we try to get things right. We manage reputational risk, and we have strict guidelines on what we will and won't do." The criticism of big banks and other financial institutions continues. But the work of Goldman Sachs in financing clean energy, green and social bonds, and other environmental assets can make a major difference in achieving a sustainable environment.

Leading with Purpose

A good example of successfully combining business and social impact is CVS Health. In 2014 the company, then known as CVS Caremark, announced that it would stop selling cigarettes and other tobacco products in its stores. At the time, CVS estimated its tobacco-related revenue at $2 billion a year. This change wasn't a single step, but rather a first move as part of a longer-term transformation. The president of CVS Pharmacy called it a "catalyst" for moving to become a true health care organization, and CEO Larry Merlo said, "Ending the sale of cigarettes and tobacco products at CVS Pharmacy is the right thing for us to do for our customers and for our company to help people on their path to better health. . . . The sale of tobacco products is inconsistent with our purpose."

That year the Campaign for Tobacco-Free Kids gave our champion's award to CVS Health for its bold action. That evening I sat next to Merlo and Eileen Howard Boone, their senior vice president for corporate social responsibility and philanthropy. They made it clear that ending tobacco sales was part of a bigger company plan.

The response from key stakeholders showed a boost in corporate reputation as well as opportunities for significant business growth. Moreover, an article in the *American Journal of Public Health* reported that the company's decision to end sales of cigarettes contributed to a drop in tobacco purchases for all retailers within three years.

In 2015—once tobacco products had been taken off the shelves—the company changed its name to CVS Health and launched a multimedia campaign called "Health Is Everything." The American Medical Association and virtually the entire health community applauded the end of tobacco sales. The company also began a series of new partnerships to help smokers quit and to encourage nonsmokers not to start. Partners included the American Lung Association, the American Cancer Society, the Campaign for Tobacco-Free Kids, the Truth Initiative, and others working in underserved communities and in reducing e-cigarette vaping among kids.

That was just the beginning. The renamed and repositioned company began a series of health-promoting steps, from eliminating chemicals in beauty products to reducing greenhouse gas emissions. In addition, CVS Pharmacy began to change its product mix, adopting, as *Fortune* magazine put it, "a much bigger focus on health and wellness products like skin care regimens and nutrition bars and other healthy food selections. The strategy behind this was to promote health, but also to get more shoppers to buy as they came in to fill prescriptions." Then the company acquired the health insurance giant Aetna. Now CVS Health is focused on transforming and innovating in health care and consumer health. One example is the introduction of HealthHUB stores, with dieticians and wellness rooms for group meetings and classes. CVS Health is itself a healthy company in terms of doing well by doing good.

Eileen Boone says she never envisioned this career path, but it fits her personal motivation to effect change. She also serves as president of the CVS Health Foundation and as an officer of the

Aetna Foundation. As a business executive, Eileen says that corporate social responsibility must stem from a company's core competency and that "you have to understand what drives your business. I look for people for my team who understand how our business works and grows." While she is the corporate leader in terms of CVS Health's triple bottom line, Eileen believes that each of the company's 300,000 employees can play a role—"store-level employees, those in packaging or procurement; everybody can have an impact on social responsibility at CVS Health." She says that the company's talent acquisition team appreciates the work she and her team do because it motivates and attracts new employees to CVS Health.

As we can see from our Georgetown students, Gallup research, and just about every other social indicator, employees and prospective employees want to take pride in the organizations where they work or seek to be employed. Many companies are responding to this challenge through employee volunteer programs and in other ways. And just being involved in doing well by doing good is itself a strong employee inducement and source of pride. For many years Procter & Gamble distributed and promoted a nonprofit product in Africa and Asia called the Pur Purifier of Water. Employees welcome this clean water initiative. As a P&G brand manager said in a business case about the program, "It is something so amazing when you are able to know your work is serving a higher purpose. The more P&G can do to give back, the more inspired people are to give of themselves to the company and community."

In their Gallup book *It's the Manager,* Jim Clifton and Jim Harter point out that today's workforce—especially younger workers—want their employment to have a real mission and purpose. I mentioned Jenny Heflin and Accenture's work in chapter 7. Another consulting firm, Deloitte, also emphasizes corporate citizenship as a strategy for recruiting and engaging employees. Like

Accenture, Deloitte invests in having its employees provide their skills to public service and nonprofit initiatives and provides grants and other assistance to the organizations they assist. Hemal Vaidya, a partner in the firm, cites as a prime example Deloitte's ambitious WorldClass program, which enables its thousands of employees around the globe, working with businesses, governments, and educators, to help provide literacy programs and other benefits to millions of people who have been "left behind . . . and lack the education, skills, and training they need." Deloitte and other firms promote their programs vigorously, and their research shows that their regard for their people and their attention to social issues are key reasons that employees choose to work and stay there. For these firms, corporate responsibility is a major *business* strategy.

Crossing the Bridge from Corporate to Nonprofit Work

Kathy Bremer says she is in her "final career," but I wouldn't bet on it. I first met her when I was at CARE and looking for a senior vice president to head marketing and development (that is, fundraising). Kathy applied for the position because, despite her success at advertising agencies, she was bored. She wanted to learn new things and do something bigger. She had climbed the ranks at three agencies, had worked on everything from copiers to coffee (managing a large ad spend for P&G's Folgers brand), and had risen to management supervisor. Kathy started our first meeting by saying, "I don't know anything about fundraising." After several conversations, I knew she was a winner and would be a success at CARE despite the huge cultural and institutional differences from the ad world. I knew because I had been there. Kathy was high on the ladder at her ad agency and had orchestrated client relations, account management, media, creative, and other functions. Nonetheless, when she came to us at CARE she found it to be a "vertical, dizzying leap." She went from a team of 8 to a

125-member department for a "sprawling global nonprofit and had 11 offices to oversee across the US." Kathy recalls working harder than she had ever worked before, including national and international travel that took her away from her small kids. Years later, her son admonished her by saying, "You spent my childhood in Rwanda." I know how she felt. Once Fran welcomed me home from a trip with, "Children, let me introduce you to your father."

After nearly eight good years at CARE, she was ready to move on. Although I was long gone from Porter Novelli, that's where Kathy went, becoming head of the Atlanta office. She described the agency as "known for its marketing prowess and for doing well by doing good" and "globally a juggernaut but tiny in Atlanta." She took care of the "tiny in Atlanta" part; after eight years she had made the office much bigger and better. What next? She became managing director of BoardWalk Consulting, a national search firm serving nonprofits, mostly recruiting CEOs, other C-suite executives, and board members. She says it's all about finding the right leader for a nonprofit, and often those leaders come from the corporate world. Kathy's life lesson: "It's possible to have both the doing well (reasonably good compensation to get our kids through college and be comfortable) and the doing good (a rewarding job in a mission-centered organization), which is a combination that is simply unbeatable."

Kathy brought her consulting and recruiting teams at Board-Walk together for an informal focus group to discuss crossing the bridge (or not) from corporate to nonprofit positions. These are seasoned search people who have seen the process from every angle. Their first conclusion is that corporate workers don't have to leave their companies to find psychic reward and make a difference. They can be, and often are expected to be, involved in their communities in many ways: board service, philanthropy, volunteerism, and being a "champion" for a nonprofit. So no, you don't have to change careers as long as you're feeling satisfied. As one

BoardWalk search person put it, "How close to the flame of the nonprofit mission do you want to be?"

Their second conclusion is that the switch—if you want to make it—can be a big challenge, just as Kathy found when she went from an ad agency to CARE. The BoardWalk team identified two factors that influence the success of such a switch: first, how well an executive's skills can meet the nonprofit's needs; and second, how well a person is equipped to lead and thrive in a culture with more stakeholders, a more ambiguous bottom line, fewer resources ("nonprofit boards typically want to see a lean organization"), and more (and more constant) work and roles to play. Like me, the BoardWalk executives believe that when these pivots aren't successful, it's often because of cultural misalignment. Nonprofits are "appropriately wary" of hiring people who lack experience in that sector and who may have trouble functioning there.

People often think the trade-off for someone considering such a move is social impact versus compensation, but as Kathy and many others have found, nonprofit compensation is usually adequate, especially for people who have done reasonably well building a nest egg during their corporate careers. There are typically two pivot points: people in their 50s who have done well in the corporate sector and want to find an off ramp to move into the social impact space ("use their skills for something bigger"), and younger workers looking for opportunities that blend career with social contributions.

The BoardWalk team's final conclusion is that the trend of moving from for-profit to nonprofit is strong and steady, and possibly growing. As they said, "For many executives, it's the route to relevance" and can be the way "to leave a legacy." And more and more nonprofits are interested in those with corporate and hybrid backgrounds.

Leslie Hortum, director of the Washington, DC, office of Spencer Stuart, the international search and recruitment firm, tends to agree with Kathy Bremer and her BoardWalk colleagues. Leslie says she has frequent conversations with corporate executives who have done well in their firms and "now want to do good in a social purpose organization." She finds that nonprofit boards are receptive to this attitude. Leslie also says that making the transition, or even thinking about the transition, can be a challenge. She cites one corporate executive who didn't understand the role of volunteers in the nonprofit organizations she was considering (there can be significant differences among various nonprofits in volunteer strategies and operations). Leslie also says that corporate leaders often have much to contribute to nonprofits *if* they take the time to understand the cultural differences between the two worlds. In addition to senior executives, Leslie also sees the millennial generation in action and believes that they certainly want purpose, but above all balance, in their lives.

These search firms are often asked to recruit corporate leaders to sit on nonprofit boards. There are three basic criteria for nonprofit board service: the duty of care (serve in good faith and with the degree of diligence that ordinarily prudent persons would exercise); the duty of loyalty (pursue the interests and goals of the nonprofit with undivided allegiance and not for personal advantage); and the responsibility of fundraising (often expressed as "give or get"). Although these criteria sound simple enough, being a good board member of a nonprofit is a demanding job. I've served on the boards of public and private corporations as well as nonprofits, and while all of them are challenging, the role of a nonprofit board member is unique. I've boiled it down to three fundamental questions. First, where's the money? That's shorthand for saying that a board member's fiduciary responsibility is paramount. You need to pay attention to financial planning, monitoring cash flow, reserves, endowments, budgets, cash burn, and so forth, whether you're on the finance or audit committee or not. Second, are we doing the right things in the right way? This is about vision, mission, policy, and strategies, not about tactics and certainly not getting down in the weeds and micromanaging. And if you are satisfied with the first two areas, the third question is, how can I help? In small organizations, that might mean assisting with marketing or legal or financial work. In larger nonprofits, which have those functions covered, it is more often about fundraising, helping with advocacy, and representing the organization to the outside world. In good governance, the most critical relationship is usually between the board and the CEO and her or his management team. A good board member is a thoughtful, constructive critic, not a naysayer or someone from the private sector there to teach everyone how management is done. Nonprofit board service is an art.

From For-Profit to Nonprofit: Success Stories

Here are four successful people—Gary Reedy, Lynn Mento, Robin Koval, and Chris Hansen—who made the switch from corporate America to the nonprofit world. Each has a different perspective on how and why they did it and how it all turned out. And each of them brings a lesson to bear.

Gary Reedy believes that you can do well by doing good in *both* the business and the nonprofit worlds, and he has proved it. Gary grew up in an Appalachian community in rural Virginia and was the first in his family to go to college. He spent 37 years in the pharmaceutical and biotech industry and eventually became worldwide vice president for government affairs and policy at Johnson & Johnson. Gary took pride in "bringing products to market that improved people's lives, enabling them to work and stay out of the hospital." And he saw his global corporate affairs initiatives as "helping to improve health and society." He liked being part of a company that "reached a billion people, every day, with four responsibilities: first to our customers, second to our employees, third to communities, and fourth to our shareholders." As he sees it, Gary's life lesson is "to make an impact, not about making dollars." He served on the board of the American Cancer Society (ACS), became board chairman, and when they began a search for a new CEO to replace John Seffrin, Gary was asked to take the position. Now he says his "doing good" is amplified, and he loves his work leading a huge nonprofit. He doesn't think of it as a job so much as the syncing of values and the opportunity to do good. The organization has a solid sense of direction, a large volunteer base, and some big ideas. Can you imagine wiping a common cancer off the face of the earth? ACS can. Cervical cancer, one of the most preventable cancers, remains a major killer. The solution is worldwide screenings and vaccinations against HPV (the human papillomavirus), which is spread through sexual contact and causes most cases of cervical cancer. ACS collaborates with the World Health Organization and others in a major call to action to eliminate cervical cancer globally. This has never happened before—eradicating a cancer—but it's possible, a truly big idea with worldwide benefits. For Gary, both the private and nonprofit sectors are social impact zones. He says with satisfaction, "Had I retired from J&J and not been fortunate enough to have this American Cancer Society position, I would still have felt I helped people to enhance their lives."

Like Kathy Bremer, both Lynn Mento and Robin Koval moved from successful advertising agency careers into nonprofit service. After a session of summer school at Columbia University, Lynn started her career by knocking on the doors of ad agency after ad agency in New York, finally getting hired as an entry-level "do anything-er." The David Ogilvy book *Confessions of an Advertising Man* inspired her as it did me. Lynn did well in her more than 20 years in the ad agency world but faced a constant dilemma: "I'm pretty good at convincing people to do something. Should I be using my persuasion talents to get people to change their detergent or steak sauce brand, or to get people to change themselves for the good of the world?" She says this troubled her for years, and she began to focus more on her firm's pro bono accounts than on paying clients, "which is not a long-term strategy at a profit-driven agency." So she jumped ship, into the nonprofit sector. As she looks back, Lynn says she "found it difficult to maintain company profit while doing good. That's just so hard. Striving for social good is a different game than striving for profit. It has different goalposts, scoring, and rules. So social-minded employees turn themselves into pretzels trying." She found her way to AARP, where she applied her marketing talents to leading the member recruitment and engagement operations. Then Lynn became the president of FONZ—Friends of the National Zoo—a stand-alone nonprofit chartered many years ago to support the Smithsonian's National Zoo in Washington, DC, and its Conservation Biology Institute. Today she is still a marketing maven but now applies her trade to promoting Spike the elephant (who was brought in to become a daddy elephant), transforming the experience of zoo visitors, and focusing on species preservation around the world. She believes she had to make the change from for-profit to nonprofit marketing to make a difference.

Robin Koval sees her transition not as a big switch so much as a "natural trajectory." For her, it's all about building brands around value systems. Whatever marketing and advertising business you're in, she says, people don't buy brands—they buy *into* brands' values. As she sees it, the difference between doing good work in the for-profit space and the nonprofit space has become fuzzier. Creating a strong commercial brand "requires a values perspective and a 'doing good' segment, which gets people on your side. This is no longer nice to do or icing on the cake; now it is an expectation, especially among young consumers, who say, You don't get my dollars if you don't respect my values." Robin (and coauthor Linda Kaplan Thaler) wrote a book, *Grit to Great*, with examples of values-driven persuasion. She and Thaler built a successful Madison Avenue ad agency, the Kaplan Thaler Group—and then the opportunity came along to become CEO of the Truth Initiative (see chapter 3) and apply her talent to persuading kids not to smoke and other youth initiatives. Robin saw it as a natural next step, not out of keeping with what she had been doing. Under Robin, the Truth Initiative applies the same rigor to its campaigns—developmental research, pre-market testing, post-evaluation—as the commercial world. She is amused by her colleagues from the for-profit marketing sector who see her social marketing as "soft and fluffy" because it's not tied to a dollar-denominated bottom line. Robin doesn't see it that way at all. She says, "What I like about it is that it's pretty bad ass. If your life is about winning in the marketplace, measuring success in lives saved is even more competitive."

Chris Hansen has his own perspective on moving from corporate America to the nonprofit sphere. It started with his father, his "life-long role model and best friend." When his father died relatively quickly from inoperable cancer, Chris was a senior vice president at the Boeing Company, where he oversaw US and international government relations. He had been involved in charitable activities outside Boeing, but now, thinking about his father, he found "an inner need to accomplish more than corporate goals and targets . . . to do something that really mattered." He made the move to AARP to head state and national policy advocacy and do what he had done so well at Boeing—work the Hill, interact with Congress and the administration, get things done. Chris looks back at how he tried to pull Boeing from the political right to the middle of the road, and then how he and I worked together to move AARP from leaning left to the "pragmatic center," as I like to call it (see chapter 4). It's that old lesson in advocacy—play political hardball, but don't be partisan. Like many other transplants from the corporate world, Chis had a tough time with nonprofit culture. What disturbed him the most was what he perceived as an attitude among many nonprofits that "the people in for-profit industries were 'evil.'" He later became president of the American Electronics Association and then went on to lead the American Cancer Society's Cancer Action Network (the society's policy advocacy arm). Chris thinks a lot about the big socioeconomic picture. He is a committed capitalist, but he rejects the current ideological fight about capitalism versus socialism among our political candidates and parties. He sees the need for blending "the efficiency and financial returns of capitalism with the greater needs of society." Chris wants a world "where business principles and market practices are employed to efficiently serve people's needs." In short, he wants a "better way." He and I still get a laugh about former Senator Jim DeMint calling us "communists" back in our AARP days (chapter 5). Chris recently stepped down into a busy "retirement" after helping make the Cancer Action Network one of the most powerful advocacy operations—corporate or nonprofit—in America. Now the top position at ACS CAN has been turned over to Lisa Lacasse, who had been deputy president to Chris and is carrying on the advocacy battles in Washington and across the country.

From Nonprofit to Corporate Life

Katya Andresen crossed the bridge in the other direction—from nonprofit work to a company, Capital One. She is senior vice president, US card customer experience, and she is absolutely certain she made the right choice. Katya and I met when we were both at CARE. Besides going overseas with CARE, Katya was a journalist for Reuters, the Associated Press, and other media in several countries. Later she worked in social marketing and at Network for Good, a nonprofit donor platform that converted to a for-profit. Now at Capital One Katya oversees 16,000 people working in research and insights, brand marketing, performance marketing, design, digital experience, call centers, and back-office operations around the world. How do you build a culture and create successful teams at that scale? Katya's answer is to "take care of the people who take care of our customers." She revels in her corporate work and sees the biggest and most important part of her job as "finding and keeping amazing people, . . . mov[ing] them around so they face new challenges and don't get bored, so they stretch and grow, and giv[ing] them incentives to help motivate them." She constantly invites in senior people from various professions just to talk, and she once hired a nonprofit executive for a marketing position because "it's much harder to get people to donate to a cause than to apply for a credit card." At the same time, she "loves to promote from within." Katya's job, as she sees it, is to "help people grow on the unique path they choose." Her motto is "Always be recruiting" (both inside and outside the company).

What about the mission of a nonprofit versus the profit-driven world of a corporation? Katya is convinced that Capital One's mission—"Changing banking for good"—is as powerful and socially relevant as any nonprofit mission, given the large scale at which the company operates. She says, "I believe that I've had more social impact in my two years at Capital One than in all my years in nonprofits in terms of workforce diversity and improving people's relationships to finance." Moreover, Katya burned out in her nonprofit work, where she thinks the progress just isn't fast enough ("international aid and development are just inching along") and there is not enough accountability. She quotes our mutual colleague, Sharyn Sutton, who said, "Nobody loses their job when diabetes rates go up, but maybe they should." Katya sees social purpose in her corporate work—for example, helping people use credit wisely and pay down credit card debt. "If people only make minimum payments, they will pay more in the long run. We have built experiences to help people understand their credit rating and protect their credit, which millions of people use. Compare that to much smaller nonprofit financial literacy programs." She defines social impact broadly: "promoting diversity, helping consumers, helping our employees, and rewarding them for serving our customers." She is working to build social impact at Capital One and also "throwing gasoline on my daughters' curiosity. They lived in the developing world, and they know how fortunate they are." Katya's journalism background serves her well. She uses data to tell compelling stories, and she says a good story really counts, especially when sound analysis goes into it. Some years ago, she wrote a book, *Robin Hood Marketing: Stealing Corporate Savvy to Sell Just Causes.* Now she's gone from stealing corporate techniques to applying them directly every day—as she sees it, to make a difference in the world.

Staying Home: Doing Well by Doing Good in Your Lifelong Sector

Nancy Brown is a nonprofit warrior all the way. She started as a special events director for a hospital, moved up to fundraising for the Michigan affiliate of the American Heart Association, and eventually went all the way to becoming AHA's chief operating officer and then CEO. One day in my AARP tenure, Cass Wheeler, then CEO of AHA and a comrade in the tobacco wars, came to introduce me to Nancy, his successor. Cass and his board had it all planned out. Nancy was groomed for the job, earned it, and was fully ready when Cass stepped down. She started fast and hasn't slowed down since. Today AHA is a global leader in cardiovascular health and stroke prevention. Nancy has set big goals: increasing scientific work (including the AHA's Institute for Precision Cardiovascular Medicine to advance personalized medicine); introducing the Research Goes Red program with an emphasis on women, who had been neglected in heart research; and launching

One Brave Idea—an $85 million research collaboration "to end coronary heart disease."

I work with Nancy and see her in action as an effective leader (she is on the boards of the Campaign for Tobacco-Free Kids and the Coalition to Transform Advanced Care). Her biggest strength, like Katya Andresen's, is attracting, nurturing, and developing talent: employees, volunteers, board, and management. Her work has led to substantial progress in AHA's revenues (up considerably in her tenure), scientific advancement, and partnerships. Nancy manages for success, and she has done it all in a nonprofit setting. She shows how leadership, learning, and development can come entirely from this sector, without the need to cross bridges from one world to another.

Pattie Yu has also built a successful career in social and environmental impact, in this case almost entirely in the private sector, with a focus on two things: public health and helping others. She began by taking dictation during the night shift at the *Washington Star* newspaper, hired because she could type fast. The *Star* soon folded, and she landed a position in public relations at the University of Maryland, where she also took classes, including one I was teaching. I remember her as an outstanding but shy student. "He would pick on me in class," she said of me. I hired her to work at Porter Novelli, where she thought she had "hit the jackpot, with a $23,000 salary and exposure to issues and campaigns that mattered to me." She recalls that she worked such long hours that her neighbors thought she should give up her dog because she was never home. Pattie went on to the public relations firm Fleishman-Hillard (now, like Porter Novelli, part of Omnicom) to build its health care, association, and social and consumer marketing businesses. She later cofounded a PR agency of her own and today has downsized into a unique boutique operation: the Yu Crew. She now spends more time mentoring young professionals and students, especially women, and taking on pro bono and volunteer projects that matter to her than she does serving paying clients. Pattie is a superb public relations practitioner and public health expert. She can still type fast, and also talk fast, work fast, and succeed fast, "all woven with purpose."

I've never met anyone to compare with Ed Zubrow. He doesn't oversee a big enterprise, doesn't have a staff, doesn't have national prominence, and doesn't need or want any of that. But Ed is an amazing role model for making a powerful difference, as well as for true modesty and humility. I first met Ed when he was the head football coach at my alma mater, the University of Pennsylvania. He held the job for three years, from 1986 to 1988, went 23 and 7, and won two Ivy League championships. He had been an assistant coach at Penn for four previous years, and when he stepped up to the top job and brought home those league titles, the alumni, the university, and the student body all thought he would bring us success for a long, long time. Instead, Ed walked away from it all. He just felt unfulfilled. To him, the work wasn't important enough. He remembers winning 10 games and being undefeated; an alumnus suggested that Penn schedule 11 games the next year. That wasn't going to do it for Ed. I recall our conversation back then about his self-assessment. He wanted to help people more directly than being a football coach. He considered running a soup kitchen. We talked about working upstream (fixing structural and policy problems to help many people) versus working downstream (direct, hands-on assistance to a few). Ed decided to go upstream, at least for a while. He took a position as special assistant to the superintendent of the Philadelphia school district to focus on drug prevention and the drug crisis among youth. He did a good job, but when the superintendent retired, he felt the bureaucracy didn't know what to do with him. He had been a football coach and a drug czar. Now what? He did some consulting, which he found unsatisfying. He worked for a while in a homeless shelter (really downstream). Ed says he remembered some advice he had received as a college intern: "Some people have the skills to change systems, and some people have the skills to change individuals. And some are cursed with the ability to do either and must choose."

Then-Pennsylvania governor Ed Rendell tried to interest him in politics, but that wasn't Ed Zubrow. He and his wife moved from Philadelphia to New Hampshire, where she is the dean at a community college in nearby Massachusetts. Ed has become a yoga teacher—in a jail and a state prison. He says he's able to connect one on one to prisoners, and he is "touched by the strength, resilience, tenderness, and kindness" he sees there. Ed is making a difference, one person at a time. He's way downstream, and he's fulfilled. He doesn't feel altruistic, just "authentic and privileged to be so rewarded." Ed is still the leader he was when he was going undefeated in the Ivy League. He says, "You can't force people to do yoga in jail. You have to persuade." He is as humble as he is effective. "I'm no saint," he says. "The saints are the ones teaching special education in North Philadelphia."

Fran and I recently returned from a homecoming football game (Penn 21, Cornell 20), and every time I step into Franklin Field I think of Ed. Early in my career, I thought about moving into a poor neighborhood with Fran and raising our kids there. I later thought of adopting a city block and contributing to community-level change. I've never followed up on any of that. I guess I'm an upstream guy, just as Ed is a downstream change agent. Henry David Thoreau wrote, "Be sure that you give the poor the aid they most need. . . . If you give money, spend yourself with it and do not merely abandon it to them." That's Ed, all the way. He spends himself as a powerful way to make a difference. Not many people do that, especially so far downstream. As I said, I've never met anybody to compare with Ed Zubrow.

Did You Hear the One about the Two Lawyers?

Lawyering is not the most popular profession. We use the term "lawyer up" to mean girding yourself with legal firepower in preparation for often nasty battles. Someone once memorably said, "We have as many lawyers in Washington as we do people." That has a double meaning if any comment ever did.

I recall a speech to a group of physicians by Joe Califano, when he was head of the US Department of Health, Education, and Welfare (now Health and Human Services). He and the docs were in a policy dispute, which Joe felt was too much about physicians' financial interests. But he wanted to mollify them, so he started out by saying, "I was determined to speak to you today about a profession that cares more about its profits than the people it serves. But you don't want to hear about lawyers." Everybody picks on lawyers—even lawyers themselves—but I like lawyers, especially the ones I work with on doing well by doing good.

Not long ago a first-year MBA student, Julia Brucks, wanted my advice on whether she should seek a dual degree in business and law because it might help her in her career path. She wants to make a difference in public affairs and social impact at the community level. I decided to seek advice for Julia from some lawyer colleagues who are prominent in social issues: John Rother, president of the National Coalition on Health Care and former policy guru at AARP; Vinny DeMarco, a well-known and successful social policy advocate in Maryland; James Siegal, CEO of Kaboom!; and Matt Myers, president of the Campaign for Tobacco-Free Kids. They pondered the question and had some thoughtful advice for Julia.

Matt Myers went to law school because he wanted to create social good, but he was unsure how to go about it. Most of his classmates were studying tax law, and he felt that bright students were likely to be funneled into big firms where there was money to be made but where it would be hard to break out of that mold. This was certainly not his interest. Eventually Matt found his way to the Federal Trade Commission, where he oversaw tobacco issues and began his work in fighting the tobacco wars. "There are very few issues where so many lives have been saved," he said. Matt told Julia that there are many paths to becoming a social change agent. He believes law is a good problem-solving discipline for thinking about issues, developing approaches, putting yourself in the shoes of those who disagree with you, and writing effectively on advocacy. However, Matt went on to say that having a first-rate mentor can accomplish almost as much, especially if you bring the right skills to the job.

John Rother told Julia that in his day a law degree was the best path into policy advocacy, especially in congressional offices on legislative issues. But today, John advised, there are several paths into advocacy, including business and economics. If her interest is policy analysis (such as health care, poverty, or tax policy), he said, then an economics degree is useful. But if she wants to focus on local community and legal advocacy, then a law degree is advisable. Like Matt, John is a believer in job experience with a strong mentor. He told Julia that if she found interesting work in a strong advocacy organization, "it may be more useful than three years in law school."

James Siegal went from law school to practicing in a big law firm, then moved to the office of the New York State attorney general to pursue his passion in public interest work. He later served in the nonprofit sector before joining the federal agency that oversees AmeriCorps, the Social Innovation Fund, and other programs, and he then went on to Kaboom! Julia was impressed with James's advice that having a background in law can be valuable in honing problem-solving skills and building large-scale, cross-sector public and private partnerships where "allocating risk through contracts is often where these partnerships can fall apart."

Vinny DeMarco has made his Maryland Citizens' Health Initiative, with his well-tested six-step action program, a powerhouse in enacting major public health legislation. He found his law school experience to be excellent training but also told Julia that he's not at all sure that it's necessary for a successful career in state and community advocacy.

Julia took all this on board and talked to other advisors as well. She found that the lawyers she consulted were less likely to recommend law school than the nonlawyers. Her decision after all this deliberation? "Somehow I decided to go to law school! I am happy with my decision. I'm thinking about how I want to bring together my community-organizing background, business skills, and now new legal skills in my career." Julia is a JD/MBA candidate for now, and she is going to make a big splash in the world.

What do today's young lawyers who are interested in public service think? Elizabeth Kelly went from being a Georgetown undergrad in health studies and an intern at our Coalition to Transform Advanced Care to law school at Penn before going on to the Boston office of Mintz. She then took a year away from the private sector and is clerking in federal court. Many of her peers say they care about social good but can do their part by making a lot of money and then donating to worthy causes. We might call this the Warren Buffett approach. Elizabeth sees things differently, even though she has student loans. She wants to work upstream, on policy change, as a way to make the biggest difference. She appreciates her firm because it has given her pro bono clients in addition to her regular billing (which often added up to more than half the long hours in a day at the office). She relates the story of a senior partner who told her that all he does is work and bill clients, which is just not satisfying. Elizabeth told him that the firm wouldn't be able to assign her pro bono clients if he weren't creating all that revenue. The senior partner thanked her for that encouragement, and they proceeded to work together on pro bono work. Today

Elizabeth is clerking at the Department of Justice and thinking ahead to her career goals.

She admires another young lawyer at Mintz named Alec Zadek, "who sat just down the hall from me and epitomizes the balance of both doing well and doing good." In his 11 years at Mintz (he made partner at age 33), Alec has already had a remarkable career. During the 2008 financial crisis the firm furloughed him for a year with reduced pay. He had huge student debt and had been recently engaged. Alec worked at the Suffolk County district attorney's office in Boston prosecuting low-level offenses, including sex offenders who failed to register with the Commonwealth. Many of these offenders were "bad guys" who were sent to jail but who also got caught up in arcane registration requirements. One of the men Alec prosecuted was sentenced to two years in jail for failing to register, but Alec later determined that there was no statutory basis for the conviction, so he appealed on behalf of the district attorney's office. The case eventually went to the Massachusetts Supreme Court, where Alec argued the case and won. He also helped a woman who was convicted of prostitution after she had been sex trafficked. He has been working on a pro bono basis ever since, helping sex-trafficking survivors, including foreign nationals. This work takes a huge amount of time (which the firm supports) in addition to his billable work. Alec says he can excel in both his commercial work (shareholder disputes and insurance coverage) and his pro bono passion. He appreciates the "balance and perspective," and he says he wants his "kids to have good lives and to do what's right." Elizabeth Kelly and Alec Zadek are making a difference.

One of the toughest, most courageous, and most hopeful people I know is a lawyer named John Kemp. We've worked together on getting people with disabilities into mainstream America, especially employment. John and I first met when I was at AARP, and we've been friends ever since. I admire his ability to rise up out of his wheelchair (he uses four prostheses), walk up to a podium, and make it real. John has excelled in two fields: business and nonprofit. He was a partner in a Washington, DC, law firm, where he built a federal legislation and lobbying practice. Now he's president and CEO of the Viscardi Center, a nonprofit that provides services to educate, employ, and support people with disabilities. John has seen it all. He's not angry and he's not bitter at the slow progress, but he is persistent, and he pushes hard for fundamental civil rights for disabled Americans. He says, "We shouldn't be exceptional, we should be ordinary. . . . We rightly belong to this culture, and we need to have an appreciation of who we are. . . . We're legitimate." John is fighting to make it so.

Good Government and Doing Good

Bill Gates once said, "The public sector's investments unlock the private sector's ingenuity." As this remark makes clear, government is an important player in the fight to achieve real change. In the Introduction of this book, I said we need good government—and good government people—to create policies and to adopt and fund innovative approaches to advance economic and social progress. Being in a government position today—federal, state, or local—is often a tough environment in which to work and do your best. Some of the most successful people in social impact have been in all three sectors: public, private, and civil society. Nick Lovegrove (formerly at McKinsey, now at Georgetown) wrote about it in an article called "Triple-Strength Leadership," in which he observes that individuals with all three experiences have unique skills and perspectives from which to make a difference.

One of the most successful triple-strength leaders I've ever worked with is Matt McKenna, who did well at a New York law firm, became a C-suite executive at PepsiCo, went to the federal government to take on a huge job, and now oversees the Rural Opportunity Initiative with our Business for Impact team at Georgetown. Matt has a unique perspective on how to make change happen. At his law firm he had many clients, diverse assignments, and smart colleagues. There he was judged by and rewarded for his individual performance. At PepsiCo, where he was senior vice president of finance, Matt built and relied on teams, had stretch goals for himself and the corporation, and found himself needing to trust colleagues who did not directly report to him. He decided he wanted to work full time on creating social impact and became the CEO of Keep America Beautiful, which presented challenges that only nonprofit leaders contend with—how to set strategies and galvanize a national organization of many semi-independent affiliates with a large number of volunteers, and how to measure progress and performance.

Matt's government challenge was even bigger. His college buddy, Tom Vilsack, head of the US Department of Agriculture (100,000 employees, $100 billion budget) in the Obama administration, enticed Matt to join him in Washington. Matt's charge was to ramp up public-private partnerships to increase economic development in rural America. He dug in and made it happen. Of all these career assignments, which one did Matt value the most? His government work. To create partnerships and get loans out, they needed local bankers and other business partners. All his career positions were essentially in top-down models, yet Matt succeeded by not being top-down, but rather by being collaborative—getting people to work together. And while he observes that "the discipline and accountability to stockholders or donors were absent in the federal government," his big takeaway was that government was the best job he ever had. Making change there was possible, and with the substantial resources at hand, Matt "had a huge opportunity to make a vast difference." Now he's working on our Business for Impact team to continue to create rural opportunity.

Tara Rice is a government employee and a Matt McKenna protégé. She represents just what America needs in our civil service.

Tara grew up in rural Montana, went to a rural county elementary school with a total student population of eight, and then off "to town" for high school. Her interest was international economic development, and she won a Fulbright scholarship after graduating from Seattle University. Then Tara went on to Yale Law School, followed by a two-year stint at USDA in rural development, where she met Matt. He advised her to join a law firm and see what she thought of private practice. What did she learn practicing law for five years in Washington, DC? That she wanted to focus full time on social and economic development. She wrote an e-mail to Montana governor Steve Bullock, got an interview, and told him why she was the right person to head the commerce department for the state of Montana. She got the job. Now, as director of the Department of Commerce, her rural roots, her experience, and her commitment to development are helping her deal with the state legislature and create business opportunities for Montana. This is government at its best.

Working in government is a tough place to be, with all the bureaucracy, the criticisms, and the slow pace. I had a tough time of it back in my Peace Corps days, even though I loved the mission. In an MBA course on leadership at Georgetown, I had a federal employee whose career goal was to go back into government and make it more efficient and better. Godspeed. We need him. Two other government people, Wendy Johnson and Jane Mosbacher Morris, decided to move into the private sector because they thought they could make a bigger dent in the universe, or at least another dent.

Wendy is the director of public affairs and public policy for Nestlé in North America. She migrated there after nearly 30 years in the public sector, "pushing individuals to make behavior change in an environment that was not supportive of the change." Most of that time she had been at the National Institutes of Health (NIH) in nutrition research and outreach. Wendy continues to maintain her public sector network, and she is convinced that the only way to change America's (and the world's) nutrition and health is to have both the public and private sectors "working toward a common goal for the people to win." Wendy believes in stirring things up. She sees herself as a "bit of a bilingual agitator" who can "speak to both sides—the public and private sectors—based on my lived experience. . . . I at least get an audience."

To her initial surprise, Wendy found that the private sector values her NIH government experience much more than public health people value her corporate experience. Anyone who knows Wendy realizes that she is in no way a cheerleader for corporations, including her own. But she believes that "industry is working very hard to impact the public's health for the better." She says, "We all bear the burden individually and corporately as we think about the total cost—human and financial—of poor health." Like many corporate executives, Wendy finds that many in the public and nonprofit world are often unwilling to work with industry on issues of common interest. And yet, she says, "we can go so much further together."

Jane Mosbacher Morris worked in the US State Department's Bureau of Counterterrorism and in the Secretary's Office of Global Women's Issues. She moved from there to a nonprofit, the McCain Institute for International Leadership (founded by the late senator John McCain and his wife, Cindy), where she oversaw their anti-human-trafficking program. Jane has seen firsthand the destruction that comes from trafficking human beings for sex and labor. She writes that "survivors of human trafficking are also at risk from their own families . . . who disown or even injure or kill a girl or woman who has been sexually exploited in an effort to reclaim the family's honor, which they believe has been soiled by the girl's lack of purity."

Jane and I serve together on VF Corporation's Responsible Sourcing Advisory Council. On a trip to Vietnam to visit VF contract factories, she organized a side trip for us to visit a family whose young daughter had been raped. The girl was ostracized by the community but was recovering as she and her mother earned a small income making goods that Jane's company sells in Western markets. The company, TO THE MARKET, which Jane founded and leads, connects businesses and consumers to ethically made products from around the world. In her book *Buy the Change You Want to See: Use Your Purchasing Power to Make the World a Better Place,* Jane writes, "We can change the world for the better with our wallets. The purchasing power of individuals and of major companies can be harnessed for good and lead to concrete improvements in people's lives . . . by empowering vulnerable communities around the world by hiring them to make the kinds of products you and I buy every day."

Jane has discovered the power of swag—the enormous quantity of materials that companies use in the office and for promotional and recruiting purposes, like coffee cups, hostess gifts, T-shirts, centerpieces, and award gifts. These companies are her customers, and she sources the products from small groups and individuals (like the girl and her mother in Vietnam) to help make a difference. Both the public and corporations are increasingly interested in this kind of "conscious consumerism"—making positive purchasing decisions with the intention of balancing some of the negative impacts that mass consumerism has on the planet. Agreeing wholeheartedly with that philosophy, Jane also focuses on helping the neediest people and families, like the girls she buys from.

Some "Retirees" Never Retire: Making an Encore Difference

George Halvorson "retired" some years ago as chairman and CEO of Kaiser Permanente, one of the largest hospital systems in America. His leadership there was legendary. One of his books, *KP Inside: 101 Letters to the People of Kaiser Permanente*, is a collection of weekly letters George wrote to his thousands of employees. He told about the successes of KP in reducing deaths from HIV/AIDS, improving health quality and service, and advancing research. But his letters were about much more than company progress. He celebrated his people: their community service, team building, diversity, and innovation. And he described the autographed World War II poster of Rosie the Riveter on his wall. She was a Kaiser employee and a KP patient. George wrote, "Rosie was one of us." *KP Inside* is a good example of leadership in a large organization, and I use it in my MBA course Managing the Enterprise. George and I worked together cochairing a colloquium on culture-driven health care at the National Academy of Medicine (I now cochair the group with Mary Naylor of Penn's School of Nursing). Immediately upon "retirement" from KP, George embarked on a new mission—promoting the health and well-being of children from birth to five years old. He became chair of First 5 California, which applies some $500 million a year (raised from tobacco taxes) to assist children and families, and he has written extensively on the importance of early brain development, with an emphasis on low-income, often disadvantaged babies and mothers. George is a persuasive man. He points out that half the births in America are to Medicaid mothers and that early childhood development is critical. He argues that we can reduce the prison population substantially by making sure every child gets the right level of brain-exercise support needed in the first years of life. George is passionate about this issue as it affects parents, families, educators, community leaders, policy makers, caregivers, and of course children—in other words, all of us. You could call George "retired," but you'd have to come up with a new definition of the word.

Don Challis, a college roommate, teammate, and lifelong buddy of mine, is another "retired" executive. After a long career in marketing communications, he serves as a volunteer business mentor with SCORE (Service Corps of Retired Executives), a national nonprofit organization dedicated to helping small businesses get off the ground and grow. Don is one of some 130 volunteer mentors in SCORE's Fairfield County chapter in Connecticut. He first went through a training program on the SCORE consulting process, which covered, among other things, understanding client needs, ways to assist clients, and the value of combining the skills of mentors from different business disciplines. Don loves his work. He often tells me about the clients he engages with and their dreams. Sometimes these dreams are not exactly business concepts ("How do I promote my cousin the rapper?"), but Don tackles them all. He describes his work as turning dreams into viable business concepts. The common thread across many of the assignments he takes on is the need to help people focus, focus, and focus. Building a business is a tough challenge, and Don revels in doing that, plus providing ongoing counseling as his dreamers move ahead.

Two other senior executives recently stepped down. Dawn Sweeney, my colleague from AARP who went on to a long and successful career as the CEO of the National Restaurant Association, just "retired." She says she has at least 10 more years of energy and drive and wants to make a significant social contribution. Dawn started down this path by recently becoming an executive in residence at our Georgetown Business for Impact initiative. And Jim Vella stepped down as the head of the Ford Fund (the Ford Motor Company's foundation). He has started an organization to foster more cooperation and effectiveness among the many nonprofits he worked with and funded while at Ford. Millions of Americans volunteer during their career years as a way to contribute to their communities, and millions more volunteer in "retirement." Our country is built on volunteerism, Ethel's "army of useful citizens."

Corporate Irresponsibility

Earlier in this chapter I mentioned McKinsey's question about where the public would come down on corporate social responsibility. Would people perceive companies' sustainable value creation as just corporate greed dressed up to look like something else? Or would businesses meet public expectations and be more trusted as corporate citizens? The answer may be some of both. It can appear that corporate misbehavior is on the increase; there's lots of news about it every day. Or does it only seem that way because the world has become so wired and transparent that companies and individuals can't hide their misbehavior anymore? After the Volkswagen emissions cheating scandal hit the headlines, Michael Schrage wrote in the *Harvard Business Review* that VW had been caught because "digital due diligence [is] emerging as the new normal . . . and networked citizen scientists" will uncover just about any cheating that occurs. "Consequently," Schrage wrote, "I believe VW's debacle signals the likely end of an era of deliberate corporate malfeasance at scale." That has not been the case.

Wells Fargo went astray, and their comeuppance was due not to today's technology, but to old-fashioned whistleblowers—employees who didn't like what was going on. In September 2016 it was revealed that large numbers of employees had opened deposit and credit-card accounts for customers who were unaware of it. As at VW, the impetus seemed to be intense pressure from above to perform—in this case to meet sales quotas. The government Consumer Financial Protection Bureau reported that the more than 2 million unauthorized accounts cost customers nearly $2.5 million in fees. One of the whistleblowers claimed he was fired several years earlier for e-mailing his human resources department to complain about the practice.

The bank was fined and required to pay back its customers. Then CEO John Stumpf said that the employees' actions were "inconsistent with the values and cultures we strive to live up to every day." The board took away Stumpf's bonus and unvested stock awards; he had a rocky time testifying before Congress and soon resigned. Later the bank was charged with illegally repossessing cars from hundreds of members of the military. The bank's troubles continued, and the next CEO also quit. Wells Fargo has a lengthy vision and values statement saying that customers come first and trust is their operating principle. But by early 2019 it was still struggling to recover its reputation and was running double-page ads in major newspapers headlined "This Is About Real Change," talking about its new leadership and its dedicated employees, and pledging to serve customers better. The ads opened with "Over the past two years we have undertaken a massive effort to transform Wells Fargo . . ." The company is working to overcome its troubles and deliver on its promise to transform itself. Recently the Wells Fargo Foundation, as part of its Diverse Community Capital program, provided a $10 million grant to establish a loan fund with the National Association for Latino Community Asset Builders and its partners. That's just one small step forward, but more appears on the way.

Elizabeth Holmes seems to be a prime example of big-league malfeasance. She dropped out of Stanford at age 19 and started a company, Theranos. Holmes began to dupe investors and big companies with the dubious claim that her technology could take a pinprick of blood from a patient and perform hundreds of sophisticated lab tests. It appeared that she was going to seriously disrupt the $60 billion lab testing industry. Holmes scammed just about everybody. At one point she said on television that, working with Johns Hopkins, Theranos had demonstrated that a blood test could show the onset of pancreatic cancer 17 years before the formation of a tumor (Hopkins later denied this). Theranos partnered with Safeway, Walgreens, and other companies, but the facts about unethical and fraudulent practices were coming out. In 2015 the *Wall Street Journal* started investigating and the FDA stepped in. Lawsuits were piling up, and the SEC and Department of Justice charged Holmes as well as the firm's president, Sunny Balwani, and the company with fraud. Now Holmes faces criminal charges claiming that she engaged in schemes to defraud investors.

And then there's just plain bad-boy behavior that seems outrageous but may not rise to the level of full-scale corporate cheating. Examples are Travis Kalanick at Uber and Adam Neumann at WeWork. Kalanick built Uber into an international company and caused upheavals in the taxicab business in many countries with his ride-sharing innovations. He admonished his people to make magic, to always be hustling, and to step on toes. He was accused of condoning sexual harassment at the firm, and he made negative headlines by screaming at an Uber driver. After prolonged controversy, Kalanick stepped down as CEO and apologized for his behavior but remained on the company's board. He has since left that position. Uber piled up financial losses as it fought off competitors and eventually went public. The initial public offering (IPO) was lackluster and negatively affected other tech company public offerings. Could Kalanick have built Uber without the scorched-earth approach, the unethical culture, including sexual harassment, and all the rest of his exploits? Maybe or maybe not, but he ranks high in the bad-boy category.

Adam Neumann stands out as another striking example. Neumann built WeWork with a "work hard, party hard" philosophy, around an offering of trendy, well-designed work spaces and cool amenities like free beer and meditation classes on the job. Like Uber, the company piled up losses but also a high valuation (some $47 billion at one point). Its IPO was delayed and then flopped. And like the Uber founder, Neumann exhibited poor behavior as an executive and a leader. He used WeWork stock as security for a $500 million personal loan. He reportedly bought property and then leased it to WeWork, and he borrowed money from the company at little or no interest. Neumann trademarked "We" and then charged the company almost $60 million for the mark, which he returned when it created a firestorm of negative news. Like Kalanick, Neumann stepped down as CEO after great controversy but remained on the board. According to the *Wall Street Journal*, Neumann gave up most of his stock in exchange for nearly $1.7 billion, including a $185 million consulting fee. The firm, renamed The We Company, has laid off a major portion of its workforce, and its stock has fallen significantly. It has a questionable future.

And then there's just plain greed. In the Introduction to this book, I referred to Clayton Christensen's question "How can I stay out of jail?" Christensen points out the great risk involved in committing an act of dishonesty "just this once." My students, and most young people, adamantly reject the philosophy of cheating, period. They don't look up to Kalanick and Neumann. But we discuss how powerful and persuasive an unethical corporate culture, which few students have yet encountered, can be. Luann Lynch and Carlos Santos of the Darden School at the University of Virginia identify three factors that contributed to the VW emissions cheating: intense pressure from the top due to management's autocratic leadership style, the opportunity to cheat because it was so easy to hide the misdeed in the millions of lines of software in modern automobiles, and the "rationalization" that even if they cheated and were caught, punishment would be light (VW had cheated in a similar way in the 1970s and been fined a mere $120,000).

So companies are sometimes seen to be acting irresponsibly, and some certainly are doing so. Still, the public—and companies' own employees—have come to expect companies to do good: to take a positive stand on social issues, to support communities, and to invest in causes and social problem solving. Despite the bad behavior among some corporations and their executives, more and more companies have come to understand and pursue this approach.

Criticisms of Corporate Social Responsibility

I see six basic and often overlapping criticisms of companies regarding corporate social responsibility. Each criticism has merit, but my bottom line is that overall we're heading in the right direction—trending toward companies serving people, planet, *and* profit.

Old Wine in New Bottles

Some say there is nothing new in corporate social responsibility; it's all been tried before, and it invariably fails because companies revert to what they always do best: make money. James O'Toole, in *The Enlightened Capitalists: Cautionary Tales of Pioneers Who Tried to Do Well by Doing Good*, claims that current social responsibility efforts (such as impact investing, social responsibility, B corporations, and conscious capitalism) are all as old as the hills. They always run into the "buzz saw of investor resistance" and a reversion to an intense focus on profits. When earnings slip, reality sinks in. And oftentimes corporate founders' good intentions go by the wayside after they pass on. All this is inevitable, the argument goes. O'Toole offers up a quote from Francesco Datini, the Merchant of Prato in the 1300s, whose motto was "In the name of God and of profit."

Is this the way it always was and always will be? Or are we in a new, more enlightened era, when companies not only *want* to achieve shared value but actually *need* to do so to attract the best talent and compete in a new marketplace? You know my answer: yes. Despite two steps forward and one step back, we are in a new era. Today's younger generations demand it, technology and transparency virtually require it, and the emergence of women business leaders (Elizabeth Holmes notwithstanding) will contribute to it. We shall see.

Milton Friedman Had It Right

The second criticism is that the business of business is still business. This argument from Milton Friedman was best stated in a 1970 article in the *New York Times Magazine*. Friedman, a Nobel Prize–winning economist, locked in the notion that the only responsibility of business is profit. He said, "There is one and only one social responsibility of business—to use its resources to engage in activities designed to increase its profits so long as it stays within the rules of the game, which is to say, engages in open and free competition without deception or fraud."

Despite what many may think, there has never been a law requiring managers to maximize share price (except when a board puts a company up for sale). No law mandates that shareholder interests supersede the long-term health of a company. What is required is that managers of corporations use the company's assets in the firm's best interest. But Friedman created a mantra that has persisted for decades. His persuasive argument has influenced the way many companies have come to operate: relentlessly pursuing earnings per share, reducing employee benefits and pensions, awarding high CEO salaries and payouts, and engaging in other practices justified by and aimed at profit performance above all. There are two persuasive counterarguments to the Friedman creed: First, times have changed, and capitalism needs revitalization to remain functional and socially relevant. Second, doing well by doing good actually accomplishes what Friedman advocates—increase profits.

A great deal has been written on the need to revitalize capitalism. Steven Pearlstein, the long-time business editor of the *Washington Post*, attacked what he believes are the negative consequences of a profit-dominated philosophy. His book's title spells it out: *Can American Capitalism Survive? Why Greed Is Not Good, Opportunity Is Not Equal, and Fairness Won't Make Us Poor.* Pearlstein, a self-described capitalist (like me), asserts that around the world free-market capitalism has helped more than a billion people rise out of poverty. But now, he says, the concentration of wealth, especially in the United States, has overwhelmingly benefited the top 10 percent, and socioeconomic inequality is obvious and rampant. Moreover, not even the father of economics, Adam Smith, believed that profit trumps all. His "invisible hand," in which every company should seek its own self-interest, is often cited as a justification for profit maximization. But as Pearlstein points out, Smith also wrote that self-interest must be balanced by an equally powerful interest in cooperation, empathy, and trust.

The second counterargument to the Friedman creed is based on the concept of shared value propounded by Michael Porter and Mark Kramer and others, including many companies included in this book (see the Introduction). This concept posits that—while profit is indeed a legitimate goal of modern companies—the best way to get there is to build social and environmental strategies into core businesses. This approach creates cost savings and revenues, consumer franchises, employee loyalty, and other avenues to profit. In other words, doing good is a money-making enterprise. And investors realize more earnings with these corporations. A 2012 study by Robert Eccles and George Serafeim showed that "high sustainability companies significantly outperformed their counterparts over an 18-year period in both stock market and accounting criteria (return on assets and equity)." And in October 2019 Serafeim and his coauthors (Porter and Kramer again) wrote, "companies that successfully implement strategies to create shared value can deliver superior shareholder returns." They pointed out that firms can't perform well merely by being in the

ESG space; they need to focus on selected social and environmental issues that are relevant to their business. That's the sweet spot. So Milton Friedman should approve.

In 2019 the Business Roundtable, composed of the CEOs of the largest companies, issued a statement defining (actually redefining) the purpose of a corporation: to promote "an economy that serves all stakeholders: customers, employees, suppliers, communities, and shareholders." The Business Roundtable asserted that putting customers first and investing in employees and communities was the most promising way to build long-term corporate value. "You can provide great returns for your shareholders and great benefits for your employees and run your business in a responsible way," said Brian Moynihan, the CEO of Bank of America and one of the Business Roundtable's leaders. The *New York Times* said the pronouncement was a "shift [that] comes at a moment of increasing distress in corporate America [the Pearlstein contention] as big companies face mounting global discontent over income inequality, harmful products and poor working conditions."

There is skepticism about the Business Roundtable's statement, which was signed by 181 CEOs. Some ask, What are they going to do to make it happen? And what authority do CEOs, who were appointed by boards representing shareholders, have to make this statement? Does this change put managers even more firmly in charge and hijack a corporation's purpose? Others say that the commitment to deliver value to all stakeholders is too vague and could result in corporations' being accountable to none of them. And David Gelles argued in the *New York Times* that reducing emphasis on profit in favor of "high-mindedness" doesn't protect CEOs "from the harsh realities of running a business." He mocked "wealthy chief executives hoping to curry favor with a public desperate to be inspired" by offering up such lofty goals as "elevate the world's consciousness," "make a bigger difference in the world," and, regarding climate change, "we owe it to our children to find the right answers." Gelles admonished, "At the end of the trading day, corporate chieftains are there to make shareholders money." The answer to all these criticisms of the Business Round-table statement—a statement that was long overdue—is yes, of course companies have to make money. Neither the Business Roundtable nor any other responsible individual or organization would argue otherwise. That's why the triple bottom line is people, planet, *profit*.

Companies Have No Soul

The harshest criticism of corporate social responsibility is that companies are essentially immoral, or rather amoral. Money trumps everything. Ethical behavior will always surrender—or simply be ignored—in the eternal quest for wealth. As the Spanish and Portuguese conquistadors pillaged and destroyed in the name of gold (and God), so too will companies chase profits no matter the consequences. It's in their DNA. Pollution, industrial accidents, obesity, low wages, global warming, and other misfortunes that may result are just collateral damage. Companies may, most of the time, observe the letter of the law, but not the spirit of the law. As you know from reading this book, I believe that's an accurate description of the tobacco industry. But what about other more legitimate industries? Are they inherently amoral? What about the giant gas and oil companies, which are often attacked for rapaciousness? There's certainly cause for criticism.

The 2010 BP oil spill in the Gulf of Mexico was the largest marine oil crisis and one of the largest environmental disasters in American history. The oil discharge, estimated to total about 5 million barrels, created enormous damage to beaches, wetlands, fishing, tourism, and wildlife. A 2013 study reported that dolphins and other marine life were continuing to die in record numbers. BP pled guilty to manslaughter and other felonies, including lying to Congress. You can't put a company in jail, but BP ended up paying more than $18 billion in fines and has so far spent more than $65 billion for cleanup, penalties, and other payments. Why did this happen? Was it avoidable? A US District court ruled that BP was primarily responsible because of its gross negligence and reckless conduct. A US government report identified defective cement on the well, with responsibility falling mostly to BP but also partly to the rig operator, Transocean, and the contractor, Halliburton. A White House commission blamed BP and its partners for cutting costs and for an inadequate safety system. It certainly seems that BP was putting profit above safety and social responsibility.

A well-publicized indictment of the oil and gas industry is Rachel Maddow's 2019 book *Blowout: Corrupted Democracy, Rogue State Russia, and the Richest, Most Destructive Industry on Earth.* Maddow, the MSNBC commentator whose progressive views are counterweights to Sean Hannity and others on Fox News, refers to the oil and gas industry as "Godzilla over downtown Tokyo" and says it is indeed amoral: when a lion kills a gazelle, says Maddow, "you really can't blame the lion. It's who she is; it's in her nature." Maddow charges that Big Oil and Gas have weakened democracies across the world, caused enormous environmental damage, and propped up Vladimir Putin (Maddow calls Russia a "second-rate, second-world piker") and other authoritarian rulers. She cites Oklahoma as an example of public harm due to earthquakes caused by fracking ("frackquakes"). After years of enduring the problem, Oklahoma's governor finally empowered a commission to order operators to shut down injection wells or prove they were not sending wastewater into basement rocks, where the added pressure could trigger earthquakes. Maddow focuses on BP, Chevron, and other big players, especially Exxon Mobil.

It's hard to observe the BP oil spill or read about the excesses of the oil and gas companies, even given the hyperbole of Maddow's book, without believing that the industry is causing worldwide problems and despoiling the planet. Exxon Mobil has also been known as a long-time leader in climate change denial, opposing regulations and funding academics and others to influence public opinion against the scientific evidence that global warming is caused in large part by the burning of fossil fuels. (More recently the company has partly reversed course and supported a carbon tax and a gasoline tax).

Action against the industry may be heating up. At the 2019 Harvard-Yale football game, climate change activists took the field at halftime to protest the universities' investments in fossil fuel companies. Some 500 people held their ground, and the game was delayed for more than an hour. More recently, Georgetown, my own school, said it will divest from fossil fuel companies. One report said that the fossil fuel divestment movement is now global, with commitments from more than a thousand organizations and tens of thousands of individuals controlling over $8 trillion in combined assets.

What does responsible corporate behavior look like in light of the charges against this industry? Ed Maibach, who oversees the Center for Climate Change Communication at George Mason University (and a Porter Novelli alumnus), identifies the industry as part of the problem, to be sure, but believes they also must be a key part of the solution. Ed says we have to accelerate the transition to a clean energy economy ("100 percent clean energy for everything—heating, cooling, transportation, manufacturing"). He argues that we need carbon-capture technologies to put the heat-trapping pollution in our skies back into the ground. And he calls for "every community, state, and nation to prepare for the unavoidable impacts of climate change that are already happening." While the energy industry should play a leading role in all this, Ed doubts that they will take the major steps that are needed. "Shell appears to be leaning into the challenge," he observes, "but their vision for what can get done falls far short of what must get done."

Mike Roman, until recently a senior executive at Exxon Mobil and now involved with the American Council for Capital Formation on international trade issues, has addressed my corporate social responsibility class on several occasions. The students were not always a friendly audience. One student challenged Mike about why Exxon Mobil was in Angola, with its corrupt government. He replied that his company operated throughout the world, where the oil is, and engaged with many governments. He said that Exxon Mobil was always careful to adhere to the US Foreign Corrupt Practices Act.

Rachel Maddow might not agree, but US companies do follow strict laws about avoiding corruption in other countries. And regarding energy sources, Mike presented a graph with Exxon Mobil's 25-year projections of the world's use of energy. It showed carbon-based fuels declining over time but still representing an important part of the world's fuel supply for decades to come. "We can talk about electric cars," he said, "but for now the auto industry is built around liquid fuels, and we have to bring new technologies along while still supporting a modern, vibrant economy." His point was that his company was about energy, not fossil energy. It is therefore working on new sources and aiming toward Ed Maibach's vision of worldwide clean energy as part of the solution.

Heather Kulp is one of the strongest proponents of corporate social responsibility I know. Now the manager of strategy and analytics for Chevron, Heather began her career with a strong belief in the power of NGOs to create social impact. She worked for an NGO called Search for Common Ground in Angola. Chevron was there working in oil extraction and engaged in what Heather saw was most important to local people—creating jobs. Her epiphany was that the private sector was critical for development. She decided to join Chevron, and when she did, "many of my NGO friends dumped me." She became part of an internal consulting group within Chevron and went to several other African countries, working with her company's business units on how to be more effective in "stakeholder and community engagement." For a time, she managed the company's Niger Delta Partnership Initiative (see chapter 7). Heather learned how to make local partnerships into a competitive advantage for Chevron and "institutionalize it" within the company. Heather says, "Other companies were engaged in this, but we were always a leader. We did it the Chevron way: people, partnerships, process."

After a few years, the company sent Heather on a six-month assignment to Richmond, California, where Chevron had a refinery. In this challenged community Kaiser Shipyards had once thrived, "but now there had been years of declining investment." Heather stayed six years. She helped fund organizations working to resolve conflicts between youth gangs and the community at large. She was reminded of the child soldiers she had encountered in Sierra Leone. As Chevron invested in trying to solve the problem, Heather decided to turn the "philanthropic model into a community development model." She found that she could take experiences from the developing world and apply them at home. Heather says that Chevron employees recognize the company's social impact efforts and are proud to participate through volunteerism, matching donations for good causes, and employee networks, including Latino, women's, and LGBTQ groups that provide scholarship funds and other community benefits. Heather started by picketing energy companies; today she sees herself as a champion of corporate responsibility for this generation. She says there's no need for a person or group to be solely in charge of Chevron's corporate responsibility because it's "baked into the company."

Rachel Maddow, Mike Roman, and Heather Kulp don't agree on social and environmental responsibility in the oil and gas industry. Maddow says the sector is "Godzilla over downtown Tokyo." Mike and Heather say the industry is responsible and moving toward a safer world. Ed Maibach says they both have valid points, but the planet is burning, and the industry needs to be a big and immediate part of solving the problem.

It's All Just Hype

The next criticism—and these attacks tend to overlap—is that the triple bottom line is just P. T. Barnum at work: a fraud, public relations, "greenwashing," big-time BS. Even my MBA students, with their focus on business, voice this criticism, and it's often true. There are lots of examples of corporate greenwashing, boasting, and bragging about being good citizens. One is Fiji Water, which is featured in a business case, *Fiji Water and Corporate Social Responsibility—Green Makeover or "Greenwashing"?* The product, natural artesian water from the Fiji Islands, was backed by a strong marketing campaign and smart distribution strategies that enabled the company to expand into new markets quickly and with little investment in physical assets. Its initial major markets were Australia and the United States. Because Fiji Water is bottled in the South Pacific and shipped thousands of miles, the company has a huge carbon footprint, which has generated lots of criticism. Consequently, Fiji Water analyzed its carbon emissions across the product life cycle; 75 percent came from its supply chain partners—no big surprise.

In response, the company planted trees and undertook other efforts to claim to offset the emissions burden and then made the questionable claim that "every drop is green." It didn't help that the Fijian government was unhappy about the company's damage to roads and bridges as well as tax issues. Meanwhile, opposition to bottled water was building on college campuses across several continents. One student summed up the criticism: "The product just doesn't make common sense. Companies are taking something that is freely accessible to everyone on . . . campus, packaging it in a non-reusable container, and then selling it under the pretense that it is somehow better than tap water." Recently I saw a colleague with a bottle of Fuji Water with the familiar square shape. She was with a nonprofit working on antipoverty programs in Texas. I didn't ask her if she thought every drop was green.

Another form of public relations is the art of communicating remorse—specifically the apology. Wells Fargo's ads don't exactly apologize but pledge to do better. BP ran continuous ads saying they would clean up the oil spill and promising to do better. After two crashes of its 737 Max 8 killed 346 people, Boeing placed newspaper advertisements saying, "We are truly sorry." Their apology does not take responsibility for the accidents but rather offers "our deepest sympathies for the families and friends who lost loved ones" and announces a $100 million relief fund.

Since there is legal liability involved, corporate apologies are tricky. Eric Dezenhall, a former Porter Novelli colleague who has a crisis management firm, offers a taxonomy of apologies for companies to choose from, only partly tongue-in-cheek. First there is the classic, Judeo-Christian apology of contrition and penance: "I did wrong, am truly sorry, and will make amends and restitution." You don't see or hear much of that. Then, there's the transactional apology: "I'm sorry that what you think happened is different from what really happened, but here's $5 million." That's most common among corporate bigwigs, athletes, and show biz types. And then there's the non-apology: "I'm sorry you're too confused to understand the situation." And finally, the marital-type apology: "OK, honey, let's just forget about it and move on."

It's Not Their Expertise

Some people argue that even if companies want to do well by doing good, they don't know how to actually perform the second part—doing good. They are ill equipped to deal with social and environmental issues and therefore should just pay their taxes, fund nonprofits, and get out of the way. Related to this is the criticism that companies and their leaders end up throwing money away when it can be applied more usefully by real experts in social impact. An example is the $100 million that Mark Zuckerberg, the head of Facebook, invested in the Newark public school system. Today his effort is regarded as largely a wasted opportunity, with much of the money spent on consultants and other expenses; little of it reached educators and students. Zuckerberg had the money but not the expertise.

This criticism may have been valid years ago, but today companies are increasingly effective at social change. When they incorporate social and environmental strategies into their core businesses, they bring expertise, resources, practical management, and a fast-track decision-making process to bear. And they often make a positive difference. As already noted, USAID, the UNDP, and CARE all work with the private sector to move low- and middle-income countries and people to "a more sustainable . . . shift in [the] journey to self-reliance." Recently the Conference Board issued a report called *Toward Standardized Social Outcomes for Companies* that concludes that most company-supported nonprofit programs in 11 social impact areas (including education, health, arts and culture, economic development, and sustainability) are effective, reaching their target goals 82 percent of the time. Measuring social impact is a continuing challenge for all sectors, but the private sector, often working in partnerships, is on the right track.

Money Distorts Decisions about the Social Good

Criticism about the distortionary effects of money applies to corporate titans and other super-wealthy individuals who turn their attention to social causes—who the hell are they to tell the rest of us what is socially valuable? They are plutocrats who believe they know best and think they have the intelligence, the experience, and the resources to reform the world and the global system. In *The Givers: Money, Power, and Philanthropy in a New Gilded Age*, David Callahan points out that the billionaires on the Forbes 400 list of the richest Americans have wealth greater than the bottom 61 percent of the population.

For some years the super-wealthy have been investing in science and in cures for disease. The scientific community often welcomes this "science philanthropy." For instance, Paul Allen, one of the cofounders of Microsoft, has made huge contributions to brain science. Steven Edwards of the American Association for the Advancement of Science remarked, "The practice of science in the twenty-first century is becoming shaped less by national priorities and more by the particular preferences of individuals with huge amounts of money. And their impact seems likely to grow, given their interests and enormous wealth."

The Gates Foundation, the Broad Foundation, and the Koch brothers spent millions of dollars at federal, state, and local levels to influence, among other things, the Obama administration's Race to the Top grant program, whose rules prohibited states from limiting the number of charter schools. In December 2018, thousands of teachers, students, and other public-school supporters marched on the Broad Museum in Los Angeles to protest Eli Broad and other billionaires who fund the growth of charter schools, because they are seen to divert funds from public schools. In a *New York Times* article by Nicholas Confessore called, "Policy-Making Billionaires," education writer and critic Diane Ravitch, author of *The Death and Life of the Great American School System*, called the charter school advocates a "billionaire boys' club" that exerted enormous influence over education policy with little accountability. Jack Ma, the very wealthy cofounder of Alibaba, the enormous Chinese e-commerce company, retired to pursue philanthropy in education. Ma, a former English teacher, said, "I love education."

In his book *Winners Take All: The Elite Charade of Changing the World*, Anand Giridharadas argues that the super-wealthy, the .001 percent who might be called "philanthropic plutocrats," seem to believe that they are saviors, helping to make things better when instead they are making things worse. And then they go to Davos and other centers of power to talk and preen about making the world a better place. Rich people putting their stamp on society is nothing new. John D. Rockefeller and Andrew Carnegie were examples back in their day. In an article in the *New York Times*, Giridharadas says, "Even as they give back, American elites generally seek to maintain the system that causes many of the problems they try to fix—and their helpfulness is part of how they pull it off. Thus, their do-gooding is an accomplice to greater, if more invisible, harm."

While the Gates Foundation has worked to reshape American public education and been challenged about its goals and accountability, it has also made hugely positive contributions to controlling malaria and other diseases. Not surprisingly, given the source of his wealth, Bill Gates himself is an unabashed capitalist. In a speech at (yes) Davos, he asserted, "The world is getting better, but it's not getting better fast enough, and it's not getting better for everyone." Gates's answer to this problem is the power of the private sector. He said, "The genius of capitalism lies in its ability to make self-interest serve the wider interest. The potential of a big financial return for innovation unleashes a broad set of talented people in pursuit of many different discoveries. This system driven by self-interest is responsible for the great innovations that have improved the lives of billions."

Thus the super-rich are spending huge amounts of money on their pet issues and causes, for good and not so good. It's a fair criticism and a problem that isn't easy to solve. When Michael Bloomberg contributes millions to reducing the incidence of vaping among adolescents, he runs up against the financial interests of the vaping industry. And when he invests millions in reducing gun violence, he is entering social territory that is even more hotly contested. The National Rifle Association and its Second Amendment adherents see it as an attack on gun freedoms they hold dear. But isn't this true of many issues? Who gets to say what is a socially beneficial cause? We all have opinions on social problems to be solved. The difference, of course, is often money, and therefore power.

Keeping Score and Preserving Principles

There is also the issue of whether companies pay their fair share through taxes to maintain our social structure. In late 2019 the left-leaning Institute on Taxation and Economic Policy issued a report claiming that some 400 of America's largest corporations paid an average federal tax rate of about 11 percent on their profits in 2018 as a result of the 2017 tax law. That law lowered the US corporate tax rate from 35 percent to 21 percent, but large companies often pay far less than that because of deductions and other tax breaks. Moreover, the report said that 91 companies in the Fortune 500 had paid no federal taxes at all in the previous year. Corporations claim they abide by the laws and are entitled—in fact, obligated—to pay the lowest taxes they can. But is this in the best interest of the nation and our well-being?

Clearly, there are conflicting views of companies and their social responsibility or irresponsibility. Companies may strive for people, planet, and profit, seeking to land on the nexus of profit and purpose, but the reality doesn't always line up. They can do good and do harm, sometimes simultaneously. And so, of course, can religious organizations, governments, nonprofits, and individuals. As employees, citizens, and voters, it's our role to keep score and to keep principles at the forefront. There are no permanent opponents, only permanent values. Larry Gostin, who teaches global health law and focuses on social justice at the Georgetown law school, agrees that to solve our problems we need big companies at the table. "But," he says, "let's make them uncomfortable." So, to make things better, we need to talk and fight, whether we're inside the organization or outside banging on the door.

CHAPTER NINE

WHAT DO WE OWE OUR GRANDCHILDREN?

For a red-blooded, patriotic American, I'm about as Italian as you can get. (Or so I thought.) All four of my grandparents came to this country from Italy (Abruzzo and Puglia). Their surnames were Novelli, Florio, DeCinque, and Bonante. Some years ago, Fran and I took my parents to the Italian village from which my dad's mother and father immigrated to America—a tiny place called Calascio, in the mountainous Abruzzo region near the Adriatic. My mother and father had never been to Italy. Fran and I had been there several times, but this was different. Seeing the village, meeting the local priest, looking for the stone house my grandfather had built, visiting the cemetery with our family names on the headstones—all gave me a deep sense of my past and of family and were a strong reminder of our responsibility to children and grandchildren.

My paternal grandfather, Raffaele, and my grandmother, Mary Josephine, married in the United States and first settled in a coal-mining town called Treveskyn, near Pittsburgh. It had a company store where my grandmother, with her limited English, would point out the things she needed for her family and payment would be subtracted from my grandfather's wages as a miner. That building is still there.

Raffaele was a strong, stocky man crippled in a coal-mining accident. He wore a straw hat and sweater much of the time, walked with two canes—which he also used to keep grandkids in line—and read Italian newspapers and books with a magnifying glass, which my brother, Jerry, has as a keepsake.

I grew up in Bridgeville, a wonderful small town near Treveskyn. It was solidly blue-collar, with lots of close-knit first- and second-generation immigrant families. There were two religions in town: Protestant and Catholic. You could tell the difference when we said the Lord's Prayer: the Catholic kids always stopped first. We said "Amen" before they did, and that was that. Bridgeville was a coal town, and when the coal gave out, the local steel mills employed many of our fathers. My dad's mill was the Universal Cyclops. Uncle Johnny worked at the Flannery Bolt. My friend Mike Ferris's father sold carpets. You get the picture.

Women worked too, but most were at home managing households and family budgets. My Aunt Sue got out of the house by taking the bus to clerk at Kaufman's department store in the "city" (Pittsburgh).

When the unions were on strike against the mills, I remember my dad and Uncle Johnny digging graves at the Cannonsburg cemetery to make ends meet. Dad went off to the steel mill at 18 and said it was "hotter than Hades in there," but at least he had finished high school and avoided following in the coal-mining footsteps of his father and oldest brother, Herman. Dad made 56 cents an hour, which he considered good money at the time, but he had to give the paycheck straight over to his father.

My mother, Celeste (DeFife) Novelli, didn't finish high school, nor did any of her or my father's sisters. Mom left school after the 10th grade to work in a sheet-metal factory, which she called "the tin mill." She was always cutting her hands as she checked big sheets of metal for flaws, and she worked in constant anxiety because her pay was docked if an imperfect sheet got by.

We had a story about her family name, DeFife. My maternal grandfather, Nicola DeCinque ("cinque" means "five" in Italian), was practicing his English on the "boat," as they called it, immigrating to America. At Ellis Island he was asked his name, and he said "de fife" in his Italian accent, meaning "de five." The official wrote it as DeFife, and that became the family name. My cousin John DeFife, our family genealogist, calls the story a myth. He thinks they just changed their name to fit in. I'm going with the myth.

My father's greatest disappointment in life was not going to college. He was offered a $125 "half scholarship" to Slippery Rock College. But as he told my son Alex the story, he said, "Where the hell was I going to find the other half?" So in our family, unlike many others, Jerry and I were going to college, period.

In that era, the newcomers were mostly Southern and Eastern Europeans, and ethnic humor was common ("the hell with US, I go to Chicago") as the different groups jostled for position in the new society. Polish and Italian and other kids traded insults and scrambled for a toehold. My father's generation never got over that. My Aunt Sue used to write letters to TV shows like the *Untouchables* if she thought they were denigrating Italian Americans. When I told my father I didn't get the job as CEO of CARE, he said, "Maybe that's because your name ends in a vowel."

Now that animosity is mostly healed, and new generations of immigrants are fighting for their place in American society.When my colleague Pattie Yu set out to trace her roots, she found herself sitting on two-by-fours in a dirt-floor house in Hangzhou, China, "to pay homage to my grandparents." She had a similar reaction to mine: "My father and mother [Michael Yung-An and Maria Chang Yu] made something of the American dream, and on that day, I understood that on a much deeper level. Their diligence, sacrifice, generosity, determination, and faith defined our [generation's] experience and left a strong legacy." Pattie remembers her childhood as eating together at a late hour when her father returned from work. "We had to get good grades, practice one or two instruments daily, and pray the rosary as a family before going to bed."

Ladan Manteghi—who was with me at AARP and was the first executive director of our Business for Impact program at Georgetown—came to the United States from Iran in the early 1970s when she was 5. Her family left Iran right before the revolution and could not return because her father had served under the shah. Ladan's key to her new country was *Sesame Street*. That's how she learned English and where she learned to fit into America. She knew she was different: "My name is weird, I spoke 'funny,' my skin and hair were darker than most kids, the food I ate looked like alien food. *Sesame Street* and my parents taught me kindness, sharing, and generosity. I was different, but not as much as I thought." Ladan points out that immigrants choose to be Americans: "Though we are not always accepted, we clutch onto our Americanism with all our might." Once when Ladan and I were in a cab in London, she entered into a conversation in Farsi with the Iranian driver. When we got to our destination, she turned to me with a smile and said, "My tribe."

Italian, Chinese, Iranian. Just how Italian am I, really? Out of curiosity, I recently took a DNA tests, and the results were fascinating. The test showed that just 57 percent of my ancestry is southeastern European, which includes Italy. OK, that's Italian. Another 11.5 percent is Sardinian, an Italian island. That's over two-thirds Italian, but what about the rest? Apparently, 3.4 percent is from the Basque region and another 3.5 percent is Ashkenazi Jewish, making me three-quarters European, mostly but not entirely Italian. The remaining quarter of my DNA is Middle Eastern and North African, including 21.4 percent Persian and 3.2 percent Bedouin. "Only in America," as Yogi Berra supposedly said when someone told him the mayor of Dublin was Jewish. I told Ladan about my Persian ancestry and said that she and I could be related (maybe descended from Cyrus the Great?). She laughed and answered, "That explains everything!"

So we're all immigrants—even Native Americans, if you go back far enough. I see Pattie's, Ladan's, and my own sense of America as based on immigrant values. Now, with my own grandkids, I think about how to impart those values to children who have so much: the importance of daily hard work, a reverence for education, strength of family, and love of America. We all believe in the American Dream. And with the benefits come the responsibilities of good citizenship and of contributing to society—to make life fairer and better for everyone. The late congresswoman Barbara Jordan said, "What people want is an America as good as its promise." That's what parents and grandparents want for their children.

My kids, Peter, Alex, and Sarah, now adults, gifted Fran and me with seven grandchildren. Peter and Mariana are raising Dominic, Christopher, and Victor out in Minneapolis. Alex and Alejandra have twins, Leo and Julia, in Rabat, Morocco. And Sarah is divorced and living right next door to us with her children, Juliana and Nathan. What do any of us "owe" our grandchildren, the generation that is coming or will come into adulthood in the coming decades of this century? The word "owe" conveys responsibility; it suggests our obligation and duty to the coming generations to leave society better than we found it. I see three things: a viable future in the face of a planet in trouble, a strengthening of the American Dream, and some practical, useful advice—often learned the hard way by making mistakes and learning from them.

A Future in a World of a Climate in Crisis

When did the Earth's climate become politicized? Why do attitudes about climate change differ substantially by party affiliation? It's an issue that has become part of the political scrum in America. As serious as other problems are—including the coronavirus and potential future pandemics—this one is at the very top of the dangers we face. We can't wait for political sanity to strike our policy makers; we need rapid change. We've wasted so much time arguing about it, and have done so little, that immediate action is now warranted. Extreme weather is common, bringing wildfires, hurricanes, heat waves, and floods. Forests are being destroyed, and ice sheets and glaciers are melting. Scientific reports are increasingly dire. The United Nations High Commissioner for Refugees and others estimate that the coming decades will produce millions of "climate refugees"—people forced to leave their homes because of sudden or long-term changes to their local environment.

A November 2019 UN report (the UN, like the climate, is also politically contentious in this country) said that global temperatures are on pace to go up as much as 7 degrees Fahrenheit by the end of the century. There are major gaps between where we are today and where we need to be to avert devastating consequences. Scientists say there is still time to act, despite all the dithering, and that if we do, we can avoid much of the devastation.

Do we want to continue to argue about this? Can it all be a hoax? I say "no" and "no." When my grandson Victor, now 12, is middle aged, many of the present coastlines, including major cities in the United States and other countries, could be under water, and severe heat could be unbearable around the world.

We must act. Recently, along with Steve Schroeder, I signed on to cochair the advisory board of the Medical Society Consortium on Climate and Health, a large alliance of organizations comprising physicians, nurses, hospitals, health care systems, and others to work with business, civil society, and government and take action on climate change. It was organized by Ed Maibach and his team at the Center for Climate Change Communication at George Mason University. That's one step forward, but much more is needed. Private companies, cities, and states have set targets to reduce carbon use. It's not nearly enough. Shall we wait for our national leaders and others around the world to find the political will to take on this enormous threat? Again, I say "no." We need to aggressively push this agenda forward in the most nonpartisan way possible.

A Fair Shot at the American Dream

The Declaration of Independence calls for life, liberty, and the pursuit of happiness. Belief in that "pursuit" is embedded in the American psyche. We believe in fairness, in opportunity, in economic security, and in optimism. It's not a guarantee, but rather a strong expectation. Work hard, play by the rules, and you will do OK. In her book *Happiness for All? Unequal Hopes and Lives in Pursuit of the American Dream,* author Carol Graham writes that of those in my generation, 90 percent of us rose to higher income levels than our parents. But of those born in 1980, only 40 percent have exceeded their parents' level of income. And in 2016 only 38 percent of Americans thought their children would be better off than themselves.

The Gallup World Poll, undertaken in many countries, asks, "Can an individual who works hard in this country [the country in which the poll is administered] get ahead?" The answers were not promising for America. The differences in positive responses between the top 20 percent and bottom 20 percent were far greater than in East Asia, Europe, and Latin America. In the United States, optimism for a brighter future is greater among African Americans and Hispanics than among poor whites. That may have changed with the racial unrest that has engulfed the United States in the wake of the deaths of George Floyd and many other men and women of color in conflicts with the police. Washington University sociologist Mark Rank adds to this picture with the finding that many American families are just one paycheck away from poverty. Some 54 percent of those aged 25 to 60 in this country will spend at least one year below the poverty line. More broadly, some 80 percent of Americans in this age group will experience poverty or financial insecurity at least one year in their lifetimes.

How is this possible in a country with so much wealth and seeming opportunity? It is not just possible; it's actually happening. This is not about lazy people who don't want to work or who are sitting on the front porch doing drugs and waiting for a welfare check. Sure, there's always some of that, but most people want to work and earn a living for themselves and their children.

So is the American Dream broken, shattered? Our Georgetown Business for Impact team is engaged in a program called the 21st Century Workforce, which is developing new approaches to providing workers with benefits, promoting employee-company engagement, and designing training and certification for today's employees that will also benefit employers, investors, and consumers. Our first target segment for research is the gig worker, who does flexible, temporary, or freelance jobs and connects with a company and customers through an online platform.

The research findings tell a lot about this new and growing cadre of American workers. They are more socioeconomically diverse than the general population. Many work full-time jobs and take gig work to earn extra income and make ends meet. They generally do not bring problems—like payment disputes—to their gig employer, and their attitudes toward this type of employment often differ by age. Older gig workers (who are most likely to be doing this type of work) are more resigned to the status quo, whereas younger, often underemployed gig workers are more disgruntled about income and working conditions and would leave gigs if they could. Gig work is growing, as is the number of American workers who work on contract without employer benefits. These people are not, by and large, living the American Dream.

In another Georgetown project we participated in a qualitative study of teens and young adults (white, African American, South Asian, East Asian, and Hispanic) in five cities across the country. The results were sobering. These young Americans are both hopeful and despairing. They see themselves as part of a changing country, and they don't see how they can get ahead. Their biggest concern is heavy debt from school and the daily cost of living. They have limitless information at their fingertips but lack opportunities to use this information to make progress. They feel daily stress about school, family, raising children, jobs—and the need for better employment. They think privilege, discrimination, and other factors are leaving them behind, and they know they are the first generation to do worse economically than their parents. They have aspirations and they work hard, but they don't believe older generations are listening or even care. I came away from this study with a real liking for these young people, as well as feeling that they have, unfortunately, a realistic perspective on how difficult their road ahead will be.

It's tougher to move up from the bottom ranks than it was in my parents' day. There are fewer well-paying jobs for young people with high school degrees and certainly fewer opportunities for those—like my mother—who didn't graduate from high school. At the same time, the future is bright for the fortunate Georgetown students and graduates I work with and for other well-educated young and middle career managers across the country.

So the American Dream is still there. But it is more unevenly distributed across our population. It depends partly on your zip code, your family advantages, and your resulting opportunities. Poor kids and poor families can still make it, but the American

Dream is less available and less fair. And it's not just about redistributing wealth and resources; it's about creating more wealth for all our citizens, about enlarging the pie.

The answers to today's challenges to the American Dream are not easy to analyze and even harder to act upon. We have good schools in many parts of America, especially in the suburbs, but we also have schools that are not graduating kids with the skills to compete in today's society. Part of the problem is where Americans live. We are a desegregated society but not an integrated one. We've never solved the problem of high concentrations of low-income, disadvantaged kids in one school district or community and high-performing students in another. Funding schools with local resources is not working equitably. Many states spend less on education on a per-student basis than before the Great Recession. We need much more investment and progress in our schools: to reduce crowding, to hire more teachers and improve teaching, and, in general, to make schools a greater priority. That's a ticket to the American Dream. At least two other issues are also important: improving the health of our citizens and paying down (and not expanding) our enormous national debt.

Health Promotion and Disease Prevention

If you were running a company called the United States of America and had finite resources, would you invest in preventing problems before they occurred, or would you spend much more money to fix things after they broke? The answer is obvious. Now think about preventing illness and disease rather than paying for treatment and continuing care. In the United States we are woefully inadequate in promoting health and preventing disease—actions that would make our people healthier and more productive and cut down drastically on health care (read "disease care") costs, which are increasingly unaffordable.

Anand Parekh, a colleague and the chief medical advisor at the Bipartisan Policy Center, wrote *Prevention First: Policymaking for a Healthier America*. He points out the shocking fact that "preventable deaths in the U.S. have increased to such an extent that the nation has been experiencing a decline in life expectancy for three years straight for the first time in a hundred years." Only about 3 percent of health expenditures go to prevention, which could save thousands of lives and billions of dollars now spent on hospital care, physician and dental services, and other costs associated with largely preventable conditions. Health care costs are virtually uncontrolled and inefficient, and they are displacing other spending needs.

Why are we so foolish and misaligned? Anand suggests it is because treatment is more urgent than prevention and because Congress is not always up to speed on prevention needs and opportunities. And he says some policymakers think prevention, such as government action against smoking, smacks of a "nanny state" at work. He also points out that prevention is funded at the national level through discretionary appropriations, which are hard to come by and easy to cut. Another reason why prevention takes a back seat to treatment is that there is less money to be made from it. It could save billions, but much of that would accrue to Medicare and Medicaid, not to the private sector. Anand has worked on national health emergencies, such as pandemics. He laments our unpreparedness, which is painfully apparent with the coronavirus crisis.

And then there's us: the public. As Anand puts it, "Many Americans would rather wait to get sick and then take a pill rather than engage in the crucial health promotion activities necessary to avoid preventable illness." I've worked on many health promotion and disease prevention programs, and I know it's a tough sell. The inclination to wait for a pill or some other easy solution is a powerful one, and overcoming it is made harder by the superb marketing practices of companies purveying soft drinks, snacks, fast foods, and other inducements that contribute to America's ever-expanding waistline.

Among the many media interviews I did at AARP, one of my favorites was with *Grand,* a magazine for grandparents. The interviewer asked if I had the power to fix just one of the vexing problems facing the United States, what it would it be. I said, "Health care: I'd work with Congress to deliver quality, affordable health care to every child and adult in the country, because virtually every other challenge we face in reinventing our society depends on our having a first-class health system for our citizens." And that system must start with prevention. We can't keep treating disease and watching health care costs go up while obesity and diabetes and hypertension and tobacco use and other risk factors drag us down. We need to be a healthier country if we are going to be able to afford and achieve a bigger and better American Dream.

The National Debt

Another deep hole that we are leaving our grandchildren is the colossal debt that they will have to pay. We are all vaguely aware of it, but the national debt (the total amount our country incurs and then owes) and annual deficits (the government budget shortfall each year) are so big that they are hard to comprehend. I saw the problem at AARP (working on entitlement programs) and then at the Bipartisan Policy Center (BPC) in Washington, DC. The BPC is aggressively bipartisan, a quality sorely lacking in policy and politics today. It was founded by four former Senate majority leaders, two Republicans (Bob Dole and Howard Baker) and two Democrats (Tom Daschle and George Mitchell), to foster bipartisanship in Congress, in presidential administrations, and throughout the country.

I became involved with the BPC by serving on their Debt Reduction Task Force, cochaired by former Senator Pete Domenici (R-NM) and Alice Rivlin, which coincided with President Obama's Simpson-Bowles Commission. Former senator Alan Simpson (R-WY) and former Clinton chief of staff Erskine Bowles said that at first they wanted to achieve debt reduction for their grandchildren. Then, as they saw how urgent it was, they resolved to solve these problems for their children. Finally, the extreme urgency made them think they needed to do it for themselves. Unfortunately, none of this got anywhere, and in the end, both political parties involved did what they do best—blamed the other side.

Today our debt and deficit problems have exploded and become far worse. Despite a strong economy, the annual deficit ballooned to almost a trillion dollars in 2019, an increase of 26 percent over 2018. It is projected to continue to grow far into the future. The total public debt of the United States is some 23 trillion dollars, a nearly incomprehensible number. But what we can understand is the annual cost of the expanding interest on that debt. Last year it was $380 billion. It will get worse, and we are leaving future generations holding the bag. Why is this happening? Because neither Republican nor Democratic leadership shows any interest in fiscal responsibility. Brian Riedl, former chief economist for Senator Rob Portman (R-OH) said, "The parties are not talking on this issue." They have abandoned their responsibility. Our grandkids are going to be paying for this throughout their lifetimes. Tax cuts are not helping. And while the recent stimulus packages passed by Congress and signed by President Trump to combat the economic downturn from the coronavirus is certainly necessary, they too will add to our problem. Can we get back to sanity? It would be a big boost to the American Dream.

While the American Dream isn't broken, it is badly tattered and bruised. Uncle Sam is walking with a decided limp. As today's generation, we need to face up to these problems of schools, health promotion and disease prevention, debt and deficits, and other challenges. We created all this. It's our responsibility, nobody else's. We owe our grandkids—and all those of their generation—a decent shot at the American Dream. They will depend on it, and the future of the United States as a strong nation will require it.

Advice to the Next Generation

Now for some advice for our kids and grandkids. We know how tiresome advice from elders can be when you're on the receiving end. The immediate directives (eat your peas, do your homework) are bad enough. But it's the "wisdom" that usually washes completely over young heads—like commencement speeches about "follow your passion, wherever it takes you"—and sometimes makes them wander off into cell phone land. So I'm going to keep this to a minimum and base it on the lessons from this book—the tobacco wars, policy fights, working in and with companies with multiple (sometimes conflicting) agendas, creating startups, dealing with students on their way up, and the missteps and mistakes I've made along the way. Here are lessons learned—just three.

Aim High and Strive Hard

We can all be better and achieve far more than we think. This is not blind luck (although good fortune is certainly part of it) or based on superior genes. It isn't about being born into privilege and going to prep school (that helps, too). It is mostly the ability and the willingness to set ambitious goals and to *strive* to achieve them. Be a competitor in whatever endeavor you choose. Striving means trying and working hard, putting your energy and effort into a goal, getting up when you're knocked down (as when we lost national tobacco control legislation), overcoming adversity, and being a little better today than you were yesterday. It's about being ambitious. If you're charming or brilliant, all the better. But you don't have to be. In fact, as I said earlier, being the smartest person in the room (or thinking you are) is probably a disadvantage.

I spent my early years overcoming a lack of confidence, working on just average speaking skills, being in too much of a hurry, and not making the best of the advice I received. We can all improve and get better, no matter where we are in our lives. At Unilever, where I started my career, I was determined to work my way into a corner executive office and to climb the corporate ladder. I worked hard at that big goal, but as I went on I came to realize that it wasn't the right goal for me after all. Over time I formed a different career goal: to make a significant contribution to solving major social problems. This strategic focus on social impact became what I worked for. At AARP, when I won the opportunity to lead a large national organization, I was determined to go big; the Three Great Goals I set for myself and for AARP were as ambitious as I could possibly make them. So the goals you strive for are critically important and go hand in hand with your willingness and drive to achieve them. Without a focus on career goals, you can drift or just settle for what's in front of you. John Gardner said, "The barnacle . . . is confronted with an existential decision about where it's going to live. Once it decides . . . it spends the rest of its life with its head cemented to a rock. For a good many of us, it comes to that." Having goals, and changing them as necessary, is to avoid the fate of the barnacle.

This is not about me, me, me. I accomplished what I did because I was able to attract and support and nurture great teams. Talented people come together because they are inspired by big goals. They see pathways to success, and they trust, believe in, and respect their teammates and their leader. Part of leading a team is giving your teammates the opportunity to challenge your ideas. And while it feels good to bring in quality people and to lead, it's not much fun to remove people from a team, especially when separating them from the organization. But that's what is necessary if a member isn't rowing in the same direction with the same commitment as everyone else. Mediocrity is a chronic disease. You can live with it for a long time, but eventually it will do you in. As business author Lou Vickery once wrote: "Nothing average ever stood as a monument to progress. When progress is looking for a partner, it doesn't turn to those who believe they are only average. It turns instead to those who are ever searching and striving to become the best they possibly can."

Another part of leading a team, or of just about anything worth doing, is to keep your ego in check. A guest once called on Abraham Lincoln at the White House and found Lincoln shining his boots. "Why Mr. President," the guest said, "you are shining your own shoes." "Well, yes," said Lincoln. "Whose shoes do you shine?" We should all shine our own shoes, and strive for humility. This also means being able to laugh at yourself and not take yourself too seriously. I once gave a speech in Thailand with simultaneous translation. That night at dinner I sat next to the translator and told her she had done a good job. She answered, "How would you know?" I pointed out that the audience had laughed at all my jokes. She said, "Oh, I don't translate humor; it doesn't work. I would say, he just told a joke. Please laugh." OK, ha, ha. But I believe humor does translate, across countries, cultures, and even across political parties.

In my early days at Porter Novelli, when someone left the firm, I used to go into a deep funk. Why is she leaving? What could have kept him on the team? But over time I came to see that this is the natural order of things. People move on. Today I am part of a large network of talented people from across my career. I call on them for help with assignments, for volunteering, for advice, for job placement for others (including Georgetown students), and for good cheer. And they call on me. That's teamwork in the larger sense.

In chapter 7 I mentioned a study of the leadership failures that led to the Great Recession of 2008. The authors concluded that competencies count a great deal, that character really matters, and that commitment is critical. Commitment is about striving. Earlier I talked about the gig workers and young adults we studied who are struggling to get ahead. Those among them who try hard, who strive to be better, and who set and adjust their goals will still probably have it tough, but they have the best chance to do well.

Be Ethical

This sounds painfully obvious and commonplace. It is, but it's also hard to do. In chapter 1 I discussed my experience of being coerced into signing political campaign contributions forms I shouldn't have. It wouldn't have been easy to get up and walk out the door, but that's what I should have done. And I mentioned the crappy TV commercial at Wells Rich Greene that I got the client to put on the air even though I knew it would not be effective. The Volkswagen and Wells Fargo employees also were essentially coerced into unethical behavior. Pressure from the top, a desire to get ahead or take shortcuts, and doing it "just this once" are powerful forces. Years ago, when I taught marketing management at the University of Maryland, I would go over the syllabus at the first session and say that we'll save ethics until the end of the semester, so it doesn't get in the way. Few students questioned that, whereas I wanted the opposite reaction—to be challenged. You can't save ethics until the end of the semester or the end of the project or the end of the day. Ethics permeates everything. It must be in our cell structure and the guts of the organization.

Greed is not good; cheating is not the way. But not everyone bothers to ask themselves "How can I be sure I'll stay out of jail?" A former Georgetown tennis coach, Gordon Ernst, was accused by prosecutors as being "the most prolific of all the coaches" caught up in the recent schemes by coaches and go-betweens to accept money from wealthy parents to get their kids into elite universities by falsely designating them as highly regarded, competitive athletes. Ernst was supposedly an entrepreneur; he not only worked with the middleman who engineered the scam but went off on his own to solicit additional parents and bribes, pocketing almost $3 million before the roof fell in. Jerome Allen, a Penn basketball star in his day who went on to become Penn's head coach, testified that he accepted hundreds of thousands of dollars from a parent to get his son into the university. Coaches at Yale and the University of Southern California were also involved. It's not just fear of jail time that is at issue here. It's about what's right. And it's about not shaming and embarrassing yourself, your family, and your organization. What will Ernst and Allen tell their mothers? Their kids?

Although these are blatant examples of bad behavior, often over the course of a career temptations come along that are less egregious. Shortcuts and questionable actions can start small, like padding an expense report, and move to bigger steps, such as fudging safety records to speed the development of a new system, a new building, or a new plane. As the old Google motto said, "Don't be evil." And far short of evil, don't be unethical.

Balance Personal Responsibility with Being Bigger Than Ourselves

We all have to make our own choices and be responsible for our own decisions. We have to accept the personal responsibility of taking care of ourselves and our families. This includes staying healthy, making financial ends meet, paying our fair share, and giving our kids and grandkids every chance to be successful citizens and adults. It's also about taking care of our elderly family members and certainly not spending down or hiding their assets so they can go into Medicaid.

These are universal responsibilities, no getting around it. But somehow personal responsibility is coming to be perceived as being selfish, as pulling up the gangplank, and more associated with

Republicans—with conservatism and libertarianism—than Democrats and liberal thinking. Some time ago I was talking to Congressman Joe Barton (R-TX), then chairman of the House Energy and Commerce Committee, about policies to improve long-term care in the United States. He said, "I'll tell you about long-term care; I take care of my mother." And well he should. (Note: America still has no long-term care system—just a hodgepodge of public and private programs that are almost impossible to understand or to navigate.)

But the other side of the equation is to be bigger than ourselves and go beyond our own personal interests and needs—to care about our communities, our country, and future generations. Democrats say, "It takes a village." Based on an African proverb, this saying essentially means that a child's upbringing belongs to the community. Hillary Clinton popularized the phrase and applied it to concepts like universal preschool. The phrase "It takes a village" has become a source of ridicule by the other party. At the 1996 Republican National Convention, Bob Dole said, "We are told it takes a village . . . and thus the state, to raise a child." As the crowd jeered, Dole said, "With all due respect, I am here to tell you it does not take a village to raise a child. It takes a family to raise a child." The concept has become associated with collectivity, common ownership without moral responsibility. It's become a "tragedy of the commons," where something that is everyone's property and therefore no one's responsibility is not cared for. President Obama once commented that successful entrepreneurs owed much of their success to the society that enabled them to thrive. That didn't go over well with the other side.

But we do need to be socially aware and involved and to help make our "villages" and nation better. We do need to help others and to care beyond ourselves. This isn't liberalism or socialism or any "ism." It's a common American value that is compatible with, and even an extension of, personal responsibility. An important part of this is helping the poor and disadvantaged, especially the youngest and oldest among us. We can all understand volunteering at the local soup kitchen or bringing toys to work for a charity that helps poor kids during the Christmas season.

But what about on a larger scale? Policy makers and political candidates frequently debate whether we should impose work requirements for safety-net programs—like food stamps and Medicaid—for low-income people. We all seem to agree that able-bodied people should work and shouldn't be given government aid (or should receive less aid) unless they do so. And work requirements can be an investment in helping welfare recipients and their families move ahead financially. But we need to get it right, and it is far more complicated than it appears. Peggy Morache, the executive director of FISH, a food bank in Washington State, said, "In our experience . . . it's the children and the elderly who eventually feel the brunt of cuts and changes. Parents are struggling as it is, and when there are further cuts and further requirements put on them, it just makes their life more difficult and therefore makes the child's life more difficult." Do we really need to make this issue a hyperpartisan political football—an argument about loafers and "takers" living off society versus collective responsibility? We want our grandkids to rise above partisan bickering and to accept both their personal responsibilities and the idea of being bigger than just themselves.

Ethel Percy Andrus, the founder of AARP, was a wise woman in this and in so many other things. She understood personal responsibility and "retired" to take care of her elderly mother. She also aimed high and provided help for others and eventually for a whole generation. She said, "What we do, we do for all." I like that. I see that attitude embodied in our attempts to tackle those big problems worthy of attack that in turn attack us back, and its's been a good North Star for me. We can balance personal responsibility with being bigger than ourselves. To be a successful society today and tomorrow, that must be our goal.

What's Next? Where Do We Go from Here?

I hope all grandkids, and certainly mine, will adopt those nuggets of advice. Now back to my generation's obligations to those who will succeed us. This book has been about doing well by doing good and combating social and environmental issues like global warming, tobacco use and vaping, health and health care, financial security and advanced illness care for older people, assistance for their caregivers, and many others.

I've been privileged and fortunate to contribute to solving major social problems—to talk, fight, and (not always, but often) to win—with Big Tobacco, international development, Congress and the White House, and in other situations. Looking back, maybe I sometimes fought too hard (or maybe not hard enough), and I sometimes may have talked too much. The balance is elusive, and today is no different. The Food and Drug Administration needs support for its regulation of the vaping and tobacco industries. And it also needs to be fought—including through legal action—to get it to do more to regulate these industries. Of course, when you follow this precept, people are going to fight back. I had to learn to toughen up under pressure. When my Aunt Jay saw us kids knocking the stuffing out of each other back in Bridgeville, she would say, "Now fight nice." But fighting nice doesn't work so well in today's world. And when I've engaged in big battles over big problems, I've often incurred the wrath of politicians.

Nancy Pelosi was so furious about the Medicare bill that she called me the worst name she could think of—"Republican" (we later made up, I think). Mitch McConnell, on the other hand, called me a "Democrat." I was meeting with him one afternoon in his office when a tornado warning sounded in the Capitol, and a security guard came to escort him to a shelter. "Do you want to come along," the Senator asked me, "or would you rather risk the tornado than hang out with Republicans?" I looked at the darkening sky outside his window and gratefully accepted his "generous" offer. Senator Jim DeMint (R-SC) called Chris Hansen and me "communists" during a discussion about Social Security. Republican, Democrat, communist—they are badges of honor. I've been assailed from the left (John Dingell, Henry Waxman, and Ted Kennedy, for example) as well as from the right (Paul Ryan, Tom DeLay, and Chuck Grassley). John McCain, on the other hand, called me a "great American," but he was known to flatter lots of people that way. It was John McCain who was the great American.

Despite all the partisan name calling, I'm still where I've always been, unattached and independent. Jim Hightower, once the agriculture commissioner in Texas and now a political commentator, famously said that the only thing you'll find in the middle of the road are yellow lines and dead armadillos. That's cute and quotable, but it's not true. Most of the voters in this country are in the broad middle. They're looking for reasonable candidates with sensible programs. And that's where I stand as an independent and a pragmatist in the practical center, where I believe problems can be analyzed and solved in a bipartisan way.

One of my all-time favorite politicians is Olympia Snowe, the former Republican senator from Maine. She was known for moderation, for crossing the aisle, and for staying calm in the face of political rancor. One day she said to me, "I don't care how much Chuck Grassley yells at me." And Senator Grassley (R-IA) is still yelling.

In 2012 Senator Snowe reached the end of her rope and decided not to run for reelection. In her book *Fighting for Common Ground*, she said that the Senate was no longer a legislative body where key issues facing the country could be resolved. She called the Congress a place of burned bridges and scorched earth. Today I see Olympia at the Bipartisan Policy Center, where she is a senior fellow and where she promotes civility as a way to bring the warring parties together.

Other people have put forth a range of ideas about how to reduce the toxic partisanship that plagues Washington and many state capitals. Some, like Olympia, call for rebuilding the sense of trust and community within our legislative bodies. Still other ideas concern term limits, encouraging a younger generation to enter politics, and getting big money and gerrymandering out of the system. All these proposals have merit.

But things just keep getting even worse. In December 2019 Senator Johnny Isakson (R-GA) gave a farewell speech. Like Olympia Snowe, Isakson is respected for his sense of bipartisanship. He was a champion of our work on advanced illness and end-of-life care. Isakson has Parkinson's disease, and he moved from a wheelchair to his desk for his final remarks. He said, "We can't continue to level brickbats at each other. . . . We've got to start listening. . . . People don't understand what 'bipartisan' means. . . . [It] is a state of mind and a state of being." The *Washington Post* commented: "If Isakson cannot halt the Senate's slow and steady fade from relevance, who can?" Good question. What should we do? What can we do when it's unforgivable to let the other party have a win? Where everything is about maneuvering for the upcoming election—and there's always an upcoming election? Where ideology stands above pragmatism? Where there's little urgency or ability among our policy makers to solve big state and national problems?

I think the best answer, really the only answer, lies in us—the companies and students and employees and "retirees" described in this book, all of us who want to make a difference. Regardless of what business or nonprofit or government agency we're in, wherever we are in our careers, we can have an impact and change society for the better. We can do well (creating economic and financial success for ourselves and our organizations) and do good for society. By discovering and fulfilling our purpose in life, we can all make a difference—we can all make our dent in the universe.

There's a lot of progress to be proud of, but the problems are colossal, and they call for aggressive action across organizations and sectors. And "fighting nice" isn't going to cut it. Like many of the examples in this book, we need to be strategic, dedicated, and aggressive. Merck, CVS Health, Walmart, Goldman Sachs, Nestlé, Unilever, Bank of America, and the other companies I discussed aren't perfect, but they are striving to do well by doing good, and their employees and customers and other stakeholders want them to succeed. Bill Matassoni, my buddy from Porter Novelli and McKinsey, likes to say that companies create value, communicate value, and capture value. That applies to the triple bottom line as much as any other part of their business. And Bill and I agree on one additional step—companies also need to share value.

Georgetown, AARP, Kidsave, the American Cancer Society, the Coalition to Transform Advanced Care, and the many other nonprofits I discussed aren't all hitting home runs, but they are moving in the right direction. And there are also many admirable leaders and employees in government who are making a difference. The people in this book are exemplars. They are showing the way.

The social and environmental problems we face that are worthy of attack really are proving their worth by attacking back. We need to work together to aim high, set big goals, create coalitions of the willing, tell powerful stories about change, mobilize and inspire grassroots cadres (like Ethel's "army of useful citizens"), exhibit leadership at the top and throughout the ranks, keep score, and have the ability to know when and how to course correct and move forward.

I started this book by saying I'm a marketing guy, and across a career in business, nonprofits, universities, and government, that's what I am and what I do. Back in the 1950s a psychologist named G. D. Wiebe asked the question, "Why can't you sell brotherhood . . . like you sell soap?" There are lots of reasons why the two aren't the same and why different approaches are called for. But as this book shows, and as I truly believe, we can definitely "sell" brotherhood. And we can build a better, stronger country for ourselves and for future generations and do well at the same time. So let's work for that. After all, our forebears created the greatest nation on Earth for us; we owe it to our children, grandchildren, and future generations to do the same.

ACKNOWLEDGMENTS

There's a story about a celebrity, a woman famous for being famous (TV talk shows and all), who let it be known at a cocktail party that she was "working on a book." A publisher overheard this and was determined to land the contract. He called in a handsome young editor and told him to get close to the woman and win the publishing rights. The celebrity booked a cruise, so the editor did the same. He managed to get close to her at lunch, dinner, walks on deck, and more. One evening he said, "How's that book coming along that you're working on?" She said, "Slow, very slow—maybe a page a day." The editor said, "Well, it isn't easy to write a book." She replied, "Oh, I'm not writing a book—I'm reading a book."

No, it isn't easy to write a book. But I had a lot of great help with this one, and I acknowledge with much appreciation those who provided outstanding counsel and assistance.

First there's Boe Workman, whom, as I said in the book, is my buddy, former speech writer, and editor of this work. Boe is gracious but no-nonsense. If something didn't fit or didn't flow, he said so. If you want to write your own book, Boe's your man.

My Georgetown colleague Leslie Crutchfield knows book writing. She's done three of them, all well received. Leslie was one of my readers and true advisors, and she knows how to get to the heart of the matter and start with that. Another helpful reader was Jennifer Swint, a former Porter Novelli executive who excels in many communications skills. Jennifer is a gentle critic but a very good critic nonetheless.

Robin Coleman at Johns Hopkins University Press turned a professional eye on the book after the initial draft and some early editing. Robin knows his craft, and he wanted more, with good reason. He was right at virtually every step. Robin's colleagues Juliana McCarthy, Kim Johnson, Hilary Jacqmin, Will Krause, Kathryn Marguy, Heidi Vincent, and Adelene Jane Medrano, as well as copy editor Heidi Fritschel, were also a big help.

In my AARP days, I retained Bob Rosenblatt, formerly of the *Los Angeles Times*, to do a postmortem on our work to get prescription drugs in Medicare (chapter 4) and protect Social Security (chapter 5). Bob did a great job and helped refresh my memory for those two chapters.

Steve Carpinelli of Porter Novelli, with his colleagues Rosy McGillan and Joe Farren, worked with me on the book and its promotion. And so did my Georgetown teammate Berry Brady and also Jane Wesman. Nothing like having dedicated pros on your team.

Two friends added a lot. Bill Matassoni, who appears in the book in several places and who wrote his own book, *Marketing Saves the World*, is a longtime sounding board of mine. If you bounce an idea off Bill, it comes back more refined and better than when you threw it to him. And the late Kirk Davidson and I had thoughtful discussions—some on beach walks—about corporate responsibility and Kirk's convictions about ethics. I miss him.

Kevin Donnellan, chief of staff at AARP, is a pragmatist. He knows the score in Washington and across the chessboard. Kevin has been a big help in creating this book and in so many other ways.

Cheryl Matheis, Diane Ty, and Marian Grant all reviewed relevant chapters and gave me good feedback. Thanks to these friends and colleagues.

Teresa Mannix and her communications team at Georgetown's McDonough School of Business keep a lot of balls in the air and have many "clients." I'm grateful to be one of them.

Since I have the tech skills of a lower primate, I'm very glad for Shannon Johnson and Lauren Beckham at Georgetown Business for Impact, as well as my daughter Sarah. They don't think I ask dumb questions, or at least pretend they don't.

Finally, my deepest thanks to Jim Clifton, chairman of Gallup, and to Jo Ann Jenkins, AARP's CEO, for writing forewords for the book. Jim runs a big operation (with the help of his chief of staff, Christine Sheehan), and he leans toward brevity. I hope I didn't disappoint. Jim's books, *The Coming Jobs War* and *It's the Manager*, are among my favorites. Jo Ann is also direct and to the point. Her book *Disrupt Aging: A Bold New Path to Living Your Best Life at Any Age* is a primer on tomorrow's society. Thanks, Jim and Jo Ann.

Note: I didn't show a draft of this book to my wife, Fran, because as I said, she's a tough critic who still doesn't laugh at my "jokes."